Cemetery Girl

BOOK THREE: HAUNTED

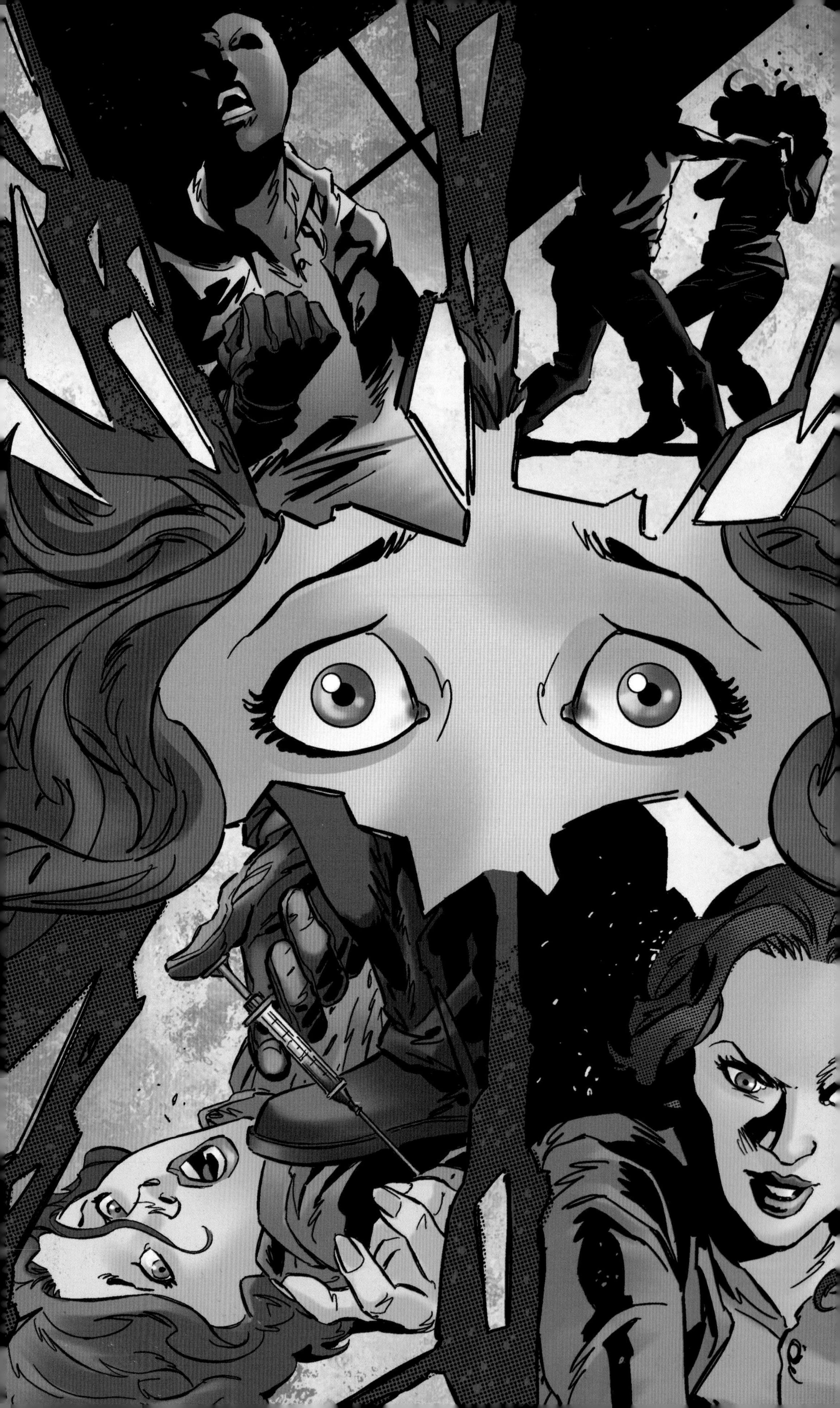

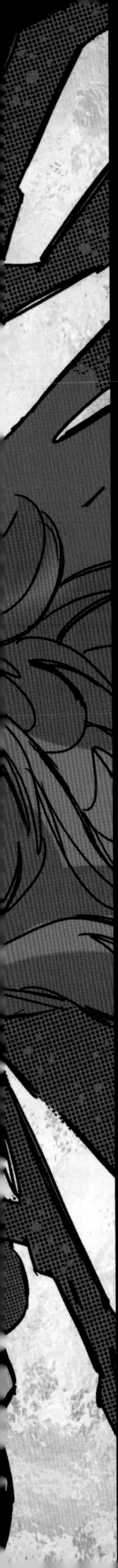

CHARLAINE HARRIS

CHRISTOPHER GOLDEN

CEMETERY GIRL

BOOK THREE: HAUNTED

ART BY GERALDO BORGES

COLORS BY MORGAN HICKMAN AND MOHAN

LETTERS BY TOM NAPOLITANO

COVER BY GERALDO BORGES AND MOHAN

EDITS BY ANTHONY MARQUES

DYNAMITE®

DYNAMITE®

NICK BARRUCCI | CEO / Publisher
JUAN COLLADO | President / COO

JOE RYBANDT | Executive Editor
MATT IDELSON | Senior Editor
ANTHONY MARQUES | Associate Editor
KEVIN KETNER | Assistant Editor

JASON ULLMEYER | Art Director
GEOFF HARKINS | Senior Graphic Designer
CATHLEEN HEARD | Graphic Designer
ALEXIS PERSSON | Production Artist
CHRIS CANIANO | Digital Associate
RACHEL KILBURY | Digital Mutimedia Associate

BRANDON DANTE PRIMAVERA | V.P. of IT and Operations
RICH YOUNG | Director of Business Development
ALAN PAYNE | V.P. of Sales and Marketing
PAT O'CONNELL | Sales Manager

www.DYNAMITE.com | Online
/Dynamitecomics | Facebook
/Dynamitecomics | Instagram
dynamitecomics.tumblr.com
@dynamitecomics | Twitter

Standard Edition ISBN13: 978-1-5241-0533-4
Signed Edition ISBN13: 978-1-5241-0537-2
First Printing 10 9 8 7 6 5 4 3 2 1

For information regarding press, media rights, foreign rights, licensing, promotions, and advertising
e-mail: marketing@dynamite.com

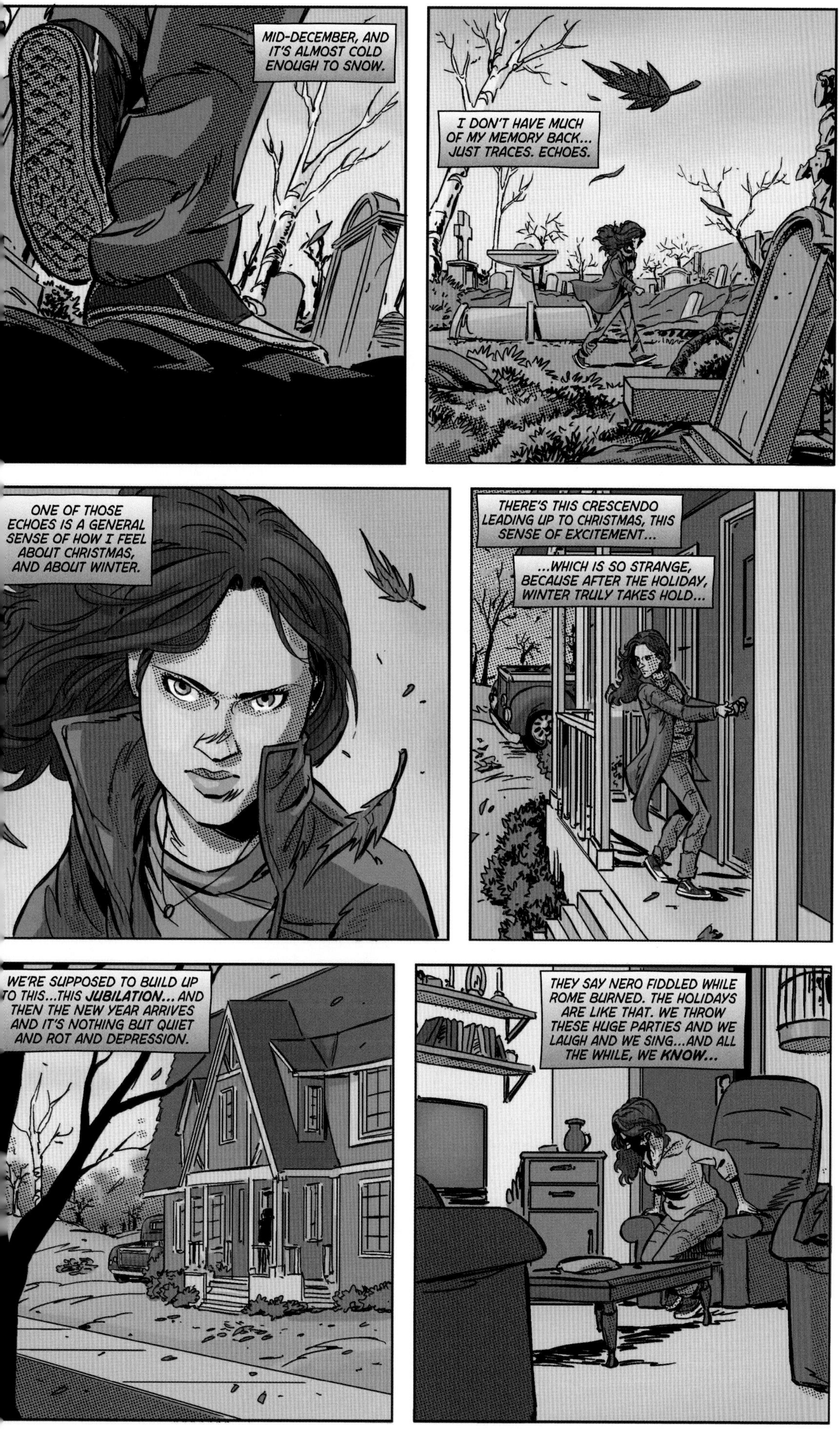
MID-DECEMBER, AND IT'S ALMOST COLD ENOUGH TO SNOW.
I DON'T HAVE MUCH OF MY MEMORY BACK... JUST TRACES. ECHOES.
ONE OF THOSE ECHOES IS A GENERAL SENSE OF HOW I FEEL ABOUT CHRISTMAS, AND ABOUT WINTER.
THERE'S THIS CRESCENDO LEADING UP TO CHRISTMAS, THIS SENSE OF EXCITEMENT...
...WHICH IS SO STRANGE, BECAUSE AFTER THE HOLIDAY, WINTER TRULY TAKES HOLD...
WE'RE SUPPOSED TO BUILD UP TO THIS...THIS JUBILATION... AND THEN THE NEW YEAR ARRIVES AND IT'S NOTHING BUT QUIET AND ROT AND DEPRESSION.
THEY SAY NERO FIDDLED WHILE ROME BURNED. THE HOLIDAYS ARE LIKE THAT. WE THROW THESE HUGE PARTIES AND WE LAUGH AND WE SING...AND ALL THE WHILE, WE KNOW...

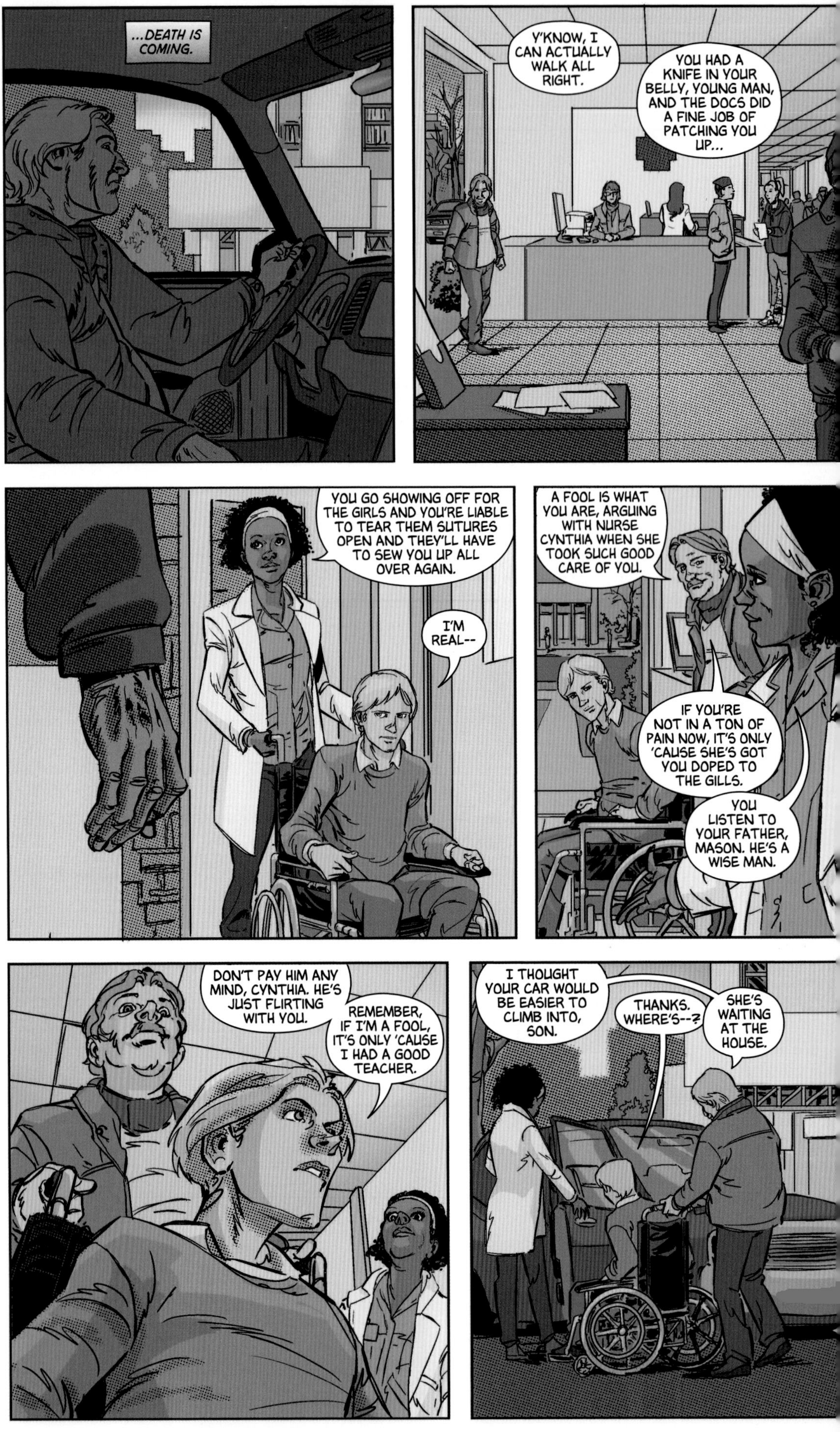
...DEATH IS COMING.
Y'KNOW, I CAN ACTUALLY WALK ALL RIGHT.
YOU HAD A KNIFE IN YOUR BELLY, YOUNG MAN, AND THE DOCS DID A FINE JOB OF PATCHING YOU UP...
YOU GO SHOWING OFF FOR THE GIRLS AND YOU'RE LIABLE TO TEAR THEM SUTURES OPEN AND THEY'LL HAVE TO SEW YOU UP ALL OVER AGAIN.
I'M REAL--
A FOOL IS WHAT YOU ARE, ARGUING WITH NURSE CYNTHIA WHEN SHE TOOK SUCH GOOD CARE OF YOU.
IF YOU'RE NOT IN A TON OF PAIN NOW, IT'S ONLY 'CAUSE SHE'S GOT YOU DOPED TO THE GILLS.
YOU LISTEN TO YOUR FATHER, MASON. HE'S A WISE MAN.
DON'T PAY HIM ANY MIND, CYNTHIA. HE'S JUST FLIRTING WITH YOU.
REMEMBER, IF I'M A FOOL, IT'S ONLY 'CAUSE I HAD A GOOD TEACHER.
I THOUGHT YOUR CAR WOULD BE EASIER TO CLIMB INTO, SON.
THANKS. WHERE'S--?
SHE'S WAITING AT THE HOUSE.

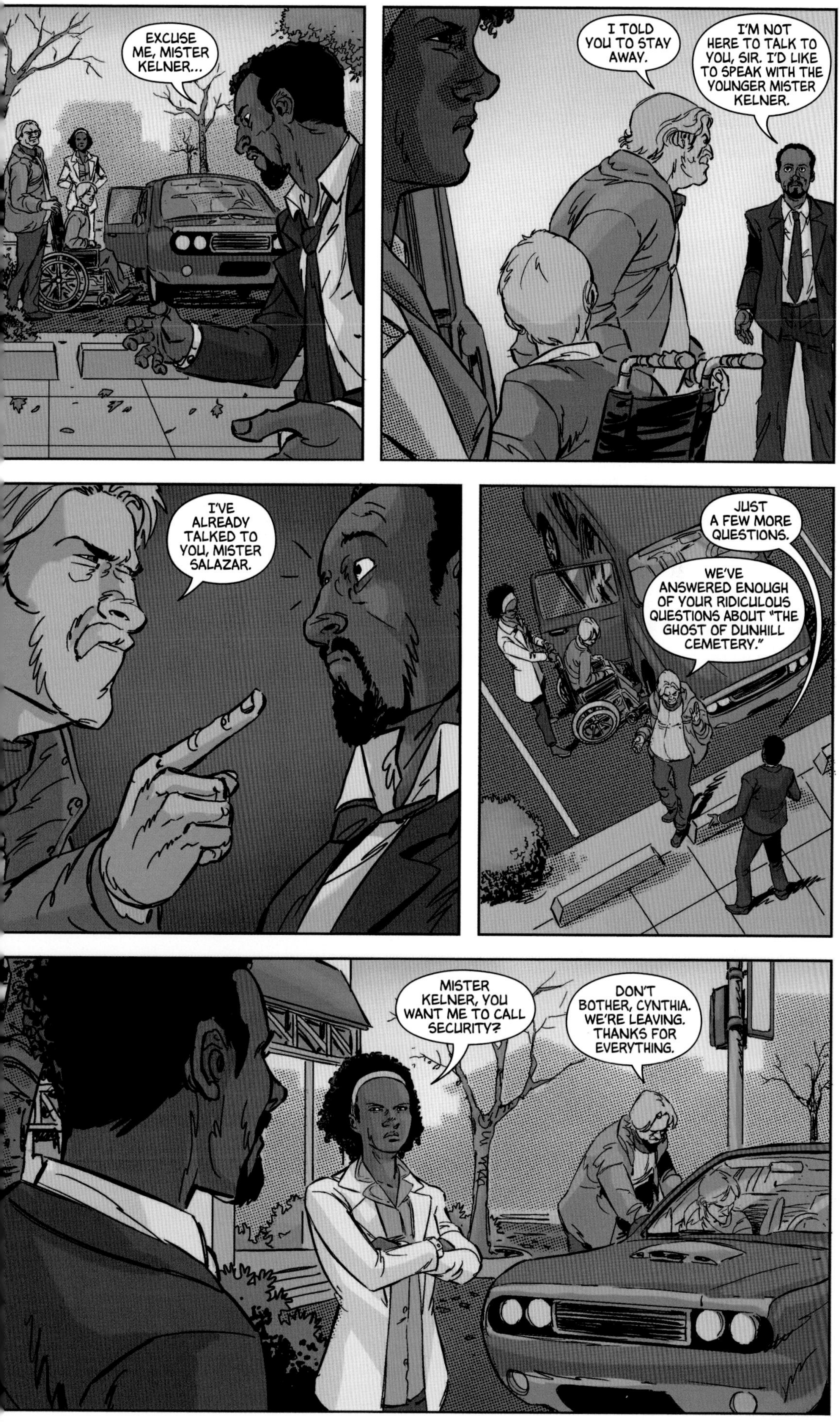
EXCUSE ME, MISTER KELNER...
I TOLD YOU TO STAY AWAY.
I'M NOT HERE TO TALK TO YOU, SIR. I'D LIKE TO SPEAK WITH THE YOUNGER MISTER KELNER.
I'VE ALREADY TALKED TO YOU, MISTER SALAZAR.
JUST A FEW MORE QUESTIONS.
WE'VE ANSWERED ENOUGH OF YOUR RIDICULOUS QUESTIONS ABOUT "THE GHOST OF DUNHILL CEMETERY."
MISTER KELNER, YOU WANT ME TO CALL SECURITY?
DON'T BOTHER, CYNTHIA. WE'RE LEAVING. THANKS FOR EVERYTHING.

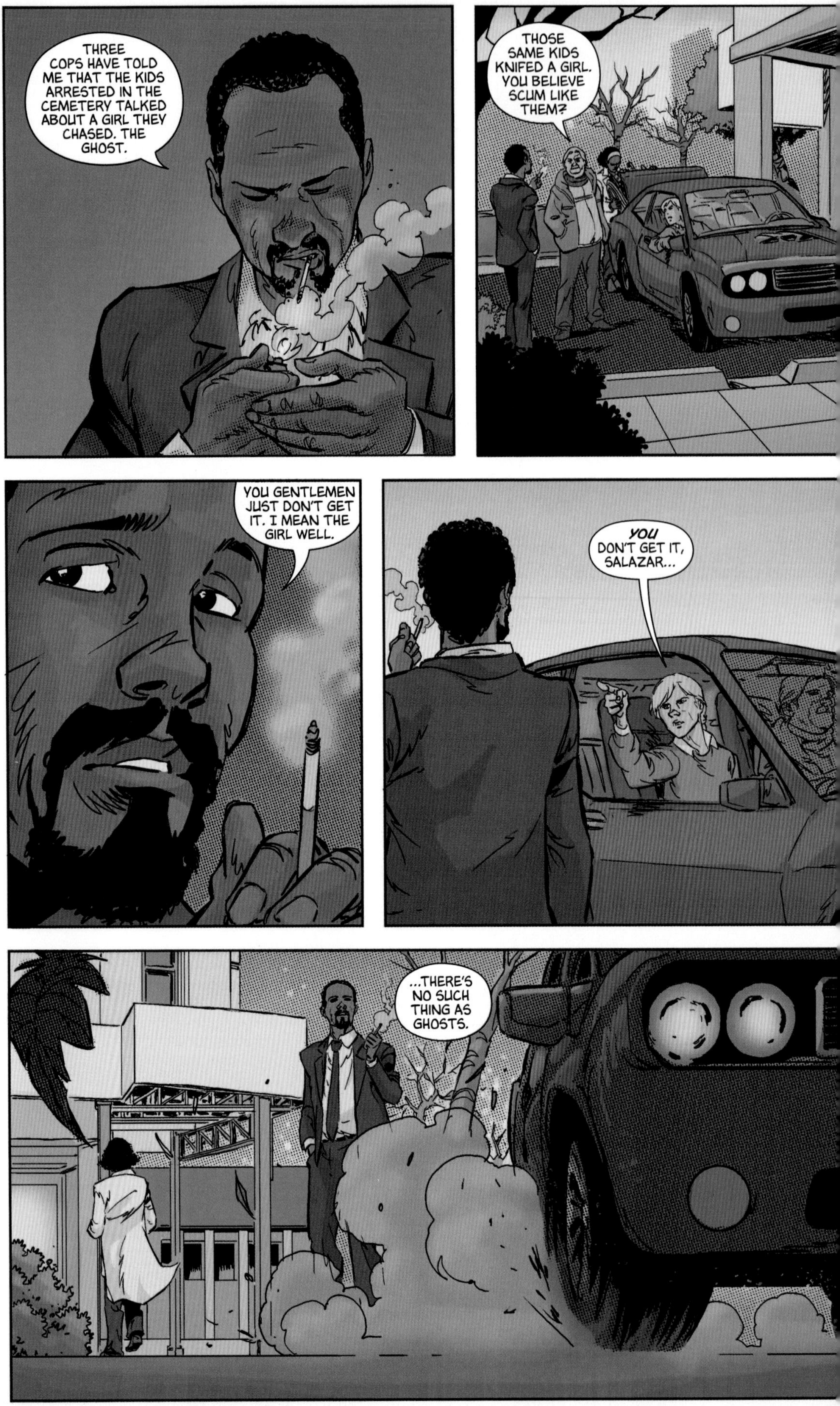
THREE COPS HAVE TOLD ME THAT THE KIDS ARRESTED IN THE CEMETERY TALKED ABOUT A GIRL THEY CHASED. THE GHOST.
THOSE SAME KIDS KNIFED A GIRL. YOU BELIEVE SCUM LIKE THEM?
YOU GENTLEMEN JUST DON'T GET IT. I MEAN THE GIRL WELL.
YOU DON'T GET IT, SALAZAR...
...THERE'S NO SUCH THING AS GHOSTS.

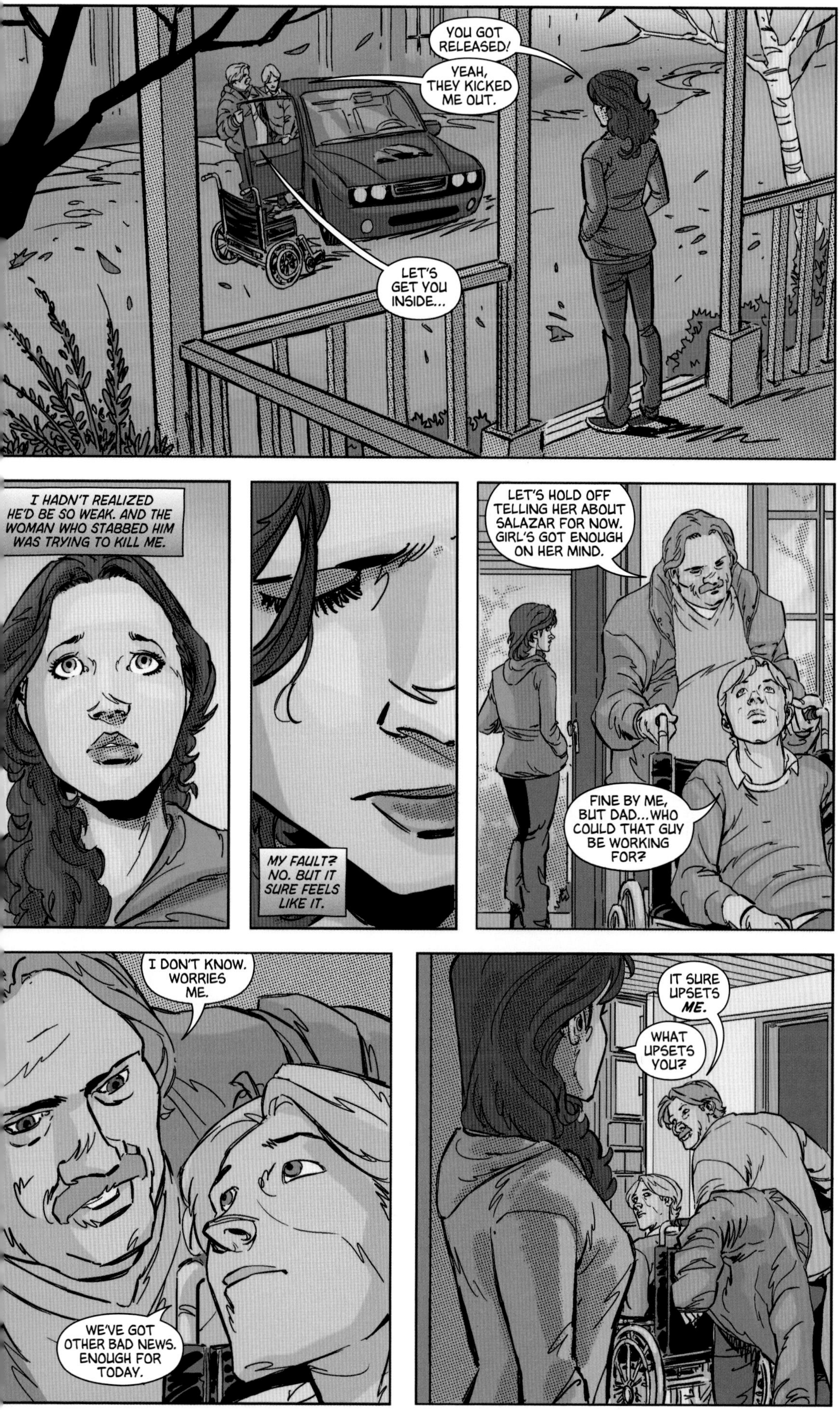
YOU GOT RELEASED!
YEAH, THEY KICKED ME OUT.
LET'S GET YOU INSIDE...
I HADN'T REALIZED HE'D BE SO WEAK. AND THE WOMAN WHO STABBED HIM WAS TRYING TO KILL ME.
MY FAULT? NO. BUT IT SURE FEELS LIKE IT.
LET'S HOLD OFF TELLING HER ABOUT SALAZAR FOR NOW. GIRL'S GOT ENOUGH ON HER MIND.
FINE BY ME, BUT DAD...WHO COULD THAT GUY BE WORKING FOR?
I DON'T KNOW. WORRIES ME.
WE'VE GOT OTHER BAD NEWS. ENOUGH FOR TODAY.
IT SURE UPSETS ME.
WHAT UPSETS YOU?

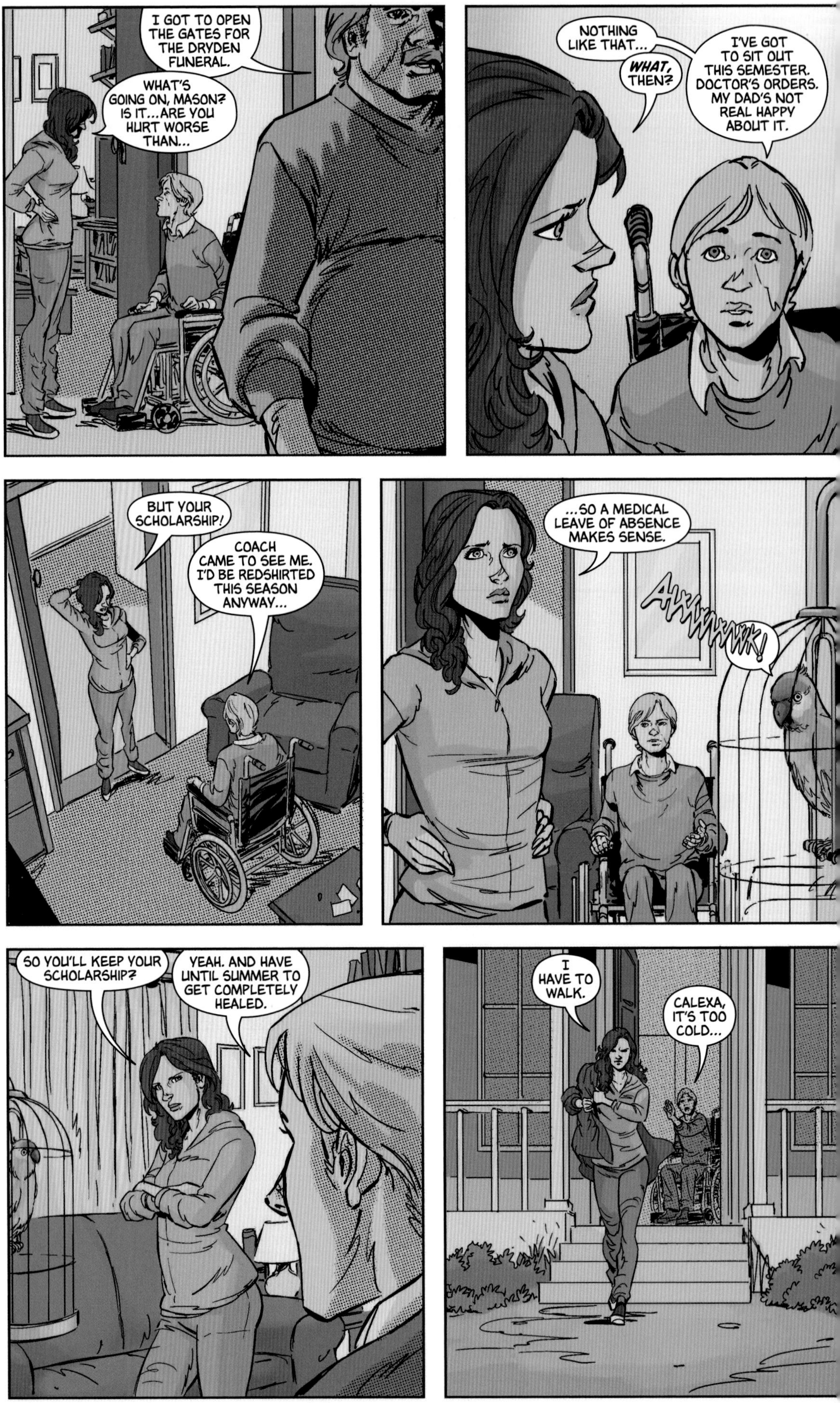
I GOT TO OPEN THE GATES FOR THE DRYDEN FUNERAL.
WHAT'S GOING ON, MASON? IS IT...ARE YOU HURT WORSE THAN...
NOTHING LIKE THAT...
WHAT, THEN?
I'VE GOT TO SIT OUT THIS SEMESTER. DOCTOR'S ORDERS. MY DAD'S NOT REAL HAPPY ABOUT IT.
BUT YOUR SCHOLARSHIP!
COACH CAME TO SEE ME. I'D BE REDSHIRTED THIS SEASON ANYWAY...
...SO A MEDICAL LEAVE OF ABSENCE MAKES SENSE.
AWWWWK!
SO YOU'LL KEEP YOUR SCHOLARSHIP?
YEAH. AND HAVE UNTIL SUMMER TO GET COMPLETELY HEALED.
I HAVE TO WALK.
CALEXA, IT'S TOO COLD...

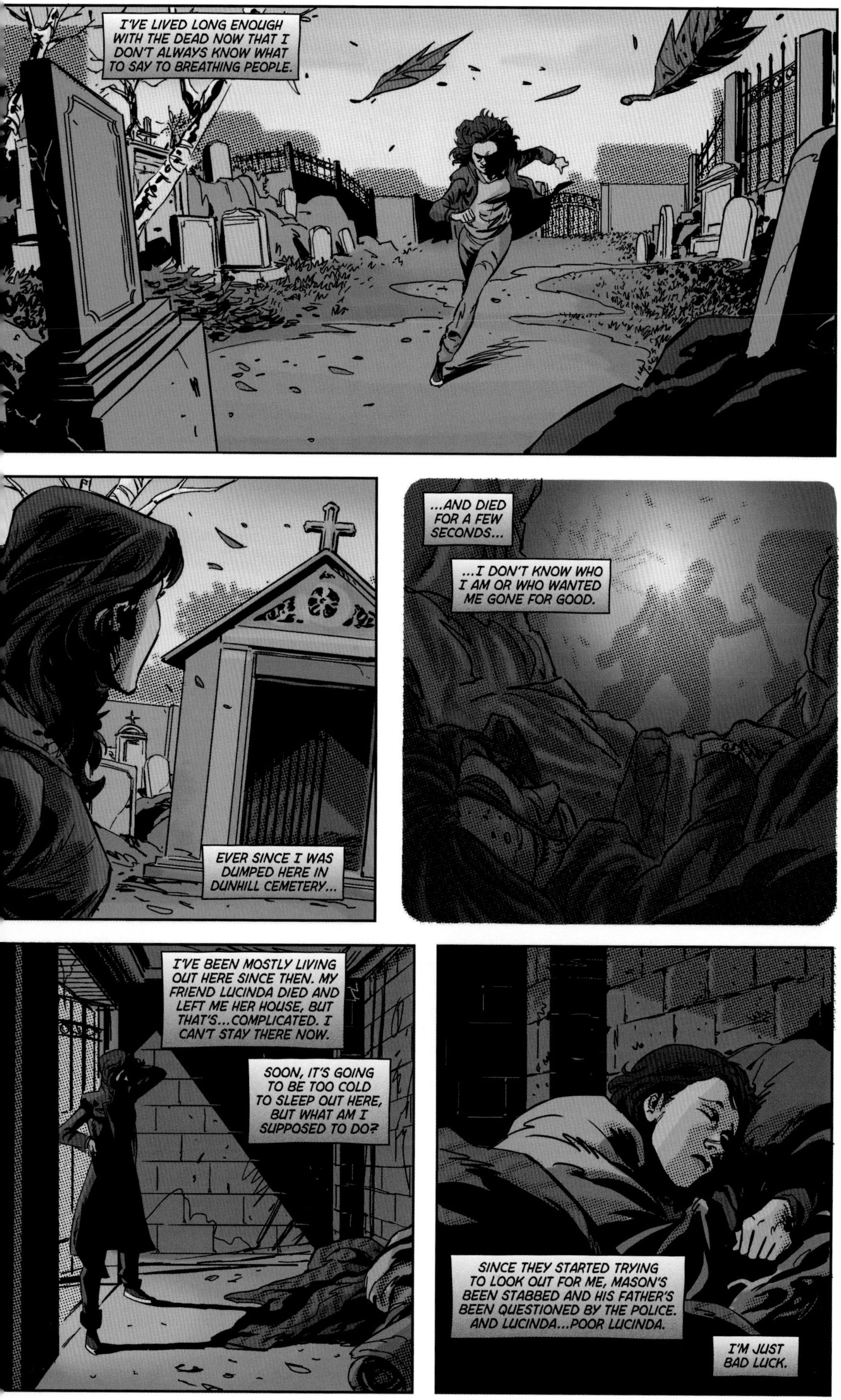
I'VE LIVED LONG ENOUGH WITH THE DEAD NOW THAT I DON'T ALWAYS KNOW WHAT TO SAY TO BREATHING PEOPLE.
EVER SINCE I WAS DUMPED HERE IN DUNHILL CEMETERY...
...AND DIED FOR A FEW SECONDS...
...I DON'T KNOW WHO I AM OR WHO WANTED ME GONE FOR GOOD.
I'VE BEEN MOSTLY LIVING OUT HERE SINCE THEN. MY FRIEND LUCINDA DIED AND LEFT ME HER HOUSE, BUT THAT'S...COMPLICATED. I CAN'T STAY THERE NOW.
SOON, IT'S GOING TO BE TOO COLD TO SLEEP OUT HERE, BUT WHAT AM I SUPPOSED TO DO?
SINCE THEY STARTED TRYING TO LOOK OUT FOR ME, MASON'S BEEN STABBED AND HIS FATHER'S BEEN QUESTIONED BY THE POLICE. AND LUCINDA...POOR LUCINDA.
I'M JUST BAD LUCK.

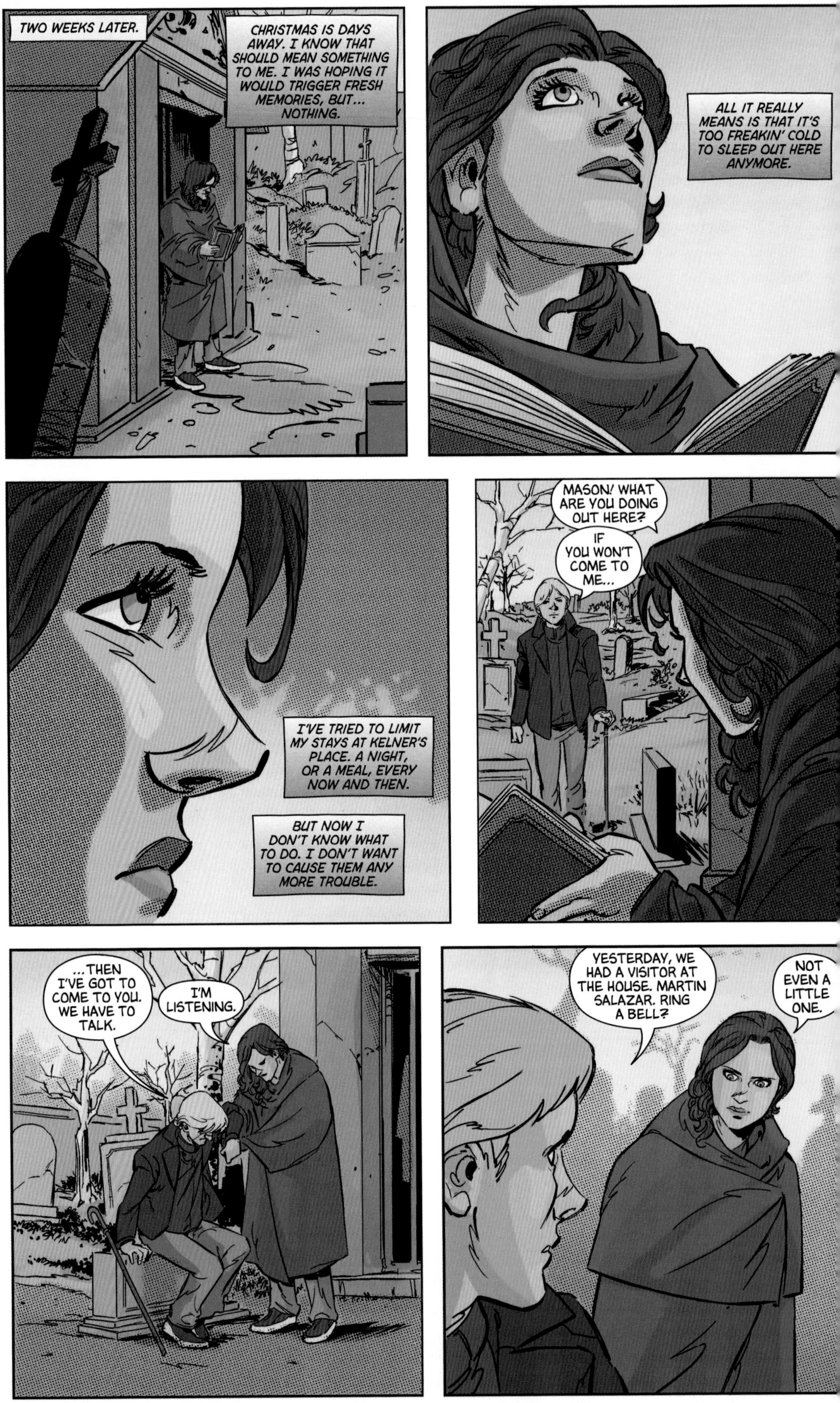
TWO WEEKS LATER.
CHRISTMAS IS DAYS AWAY. I KNOW THAT SHOULD MEAN SOMETHING TO ME. I WAS HOPING IT WOULD TRIGGER FRESH MEMORIES, BUT... NOTHING.
ALL IT REALLY MEANS IS THAT IT'S TOO FREAKIN' COLD TO SLEEP OUT HERE ANYMORE.
I'VE TRIED TO LIMIT MY STAYS AT KELNER'S PLACE. A NIGHT, OR A MEAL, EVERY NOW AND THEN.
BUT NOW I DON'T KNOW WHAT TO DO. I DON'T WANT TO CAUSE THEM ANY MORE TROUBLE.
MASON! WHAT ARE YOU DOING OUT HERE?
IF YOU WON'T COME TO ME...
...THEN I'VE GOT TO COME TO YOU. WE HAVE TO TALK.
I'M LISTENING.
YESTERDAY, WE HAD A VISITOR AT THE HOUSE. MARTIN SALAZAR. RING A BELL?
NOT EVEN A LITTLE ONE.

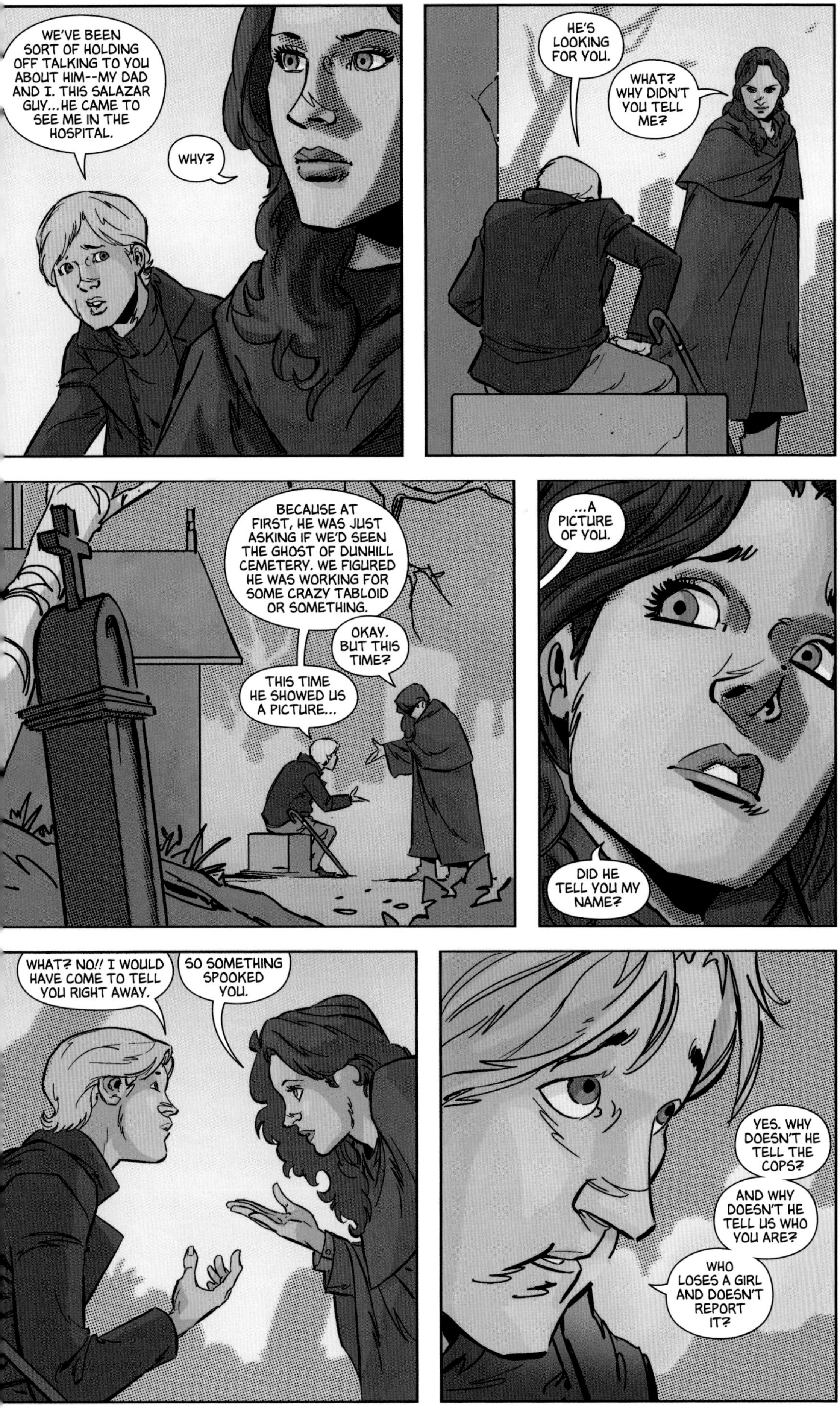
WE'VE BEEN SORT OF HOLDING OFF TALKING TO YOU ABOUT HIM--MY DAD AND I. THIS SALAZAR GUY...HE CAME TO SEE ME IN THE HOSPITAL.
WHY?
HE'S LOOKING FOR YOU.
WHAT? WHY DIDN'T YOU TELL ME?
BECAUSE AT FIRST, HE WAS JUST ASKING IF WE'D SEEN THE GHOST OF DUNHILL CEMETERY. WE FIGURED HE WAS WORKING FOR SOME CRAZY TABLOID OR SOMETHING.
OKAY. BUT THIS TIME?
THIS TIME HE SHOWED US A PICTURE...
...A PICTURE OF YOU.
DID HE TELL YOU MY NAME?
WHAT? NO!! I WOULD HAVE COME TO TELL YOU RIGHT AWAY.
SO SOMETHING SPOOKED YOU.
YES. WHY DOESN'T HE TELL THE COPS?
AND WHY DOESN'T HE TELL US WHO YOU ARE?
WHO LOSES A GIRL AND DOESN'T REPORT IT?

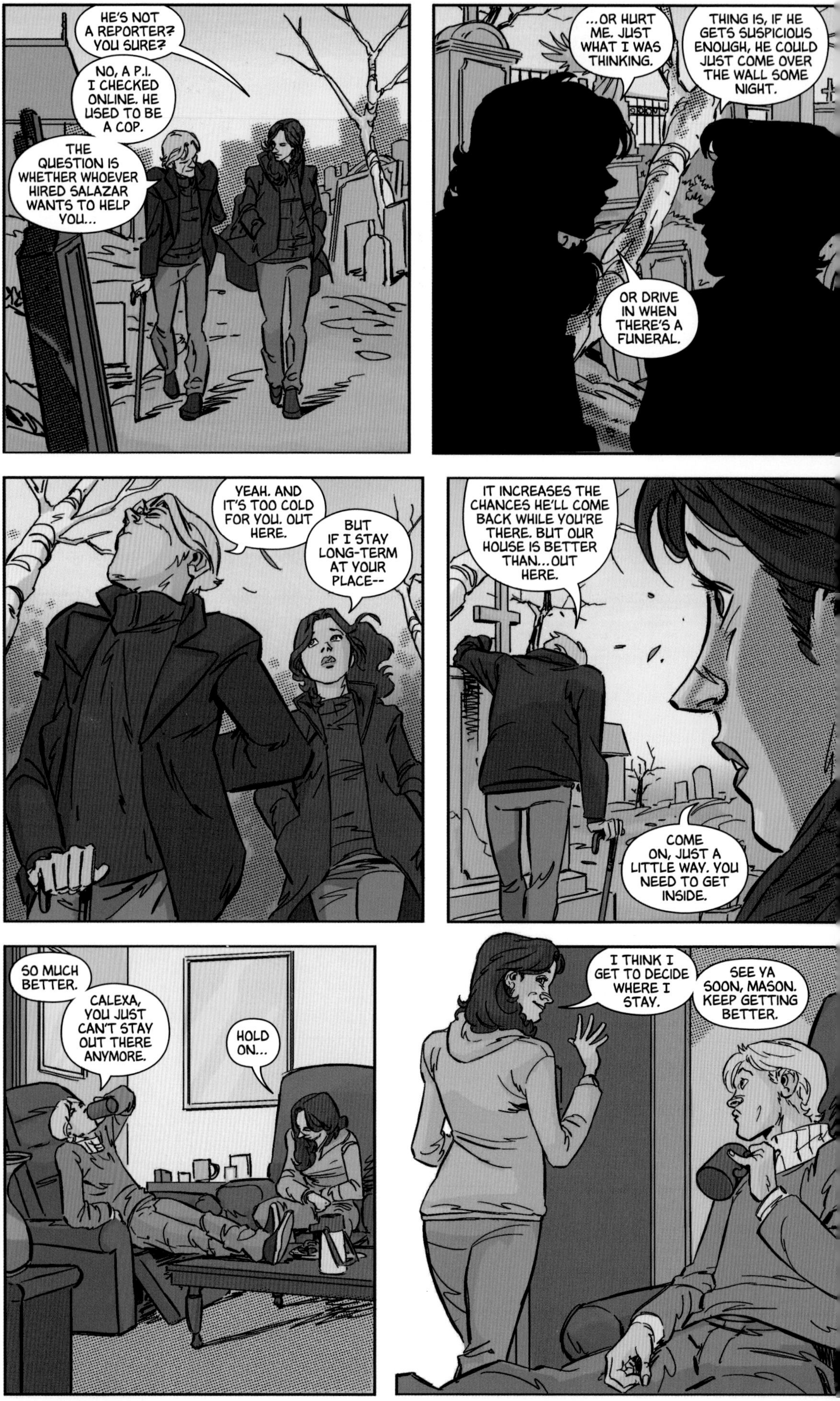
HE'S NOT A REPORTER? YOU SURE?
NO, A P.I. I CHECKED ONLINE. HE USED TO BE A COP.
THE QUESTION IS WHETHER WHOEVER HIRED SALAZAR WANTS TO HELP YOU...
...OR HURT ME. JUST WHAT I WAS THINKING.
THING IS, IF HE GETS SUSPICIOUS ENOUGH, HE COULD JUST COME OVER THE WALL SOME NIGHT.
OR DRIVE IN WHEN THERE'S A FUNERAL.
YEAH. AND IT'S TOO COLD FOR YOU. OUT HERE.
BUT IF I STAY LONG-TERM AT YOUR PLACE--
IT INCREASES THE CHANCES HE'LL COME BACK WHILE YOU'RE THERE. BUT OUR HOUSE IS BETTER THAN...OUT HERE.
COME ON, JUST A LITTLE WAY. YOU NEED TO GET INSIDE.
SO MUCH BETTER.
CALEXA, YOU JUST CAN'T STAY OUT THERE ANYMORE.
HOLD ON...
I THINK I GET TO DECIDE WHERE I STAY.
SEE YA SOON, MASON. KEEP GETTING BETTER.

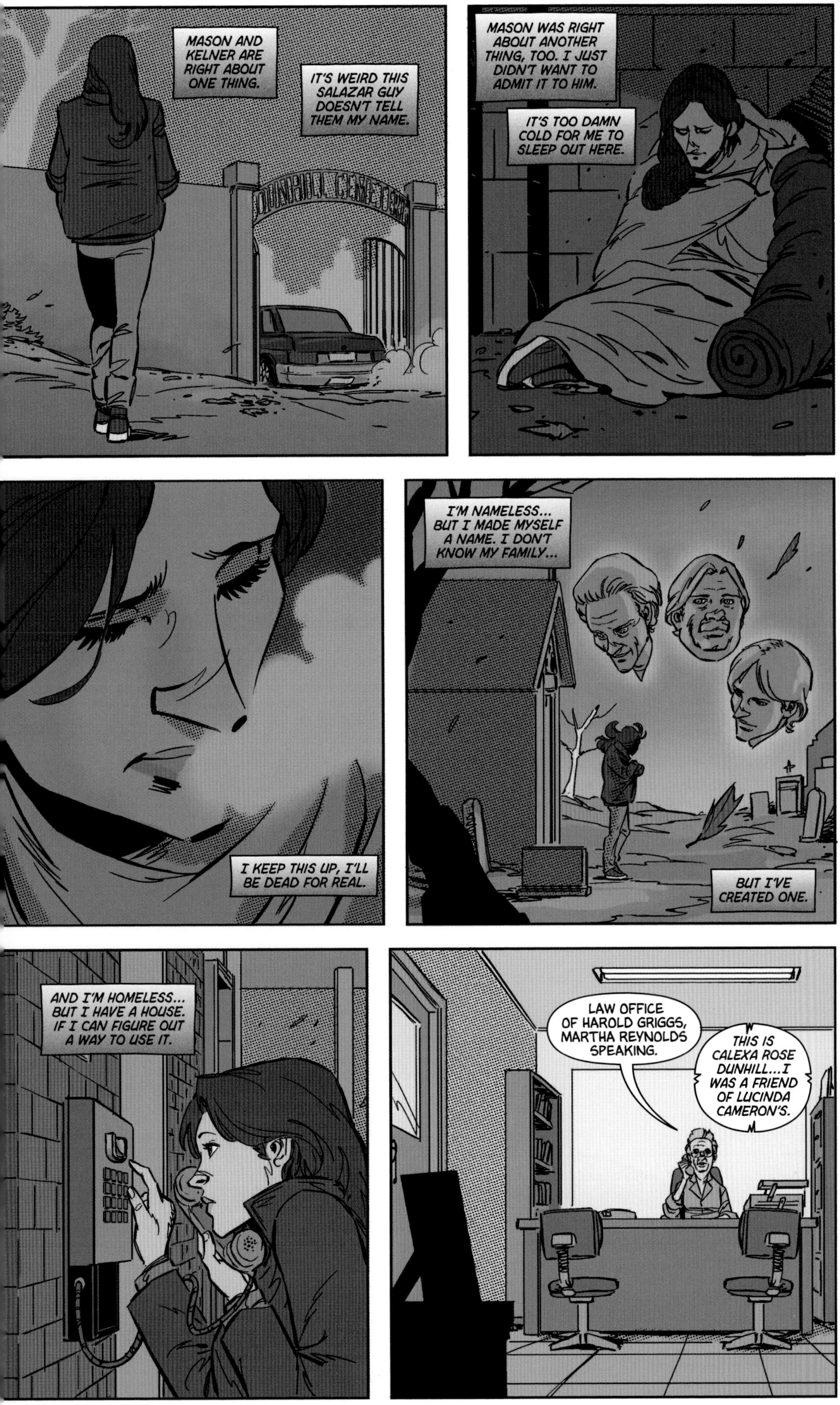
MASON AND KELNER ARE RIGHT ABOUT ONE THING.
IT'S WEIRD THIS SALAZAR GUY DOESN'T TELL THEM MY NAME.
DUNHILL CEMETERY
MASON WAS RIGHT ABOUT ANOTHER THING, TOO. I JUST DIDN'T WANT TO ADMIT IT TO HIM.
IT'S TOO DAMN COLD FOR ME TO SLEEP OUT HERE.
I KEEP THIS UP, I'LL BE DEAD FOR REAL.
I'M NAMELESS... BUT I MADE MYSELF A NAME. I DON'T KNOW MY FAMILY...
BUT I'VE CREATED ONE.
AND I'M HOMELESS... BUT I HAVE A HOUSE. IF I CAN FIGURE OUT A WAY TO USE IT.
LAW OFFICE OF HAROLD GRIGGS, MARTHA REYNOLDS SPEAKING.
THIS IS CALEXA ROSE DUNHILL...I WAS A FRIEND OF LUCINDA CAMERON'S.

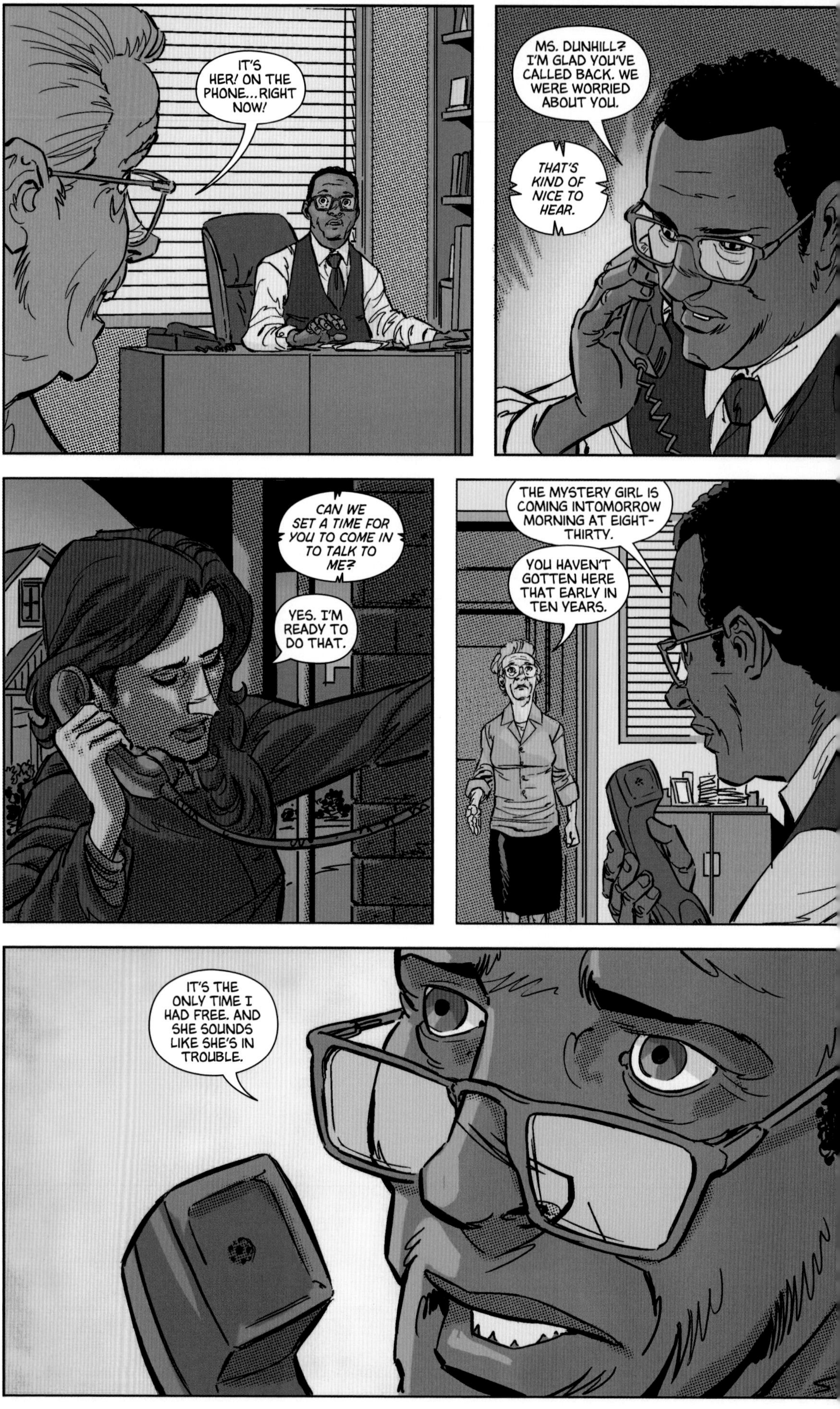
IT'S HER! ON THE PHONE... RIGHT NOW!
MS. DUNHILL? I'M GLAD YOU'VE CALLED BACK. WE WERE WORRIED ABOUT YOU.
THAT'S KIND OF NICE TO HEAR.
CAN WE SET A TIME FOR YOU TO COME IN TO TALK TO ME?
YES. I'M READY TO DO THAT.
THE MYSTERY GIRL IS COMING INTOMORROW MORNING AT EIGHT-THIRTY.
YOU HAVEN'T GOTTEN HERE THAT EARLY IN TEN YEARS.
IT'S THE ONLY TIME I HAD FREE. AND SHE SOUNDS LIKE SHE'S IN TROUBLE.

WE CAN'T JUST LEAVE HER OUT THERE.

WE CAN'T FORCE HER, EITHER.

TEMPERATURE'S GOING TO DROP TOMORROW NIGHT. WORD IS WE COULD HAVE A HELL OF A SNOWSTORM. I'M NOT GOING TO SIT IN HERE, SAFE AND WARM, WITH HER OUT THERE.

NO... I GUESS I'M NOT EITHER.

IF SHE DOESN'T COME TO HER SENSES TONIGHT, WE'LL GO AND TALK TO HER IN THE MORNING.

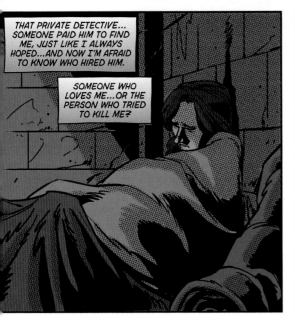

THAT PRIVATE DETECTIVE... SOMEONE PAID HIM TO FIND ME, JUST LIKE I ALWAYS HOPED...AND NOW I'M AFRAID TO KNOW WHO HIRED HIM.

SOMEONE WHO LOVES ME...OR THE PERSON WHO TRIED TO KILL ME?

GOING TO SEE MR. GRIGGS SEEMS LIKE THE ONLY CHOICE, BUT I'M SO SCARED.

SO SCARED...AND SO, SO COLD.

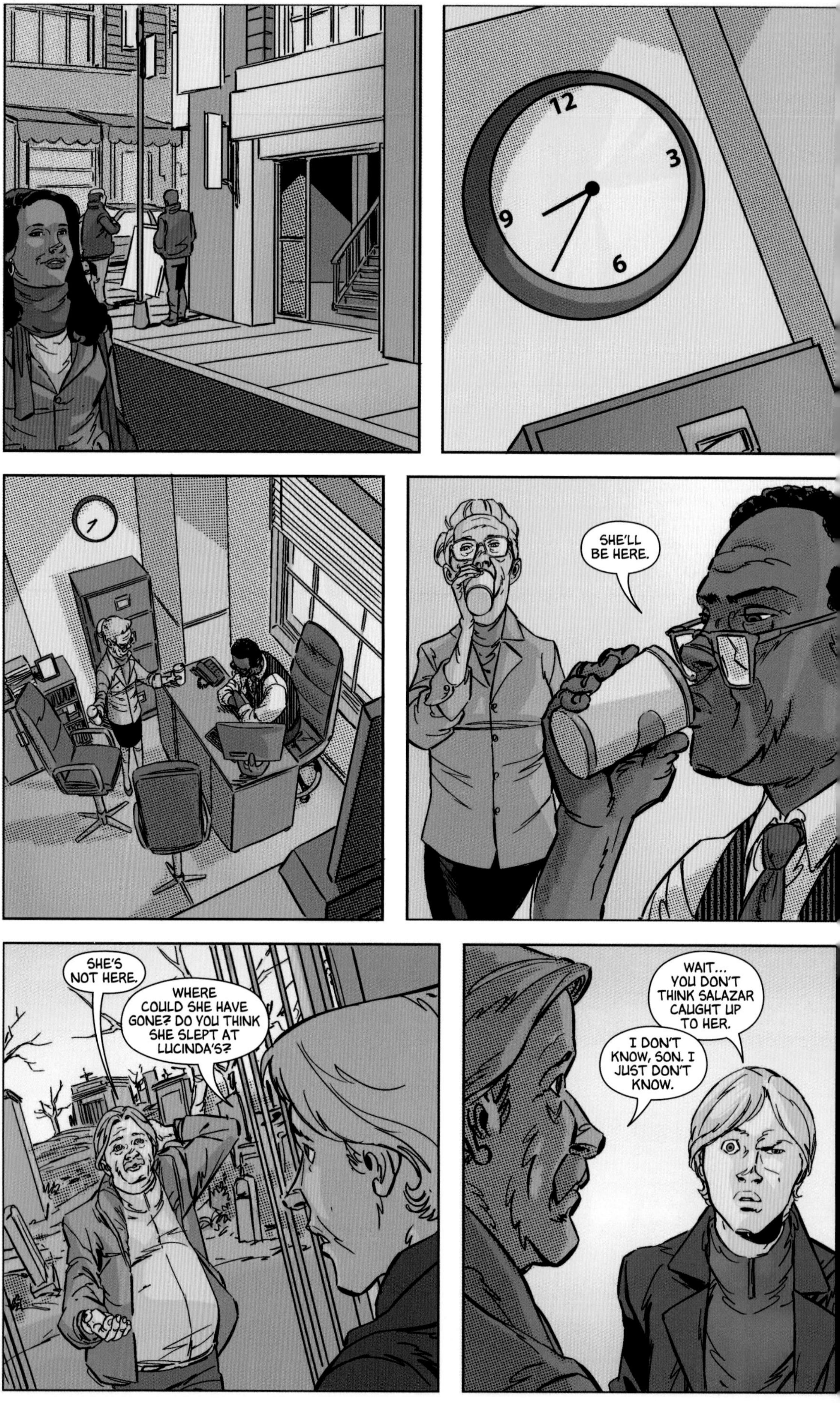
12
3
9
6
SHE'LL BE HERE.
SHE'S NOT HERE.
WHERE COULD SHE HAVE GONE? DO YOU THINK SHE SLEPT AT LUCINDA'S?
WAIT... YOU DON'T THINK SALAZAR CAUGHT UP TO HER.
I DON'T KNOW, SON. I JUST DON'T KNOW.

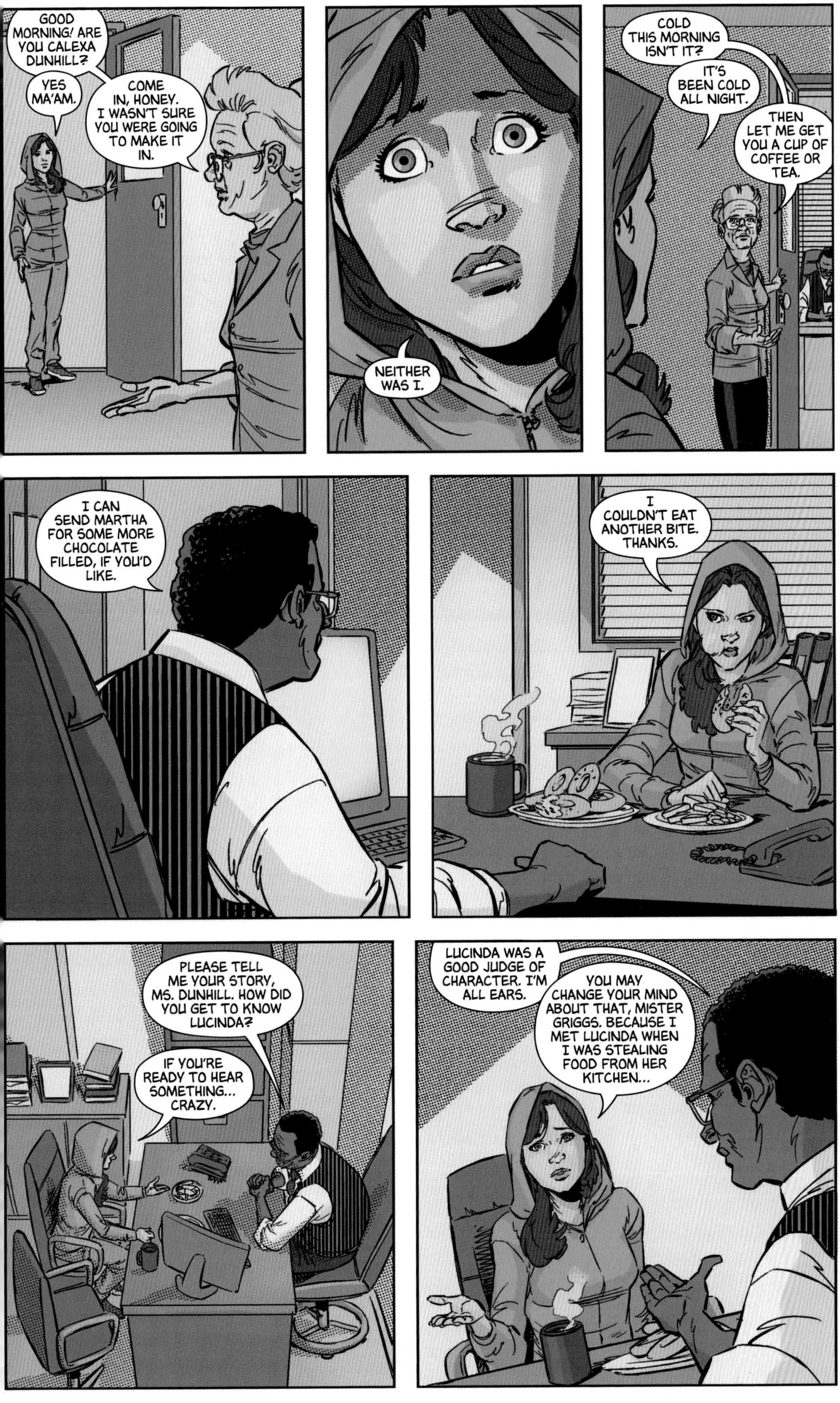
GOOD MORNING! ARE YOU CALEXA DUNHILL?
YES MA'AM.
COME IN, HONEY. I WASN'T SURE YOU WERE GOING TO MAKE IT IN.
NEITHER WAS I.
COLD THIS MORNING ISN'T IT?
IT'S BEEN COLD ALL NIGHT.
THEN LET ME GET YOU A CUP OF COFFEE OR TEA.
I CAN SEND MARTHA FOR SOME MORE CHOCOLATE FILLED, IF YOU'D LIKE.
I COULDN'T EAT ANOTHER BITE. THANKS.
PLEASE TELL ME YOUR STORY, MS. DUNHILL. HOW DID YOU GET TO KNOW LUCINDA?
IF YOU'RE READY TO HEAR SOMETHING... CRAZY.
LUCINDA WAS A GOOD JUDGE OF CHARACTER. I'M ALL EARS.
YOU MAY CHANGE YOUR MIND ABOUT THAT, MISTER GRIGGS. BECAUSE I MET LUCINDA WHEN I WAS STEALING FOOD FROM HER KITCHEN...

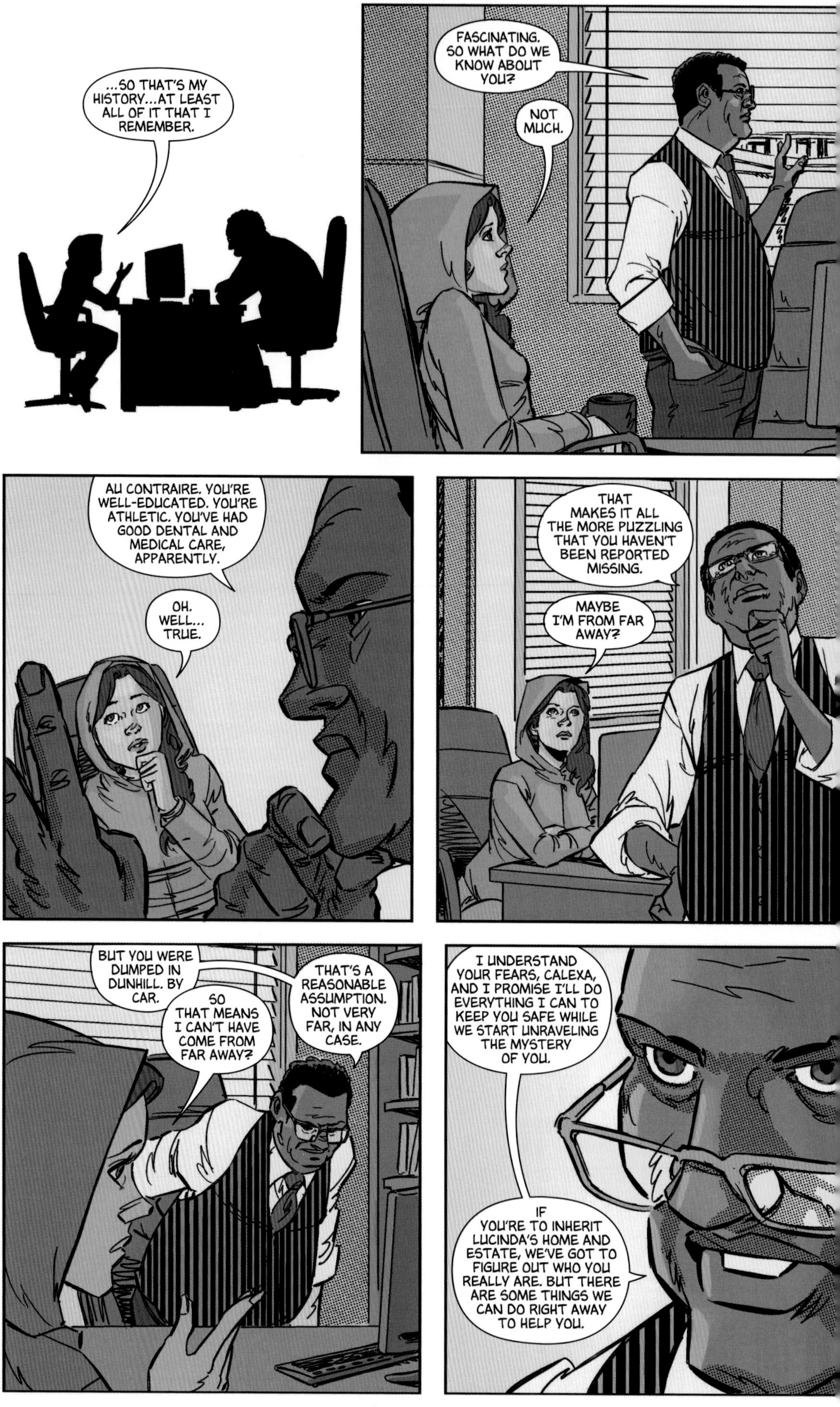
...SO THAT'S MY HISTORY...AT LEAST ALL OF IT THAT I REMEMBER.
FASCINATING. SO WHAT DO WE KNOW ABOUT YOU?
NOT MUCH.
AU CONTRAIRE. YOU'RE WELL-EDUCATED. YOU'RE ATHLETIC. YOU'VE HAD GOOD DENTAL AND MEDICAL CARE, APPARENTLY.
OH. WELL... TRUE.
THAT MAKES IT ALL THE MORE PUZZLING THAT YOU HAVEN'T BEEN REPORTED MISSING.
MAYBE I'M FROM FAR AWAY?
BUT YOU WERE DUMPED IN DUNHILL. BY CAR.
SO THAT MEANS I CAN'T HAVE COME FROM FAR AWAY?
THAT'S A REASONABLE ASSUMPTION. NOT VERY FAR, IN ANY CASE.
I UNDERSTAND YOUR FEARS, CALEXA, AND I PROMISE I'LL DO EVERYTHING I CAN TO KEEP YOU SAFE WHILE WE START UNRAVELING THE MYSTERY OF YOU.
IF YOU'RE TO INHERIT LUCINDA'S HOME AND ESTATE, WE'VE GOT TO FIGURE OUT WHO YOU REALLY ARE. BUT THERE ARE SOME THINGS WE CAN DO RIGHT AWAY TO HELP YOU.

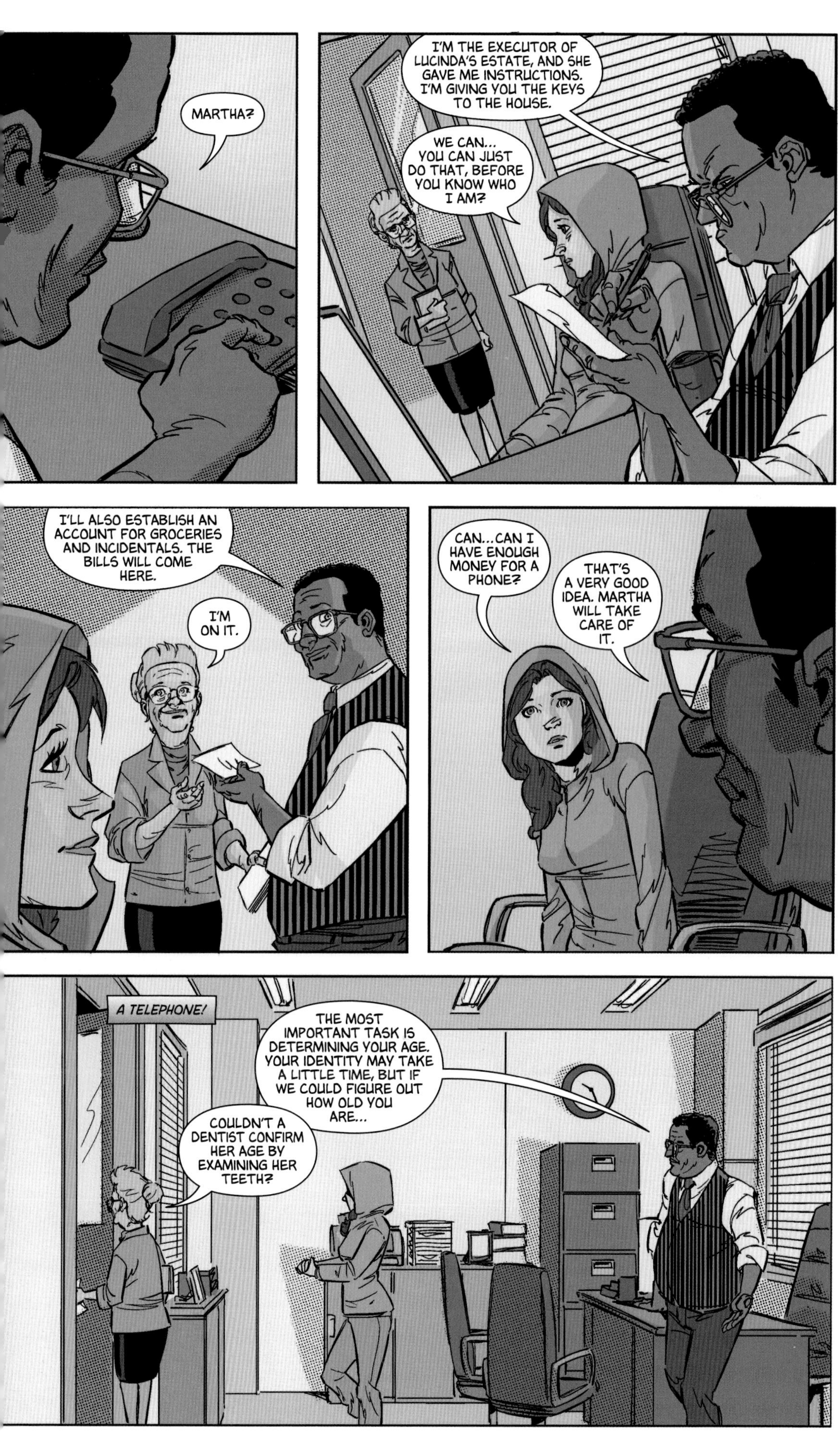
MARTHA?
I'M THE EXECUTOR OF LUCINDA'S ESTATE, AND SHE GAVE ME INSTRUCTIONS. I'M GIVING YOU THE KEYS TO THE HOUSE.
WE CAN... YOU CAN JUST DO THAT, BEFORE YOU KNOW WHO I AM?
I'LL ALSO ESTABLISH AN ACCOUNT FOR GROCERIES AND INCIDENTALS. THE BILLS WILL COME HERE.
I'M ON IT.
CAN...CAN I HAVE ENOUGH MONEY FOR A PHONE?
THAT'S A VERY GOOD IDEA. MARTHA WILL TAKE CARE OF IT.
A TELEPHONE!
THE MOST IMPORTANT TASK IS DETERMINING YOUR AGE. YOUR IDENTITY MAY TAKE A LITTLE TIME, BUT IF WE COULD FIGURE OUT HOW OLD YOU ARE...
COULDN'T A DENTIST CONFIRM HER AGE BY EXAMINING HER TEETH?

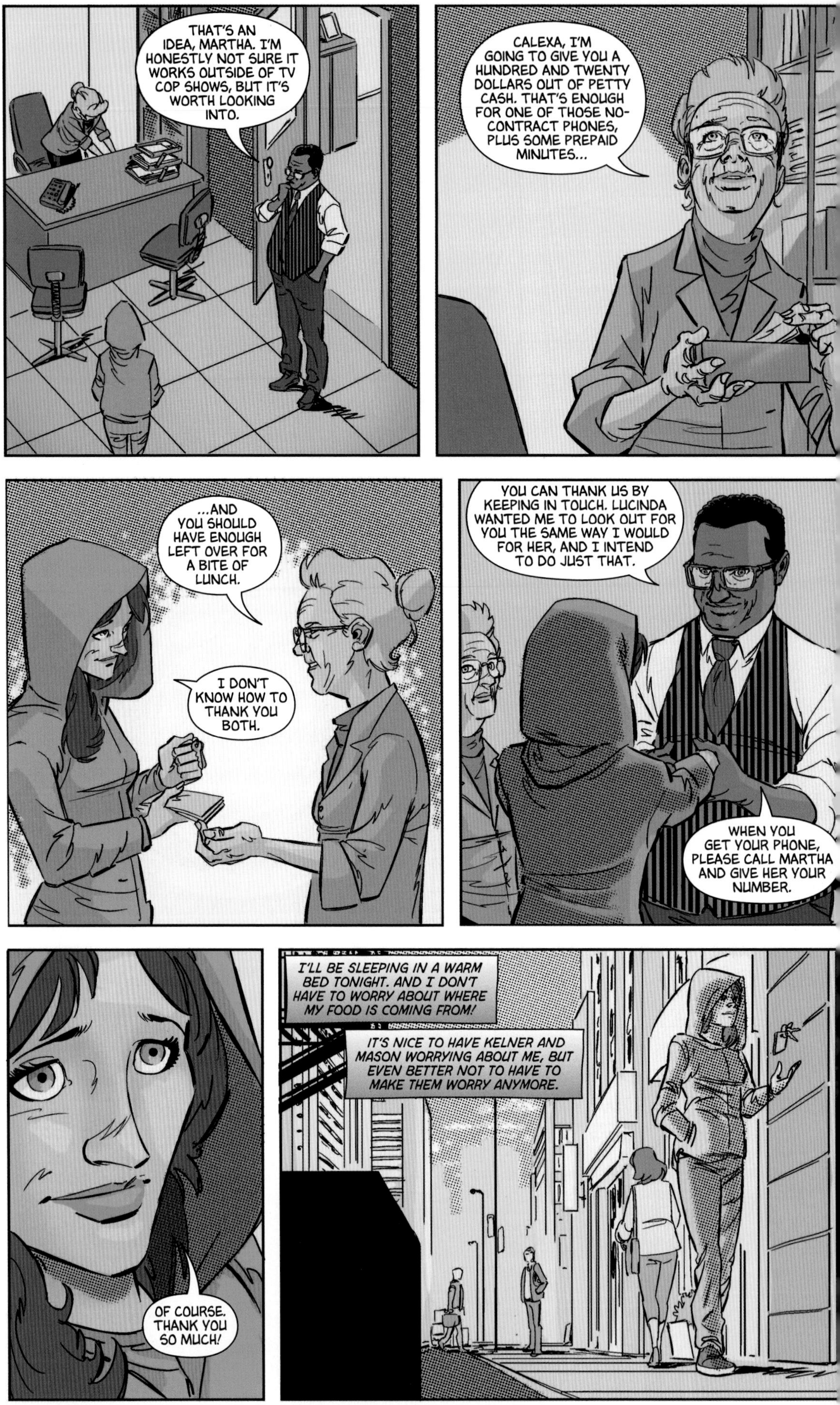
THAT'S AN IDEA, MARTHA. I'M HONESTLY NOT SURE IT WORKS OUTSIDE OF TV COP SHOWS, BUT IT'S WORTH LOOKING INTO.
CALEXA, I'M GOING TO GIVE YOU A HUNDRED AND TWENTY DOLLARS OUT OF PETTY CASH. THAT'S ENOUGH FOR ONE OF THOSE NO-CONTRACT PHONES, PLUS SOME PREPAID MINUTES...
...AND YOU SHOULD HAVE ENOUGH LEFT OVER FOR A BITE OF LUNCH.
I DON'T KNOW HOW TO THANK YOU BOTH.
YOU CAN THANK US BY KEEPING IN TOUCH. LUCINDA WANTED ME TO LOOK OUT FOR YOU THE SAME WAY I WOULD FOR HER, AND I INTEND TO DO JUST THAT.
WHEN YOU GET YOUR PHONE, PLEASE CALL MARTHA AND GIVE HER YOUR NUMBER.
OF COURSE. THANK YOU SO MUCH!
I'LL BE SLEEPING IN A WARM BED TONIGHT. AND I DON'T HAVE TO WORRY ABOUT WHERE MY FOOD IS COMING FROM!
IT'S NICE TO HAVE KELNER AND MASON WORRYING ABOUT ME, BUT EVEN BETTER NOT TO HAVE TO MAKE THEM WORRY ANYMORE.

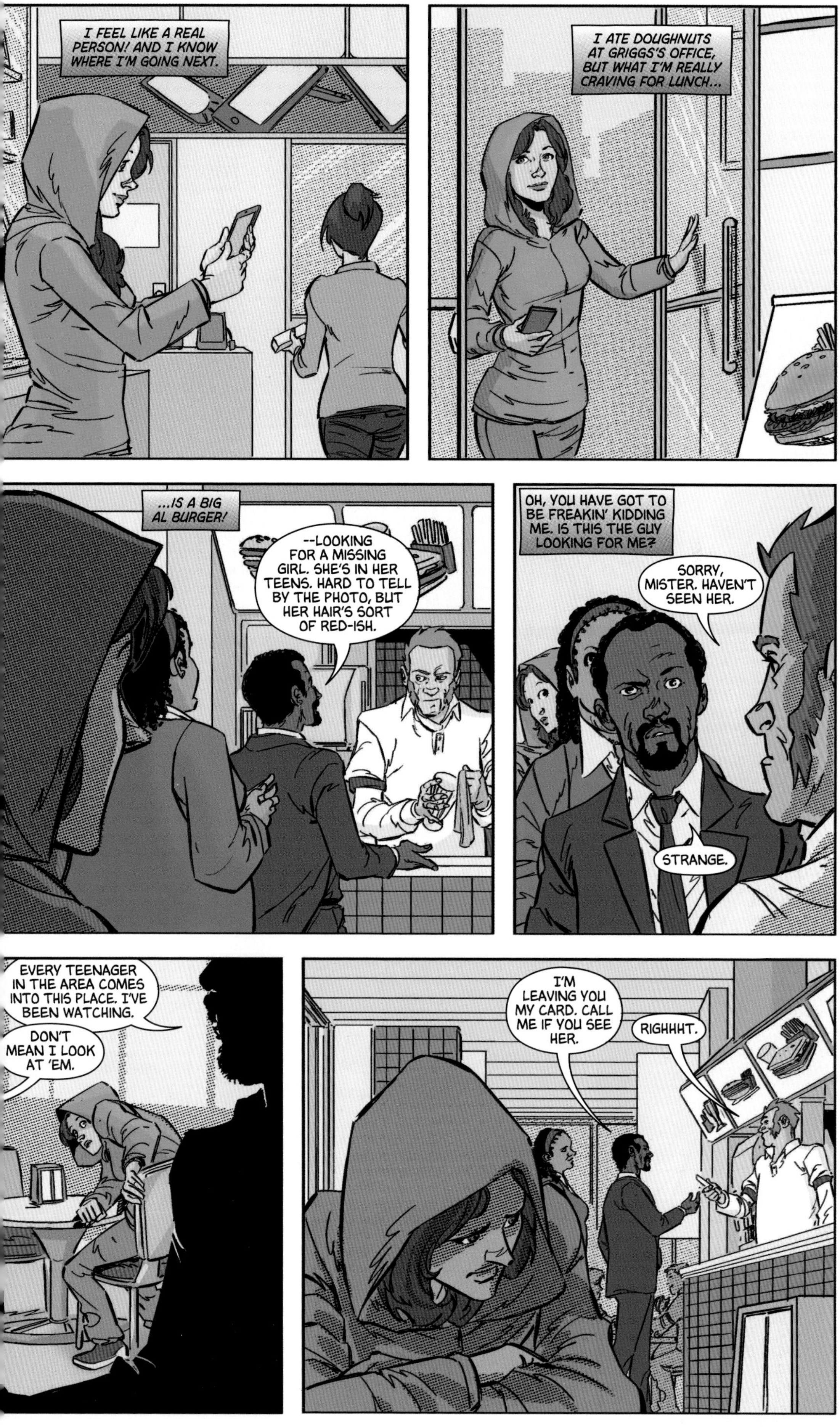

I FEEL LIKE A REAL PERSON! AND I KNOW WHERE I'M GOING NEXT.
I ATE DOUGHNUTS AT GRIGGS'S OFFICE, BUT WHAT I'M REALLY CRAVING FOR LUNCH...
...IS A BIG AL BURGER!
--LOOKING FOR A MISSING GIRL. SHE'S IN HER TEENS. HARD TO TELL BY THE PHOTO, BUT HER HAIR'S SORT OF RED-ISH.
OH, YOU HAVE GOT TO BE FREAKIN' KIDDING ME. IS THIS THE GUY LOOKING FOR ME?
SORRY, MISTER. HAVEN'T SEEN HER.
STRANGE.
EVERY TEENAGER IN THE AREA COMES INTO THIS PLACE. I'VE BEEN WATCHING.
DON'T MEAN I LOOK AT 'EM.
I'M LEAVING YOU MY CARD. CALL ME IF YOU SEE HER.
RIGHHHT.

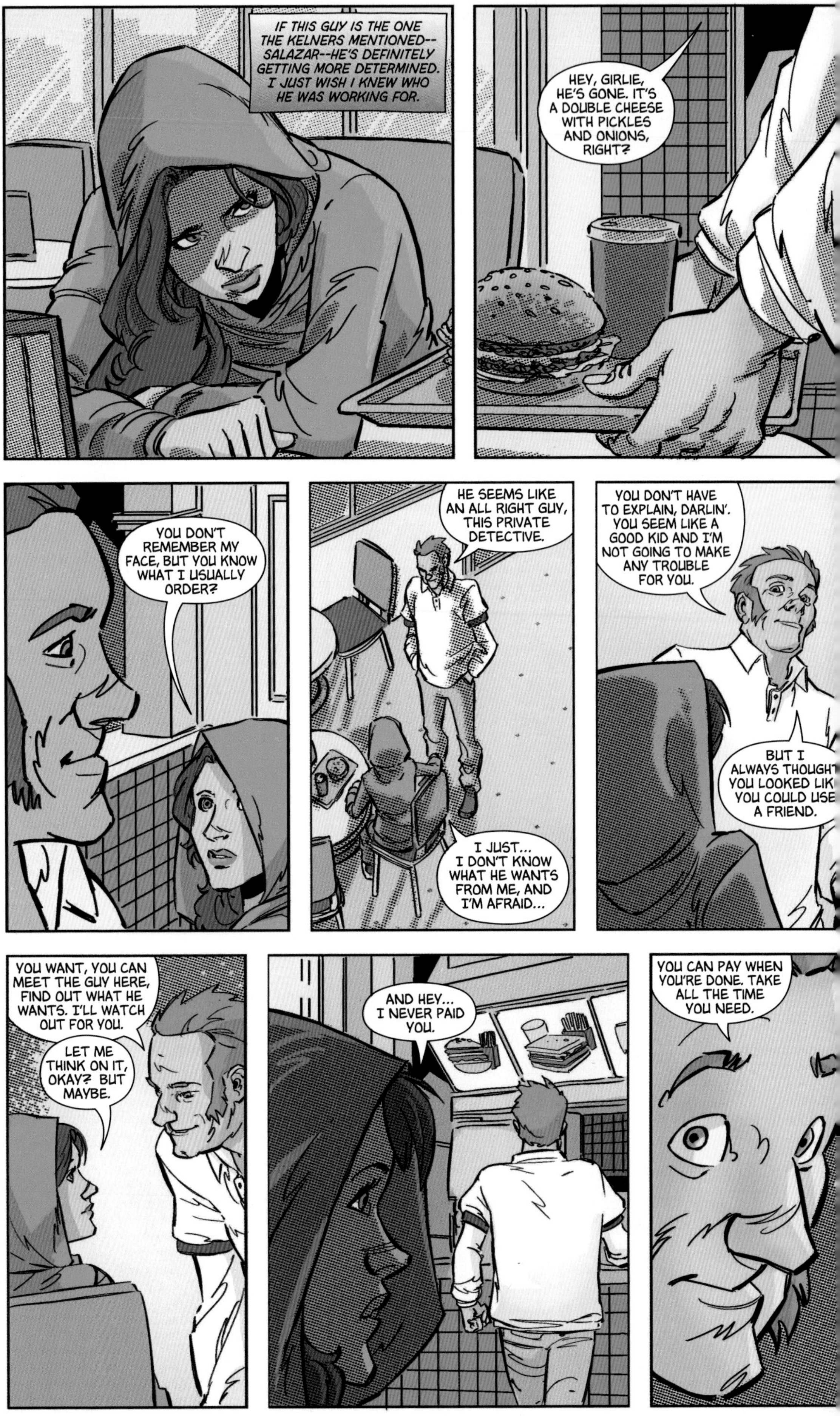

IF THIS GUY IS THE ONE THE KELNERS MENTIONED--SALAZAR--HE'S DEFINITELY GETTING MORE DETERMINED. I JUST WISH I KNEW WHO HE WAS WORKING FOR.
HEY, GIRLIE, HE'S GONE. IT'S A DOUBLE CHEESE WITH PICKLES AND ONIONS, RIGHT?
YOU DON'T REMEMBER MY FACE, BUT YOU KNOW WHAT I USUALLY ORDER?
HE SEEMS LIKE AN ALL RIGHT GUY, THIS PRIVATE DETECTIVE.
I JUST... I DON'T KNOW WHAT HE WANTS FROM ME, AND I'M AFRAID...
YOU DON'T HAVE TO EXPLAIN, DARLIN'. YOU SEEM LIKE A GOOD KID AND I'M NOT GOING TO MAKE ANY TROUBLE FOR YOU.
BUT I ALWAYS THOUGHT YOU LOOKED LIK YOU COULD USE A FRIEND.
YOU WANT, YOU CAN MEET THE GUY HERE, FIND OUT WHAT HE WANTS. I'LL WATCH OUT FOR YOU.
LET ME THINK ON IT, OKAY? BUT MAYBE.
AND HEY... I NEVER PAID YOU.
YOU CAN PAY WHEN YOU'RE DONE. TAKE ALL THE TIME YOU NEED.

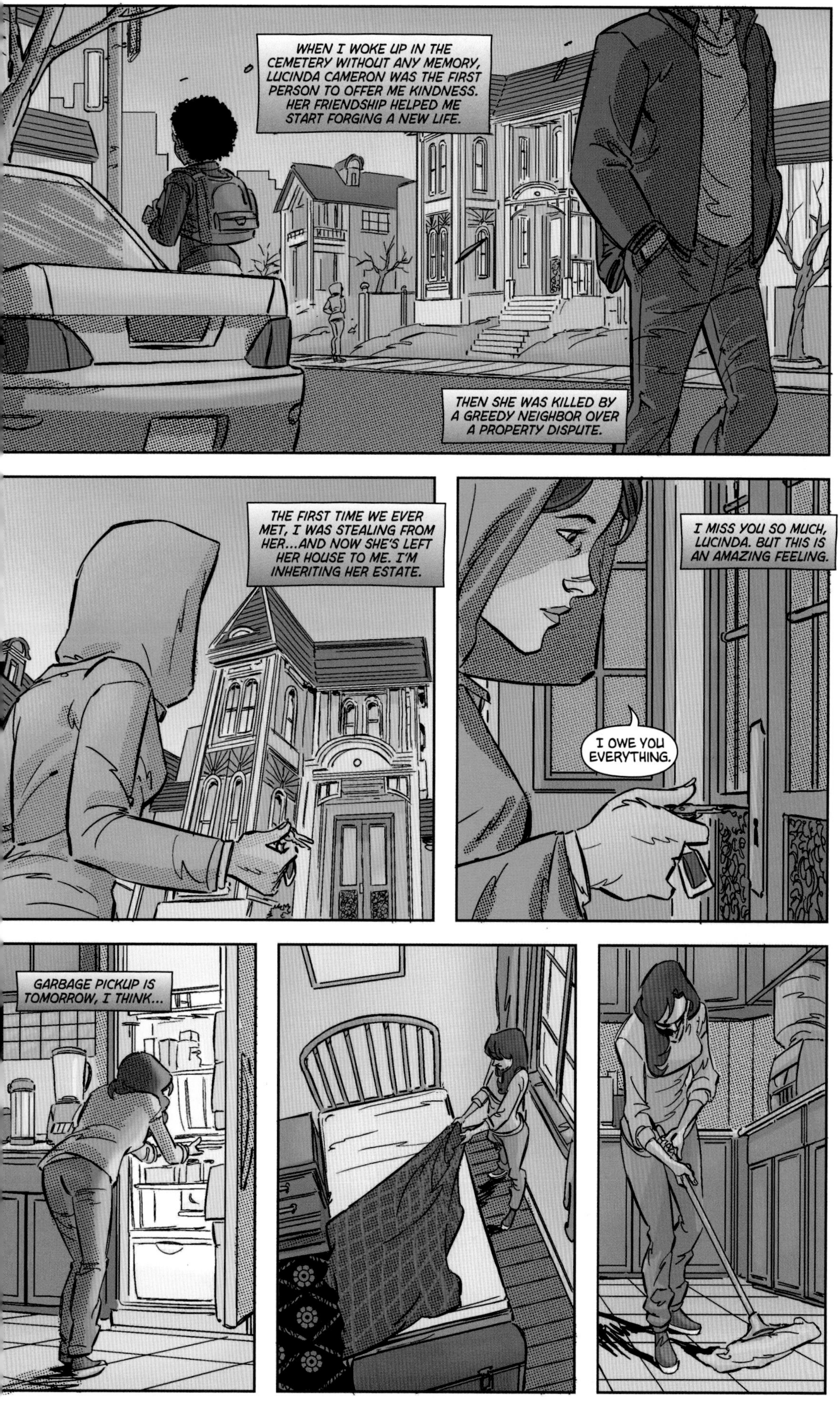
WHEN I WOKE UP IN THE CEMETERY WITHOUT ANY MEMORY, LUCINDA CAMERON WAS THE FIRST PERSON TO OFFER ME KINDNESS. HER FRIENDSHIP HELPED ME START FORGING A NEW LIFE.
THEN SHE WAS KILLED BY A GREEDY NEIGHBOR OVER A PROPERTY DISPUTE.
THE FIRST TIME WE EVER MET, I WAS STEALING FROM HER...AND NOW SHE'S LEFT HER HOUSE TO ME. I'M INHERITING HER ESTATE.
I MISS YOU SO MUCH, LUCINDA. BUT THIS IS AN AMAZING FEELING.
I OWE YOU EVERYTHING.
GARBAGE PICKUP IS TOMORROW, I THINK...

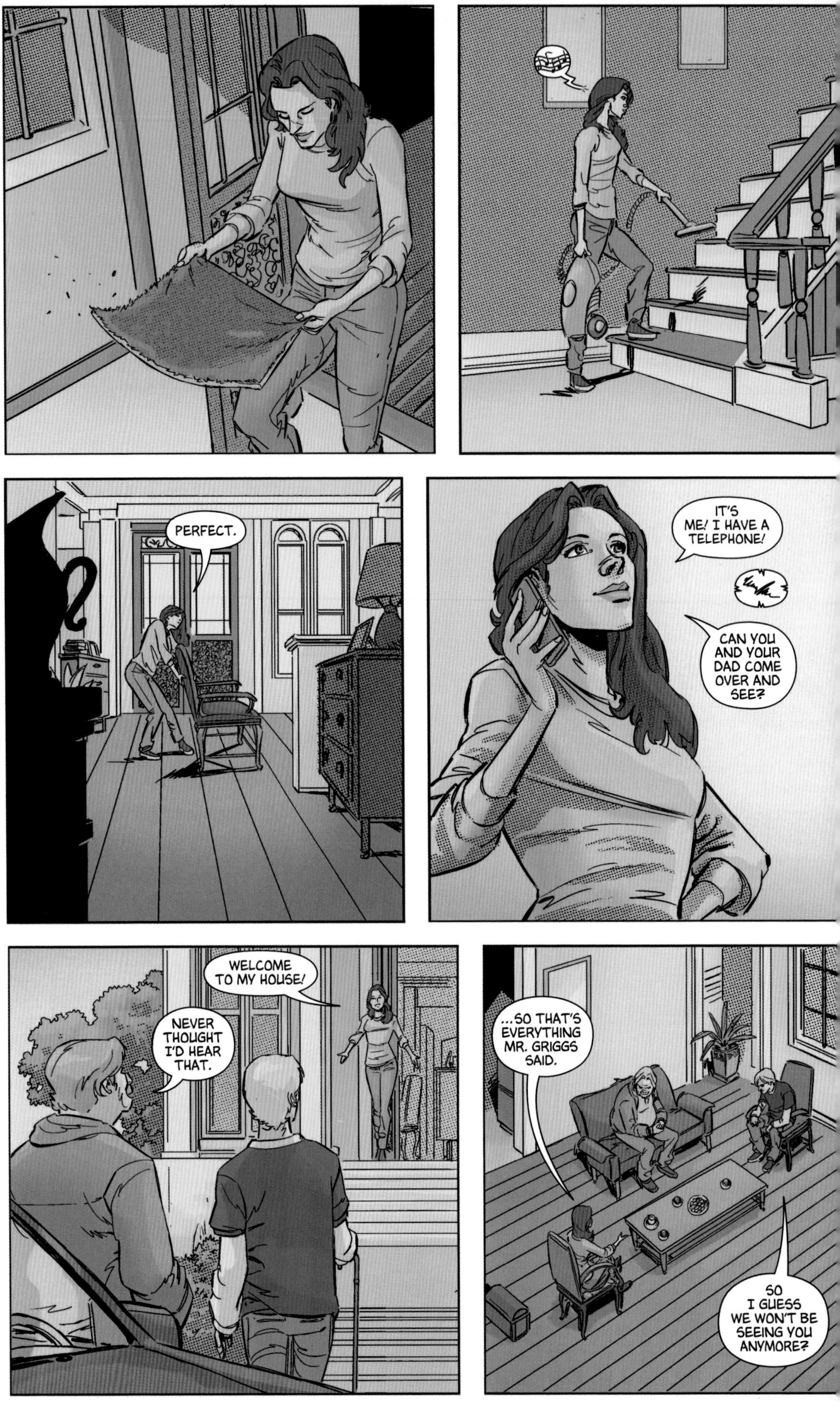
PERFECT.
IT'S ME! I HAVE A TELEPHONE!
CAN YOU AND YOUR DAD COME OVER AND SEE?
WELCOME TO MY HOUSE!
NEVER THOUGHT I'D HEAR THAT.
...SO THAT'S EVERYTHING MR. GRIGGS SAID.
SO I GUESS WE WON'T BE SEEING YOU ANYMORE?

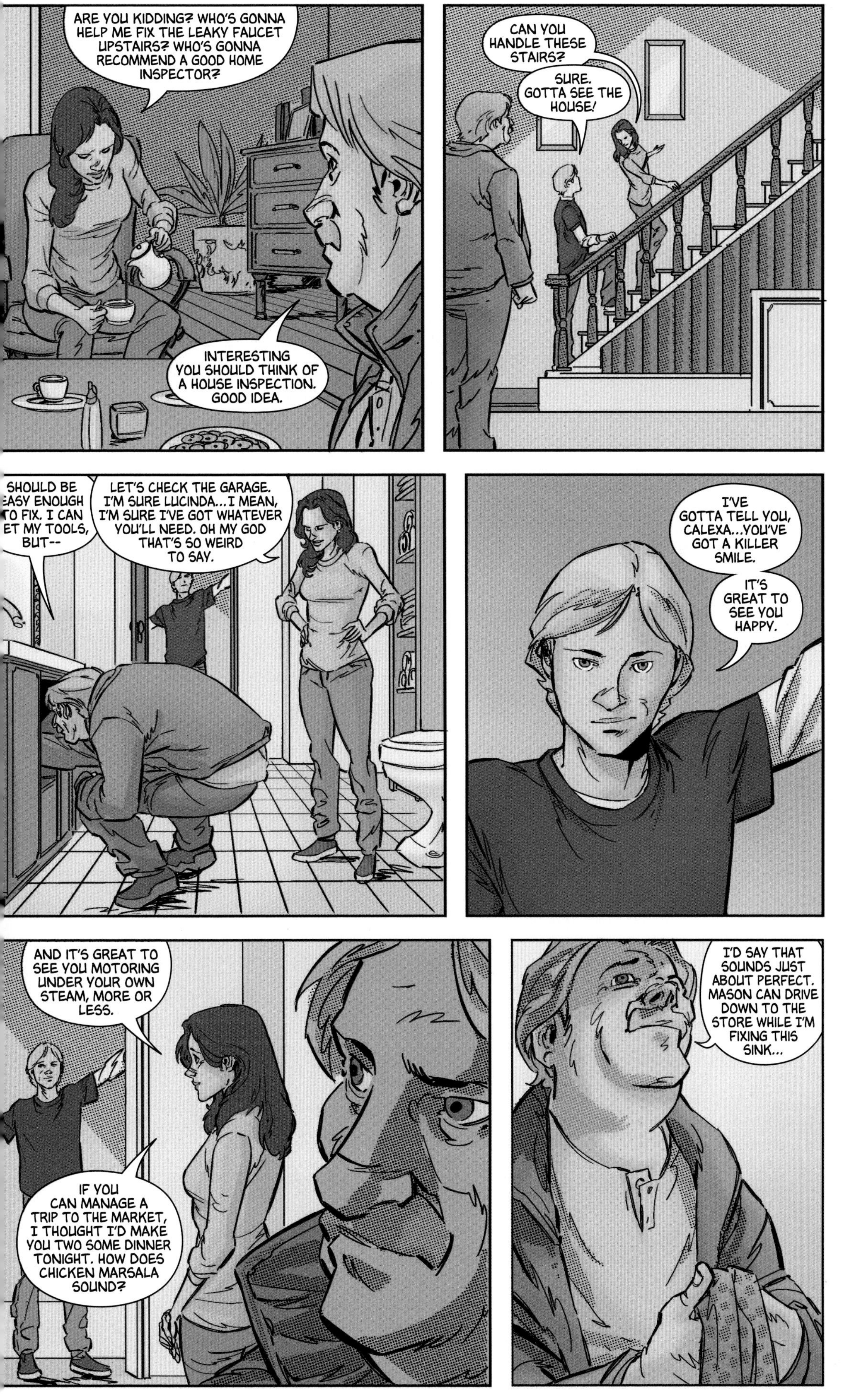
ARE YOU KIDDING? WHO'S GONNA HELP ME FIX THE LEAKY FAUCET UPSTAIRS? WHO'S GONNA RECOMMEND A GOOD HOME INSPECTOR?
INTERESTING YOU SHOULD THINK OF A HOUSE INSPECTION. GOOD IDEA.
CAN YOU HANDLE THESE STAIRS?
SURE. GOTTA SEE THE HOUSE!
SHOULD BE EASY ENOUGH TO FIX. I CAN GET MY TOOLS, BUT--
LET'S CHECK THE GARAGE. I'M SURE LUCINDA... I MEAN, I'M SURE I'VE GOT WHATEVER YOU'LL NEED. OH MY GOD THAT'S SO WEIRD TO SAY.
I'VE GOTTA TELL YOU, CALEXA...YOU'VE GOT A KILLER SMILE.
IT'S GREAT TO SEE YOU HAPPY.
AND IT'S GREAT TO SEE YOU MOTORING UNDER YOUR OWN STEAM, MORE OR LESS.
IF YOU CAN MANAGE A TRIP TO THE MARKET, I THOUGHT I'D MAKE YOU TWO SOME DINNER TONIGHT. HOW DOES CHICKEN MARSALA SOUND?
I'D SAY THAT SOUNDS JUST ABOUT PERFECT. MASON CAN DRIVE DOWN TO THE STORE WHILE I'M FIXING THIS SINK...

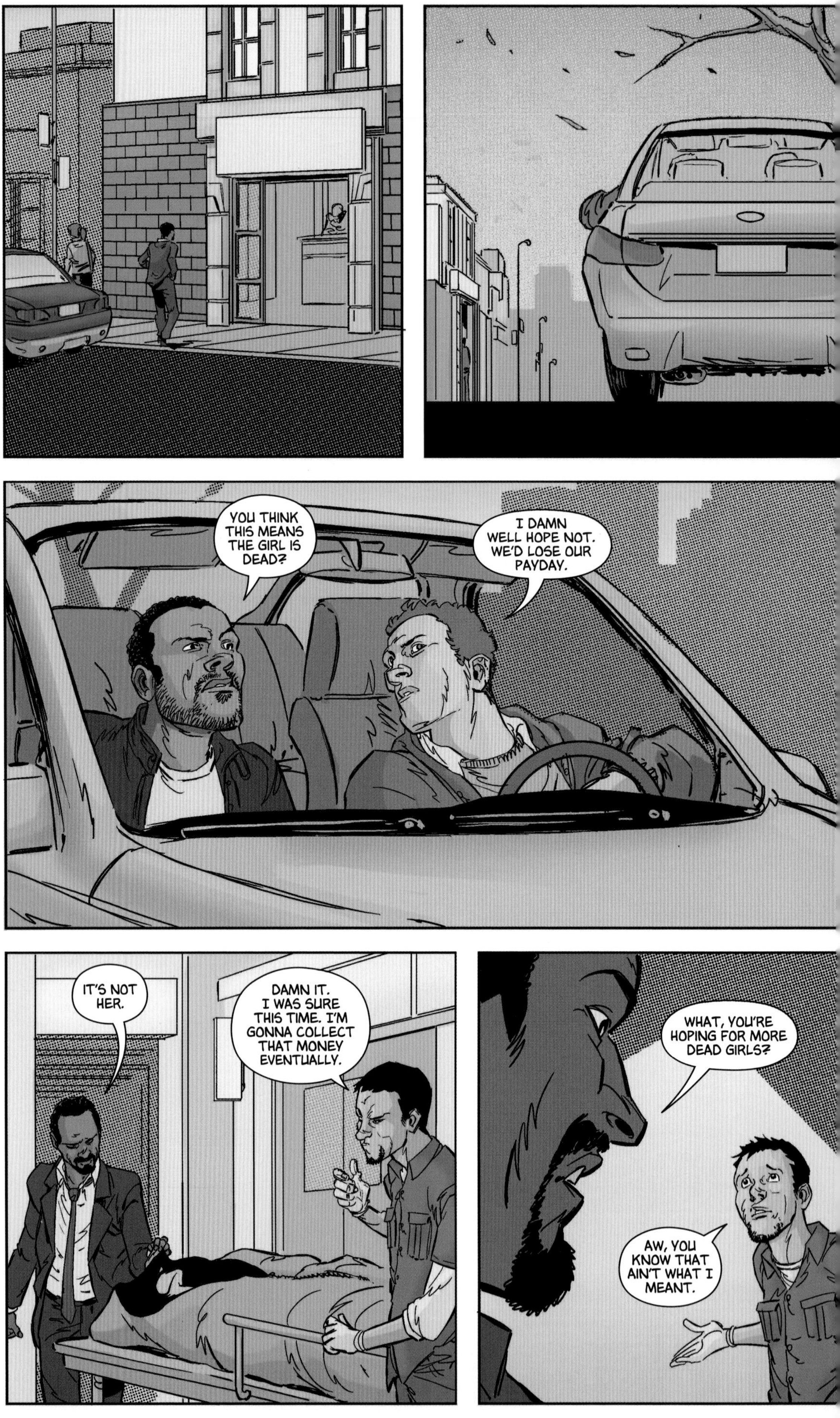
YOU THINK THIS MEANS THE GIRL IS DEAD?
I DAMN WELL HOPE NOT. WE'D LOSE OUR PAYDAY.
IT'S NOT HER.
DAMN IT. I WAS SURE THIS TIME. I'M GONNA COLLECT THAT MONEY EVENTUALLY.
WHAT, YOU'RE HOPING FOR MORE DEAD GIRLS?
AW, YOU KNOW THAT AIN'T WHAT I MEANT.

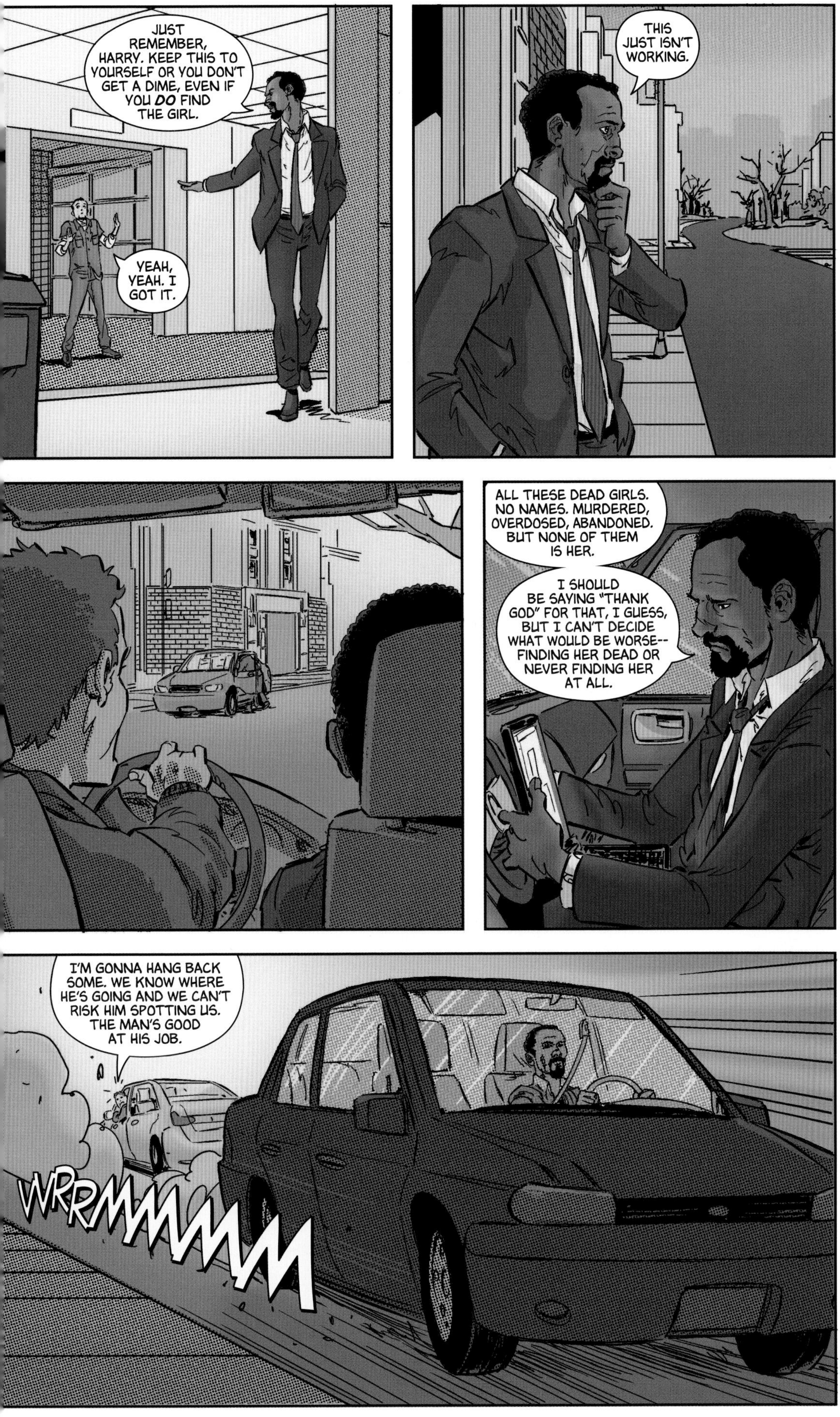
JUST REMEMBER, HARRY. KEEP THIS TO YOURSELF OR YOU DON'T GET A DIME, EVEN IF YOU *DO* FIND THE GIRL.
YEAH, YEAH. I GOT IT.
THIS JUST ISN'T WORKING.
ALL THESE DEAD GIRLS. NO NAMES. MURDERED, OVERDOSED, ABANDONED. BUT NONE OF THEM IS HER.
I SHOULD BE SAYING "THANK GOD" FOR THAT, I GUESS, BUT I CAN'T DECIDE WHAT WOULD BE WORSE--FINDING HER DEAD OR NEVER FINDING HER AT ALL.
I'M GONNA HANG BACK SOME. WE KNOW WHERE HE'S GOING AND WE CAN'T RISK HIM SPOTTING US. THE MAN'S GOOD AT HIS JOB.
WRRMMMMMM

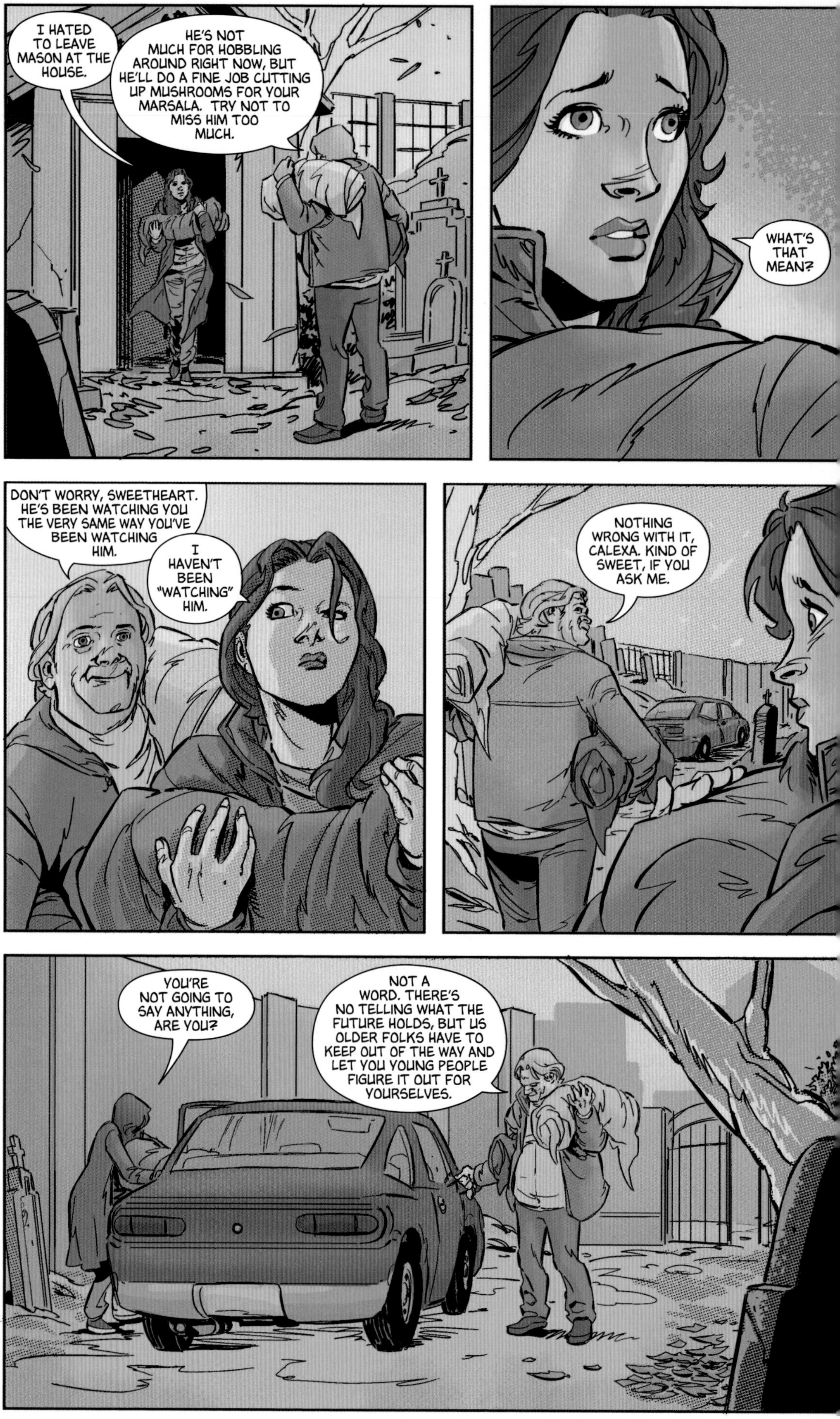
I HATED TO LEAVE MASON AT THE HOUSE.
HE'S NOT MUCH FOR HOBBLING AROUND RIGHT NOW, BUT HE'LL DO A FINE JOB CUTTING UP MUSHROOMS FOR YOUR MARSALA. TRY NOT TO MISS HIM TOO MUCH.
WHAT'S THAT MEAN?
DON'T WORRY, SWEETHEART. HE'S BEEN WATCHING YOU THE VERY SAME WAY YOU'VE BEEN WATCHING HIM.
I HAVEN'T BEEN "WATCHING" HIM.
NOTHING WRONG WITH IT, CALEXA. KIND OF SWEET, IF YOU ASK ME.
YOU'RE NOT GOING TO SAY ANYTHING, ARE YOU?
NOT A WORD. THERE'S NO TELLING WHAT THE FUTURE HOLDS, BUT US OLDER FOLKS HAVE TO KEEP OUT OF THE WAY AND LET YOU YOUNG PEOPLE FIGURE IT OUT FOR YOURSELVES.

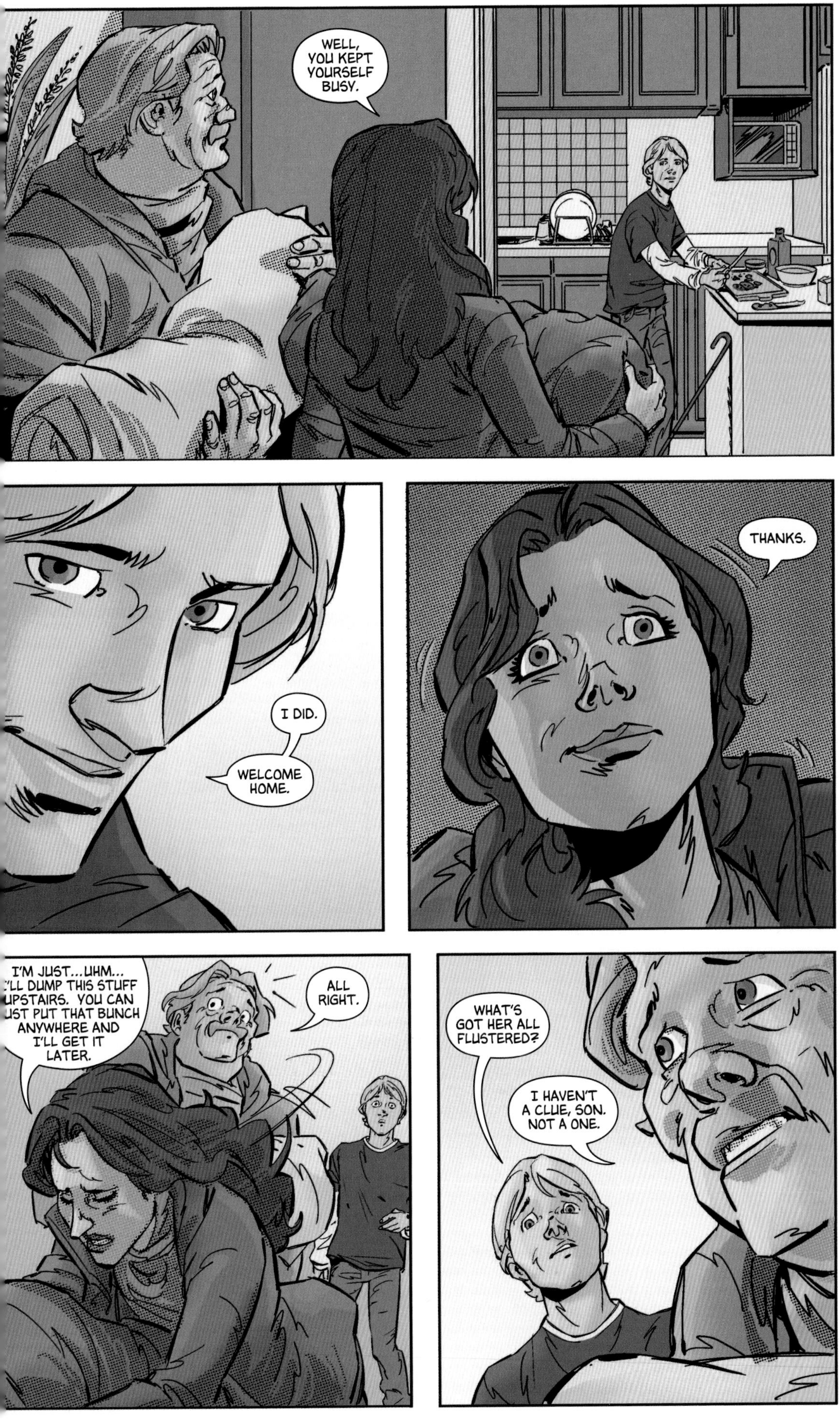
WELL, YOU KEPT YOURSELF BUSY.
I DID.
WELCOME HOME.
THANKS.
I'M JUST...UHM... I'LL DUMP THIS STUFF UPSTAIRS. YOU CAN JUST PUT THAT BUNCH ANYWHERE AND I'LL GET IT LATER.
ALL RIGHT.
WHAT'S GOT HER ALL FLUSTERED?
I HAVEN'T A CLUE, SON. NOT A ONE.

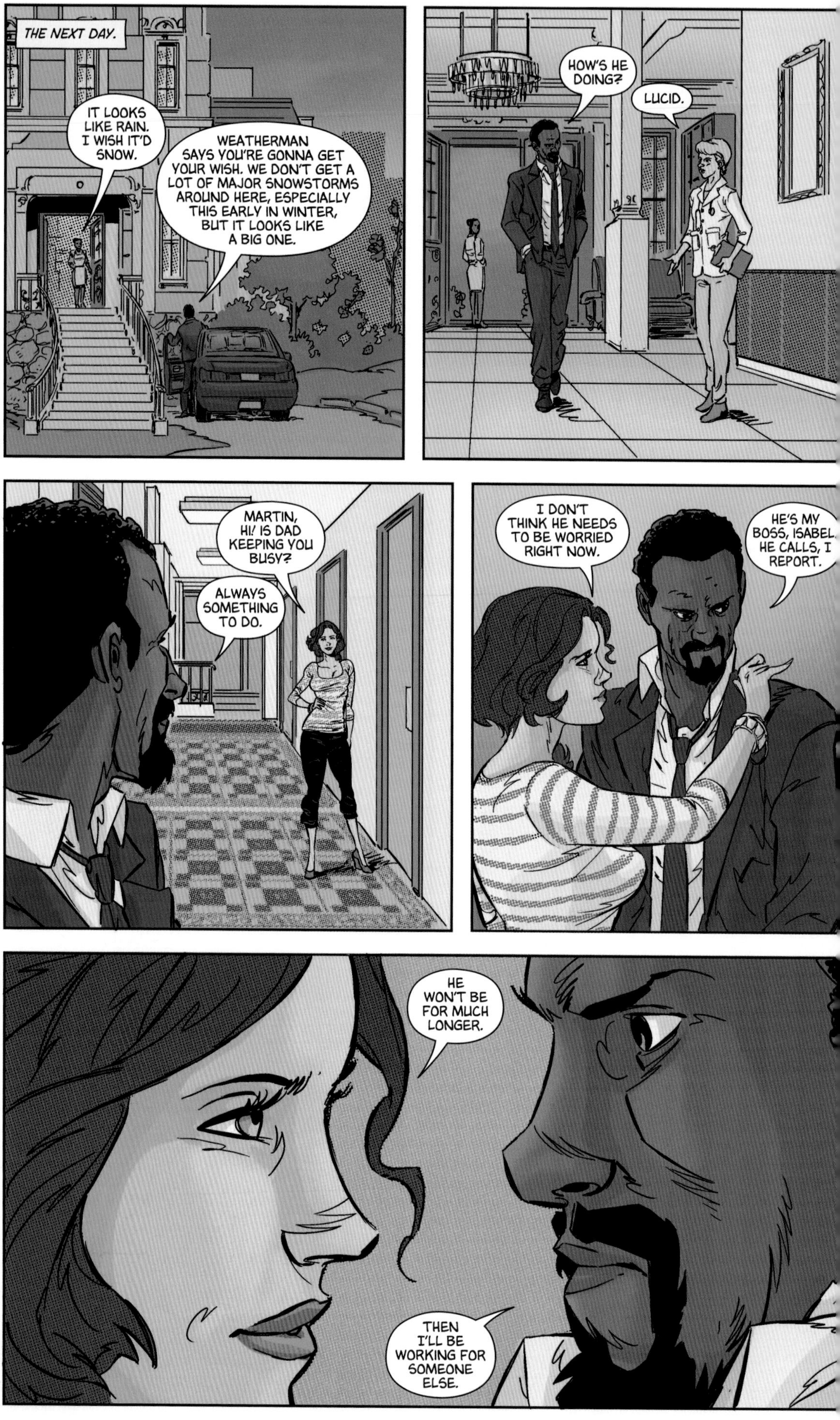
THE NEXT DAY.
IT LOOKS LIKE RAIN. I WISH IT'D SNOW.
WEATHERMAN SAYS YOU'RE GONNA GET YOUR WISH. WE DON'T GET A LOT OF MAJOR SNOWSTORMS AROUND HERE, ESPECIALLY THIS EARLY IN WINTER, BUT IT LOOKS LIKE A BIG ONE.
HOW'S HE DOING?
LUCID.
MARTIN, HI! IS DAD KEEPING YOU BUSY?
ALWAYS SOMETHING TO DO.
I DON'T THINK HE NEEDS TO BE WORRIED RIGHT NOW.
HE'S MY BOSS, ISABEL. HE CALLS, I REPORT.
HE WON'T BE FOR MUCH LONGER.
THEN I'LL BE WORKING FOR SOMEONE ELSE.

THAT SOMEONE'S GONNA BE ME.

HE'S WAITING, MR. SALAZAR.

MR. DABNEY? HOW ARE YOU DOING?

DYING, AS YOU CAN SEE. WHAT NEWS?

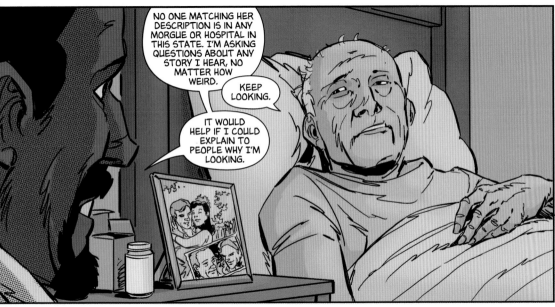

NO ONE MATCHING HER DESCRIPTION IS IN ANY MORGUE OR HOSPITAL IN THIS STATE. I'M ASKING QUESTIONS ABOUT ANY STORY I HEAR, NO MATTER HOW WEIRD.

KEEP LOOKING.

IT WOULD HELP IF I COULD EXPLAIN TO PEOPLE WHY I'M LOOKING.

NO! YOU KNOW THIS, MARTIN! NO ONE CAN KNOW SHE'S MISSING. I WON'T HAVE THIS IN THE PRESS, WHERE THE WORLD CAN SEE WHAT'S BECOME OF ME!

MR. DABNEY... WHY NOT INVOLVE THE POLICE? SO MANY MORE EYES LOOKING! THEY COULD WORK IT QUIETLY--

I DON'T TRUST ANYONE NOT ON MY PAYROLL.

SO YOUR PRIDE IS MORE IMPORTANT THAN YOUR DAUGHTER?

WHAT IF I BRIBED A COP TO LOOK INTO IT, PAID HIM TO SHARE INFORMATION ONLY WITH US?

NO ONE MORE CROOKED THAN A COP ON THE TAKE. NO.

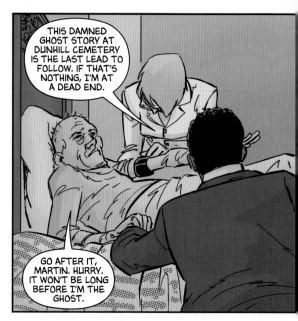

THIS DAMNED GHOST STORY AT DUNHILL CEMETERY IS THE LAST LEAD TO FOLLOW. IF THAT'S NOTHING, I'M AT A DEAD END.

GO AFTER IT, MARTIN. HURRY. IT WON'T BE LONG BEFORE I'M THE GHOST.

WAS HE CALLING FOR ME?

I THOUGHT I HEARD HIM, BUT I GUESS NOT. HE'S JUST LOSING PATIENCE WITH SALAZAR.

SALAZAR'S GOING TO BE LEAVING IN A MINUTE. FOLLOW HIM.

GRAB HER IF YOU SEE HER! DON'T SCREW THIS UP, MCKEE.

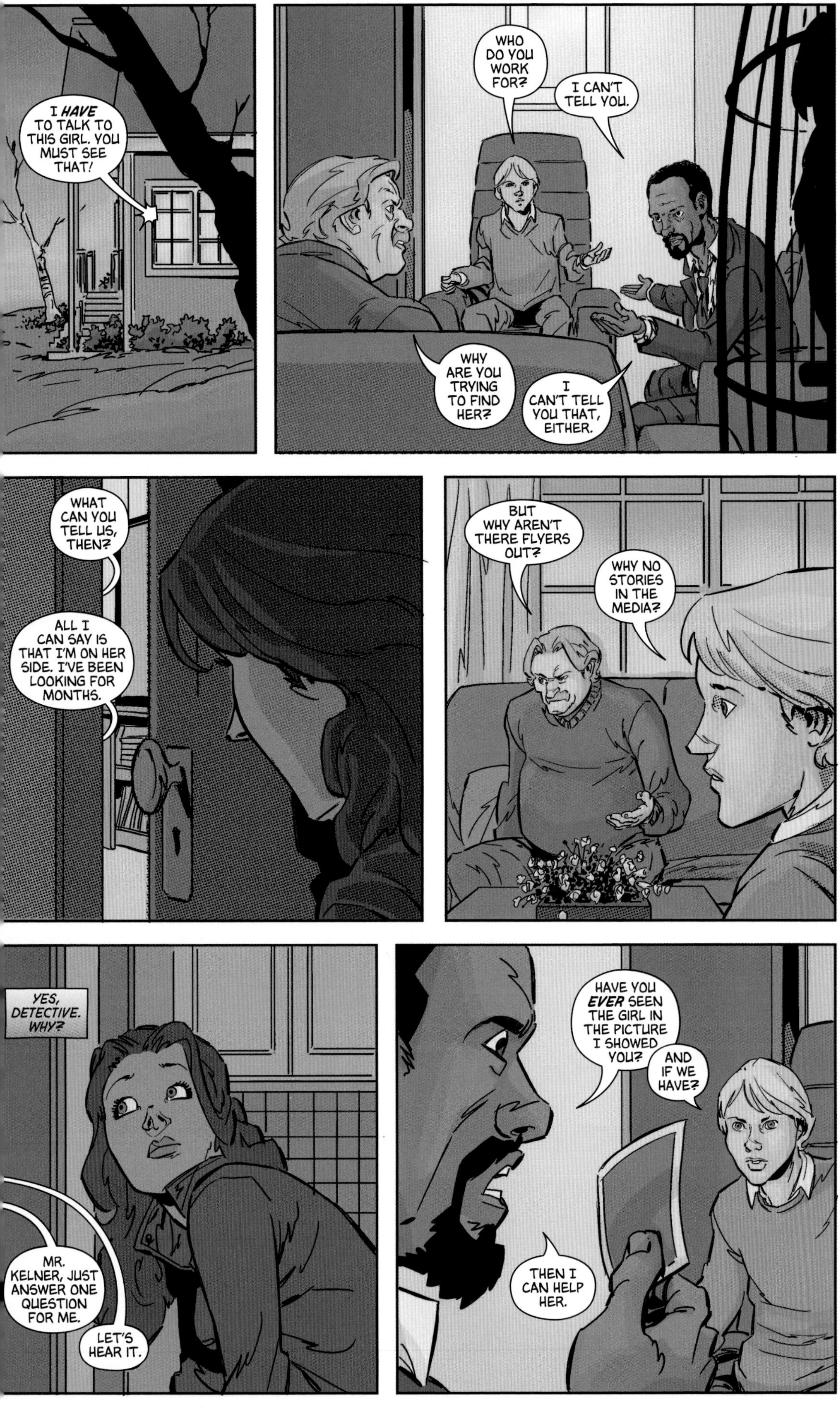
I HAVE TO TALK TO THIS GIRL. YOU MUST SEE THAT!
WHO DO YOU WORK FOR?
I CAN'T TELL YOU.
WHY ARE YOU TRYING TO FIND HER?
I CAN'T TELL YOU THAT, EITHER.
WHAT CAN YOU TELL US, THEN?
ALL I CAN SAY IS THAT I'M ON HER SIDE. I'VE BEEN LOOKING FOR MONTHS.
BUT WHY AREN'T THERE FLYERS OUT?
WHY NO STORIES IN THE MEDIA?
YES, DETECTIVE. WHY?
MR. KELNER, JUST ANSWER ONE QUESTION FOR ME.
LET'S HEAR IT.
HAVE YOU EVER SEEN THE GIRL IN THE PICTURE I SHOWED YOU?
AND IF WE HAVE?
THEN I CAN HELP HER.

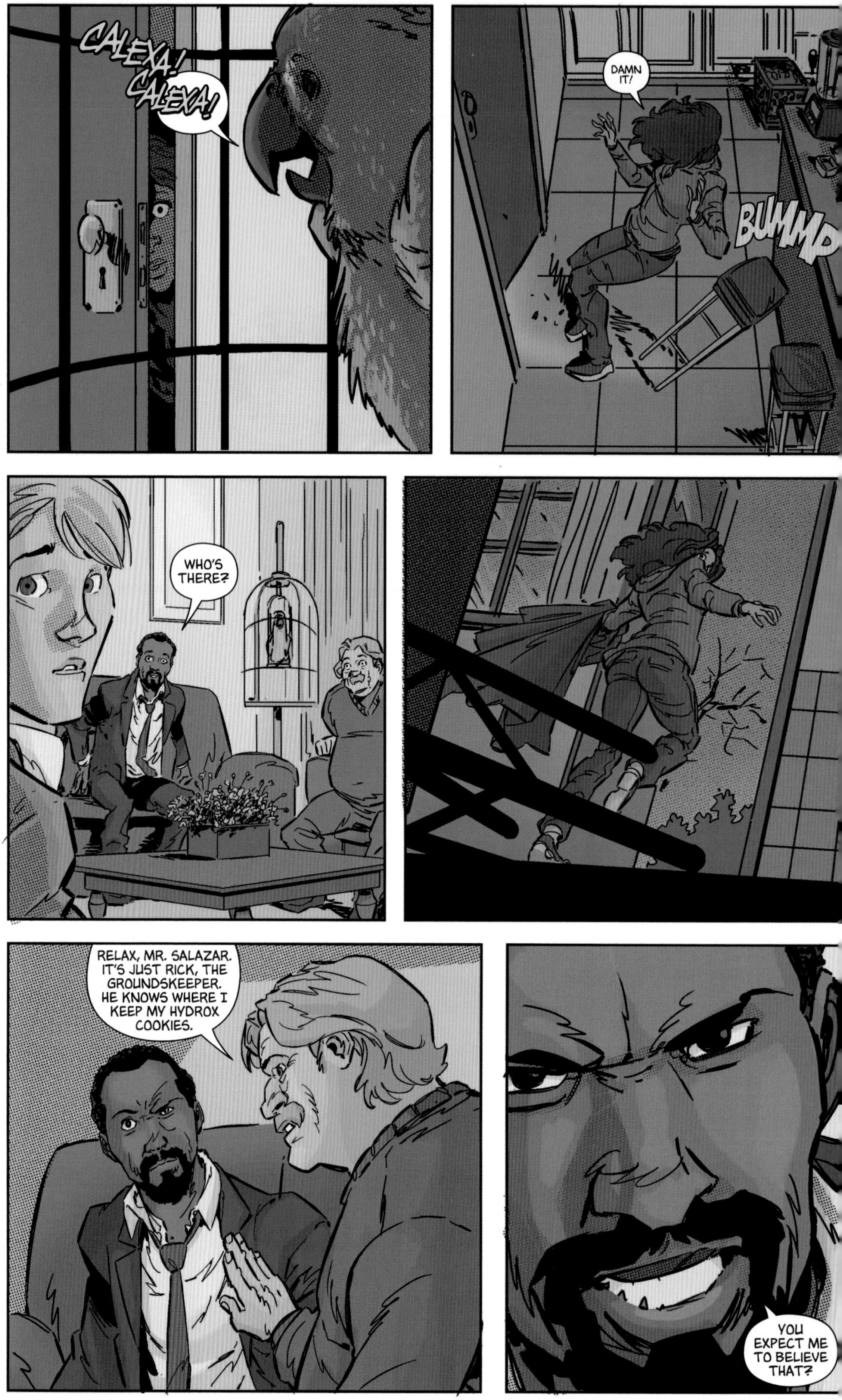
CALEXA! CALEXA!
DAMN IT!
BUMMP
WHO'S THERE?
RELAX, MR. SALAZAR. IT'S JUST RICK, THE GROUNDSKEEPER. HE KNOWS WHERE I KEEP MY HYDROX COOKIES.
YOU EXPECT ME TO BELIEVE THAT?

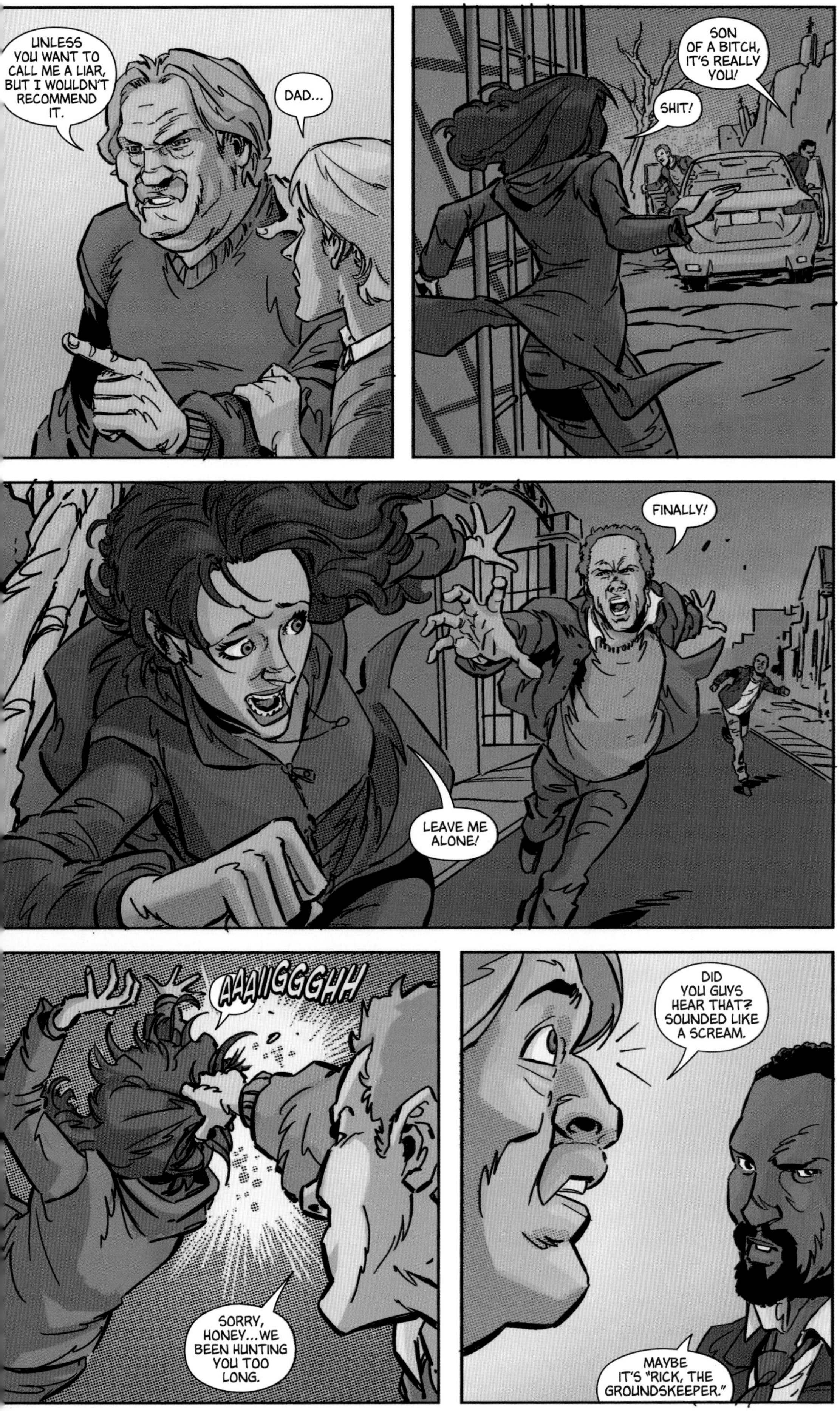
UNLESS YOU WANT TO CALL ME A LIAR, BUT I WOULDN'T RECOMMEND IT.
DAD...
SON OF A BITCH, IT'S REALLY YOU!
SHIT!
FINALLY!
LEAVE ME ALONE!
AAAIIGGGHH
SORRY, HONEY...WE BEEN HUNTING YOU TOO LONG.
DID YOU GUYS HEAR THAT? SOUNDED LIKE A SCREAM.
MAYBE IT'S "RICK, THE GROUNDSKEEPER."

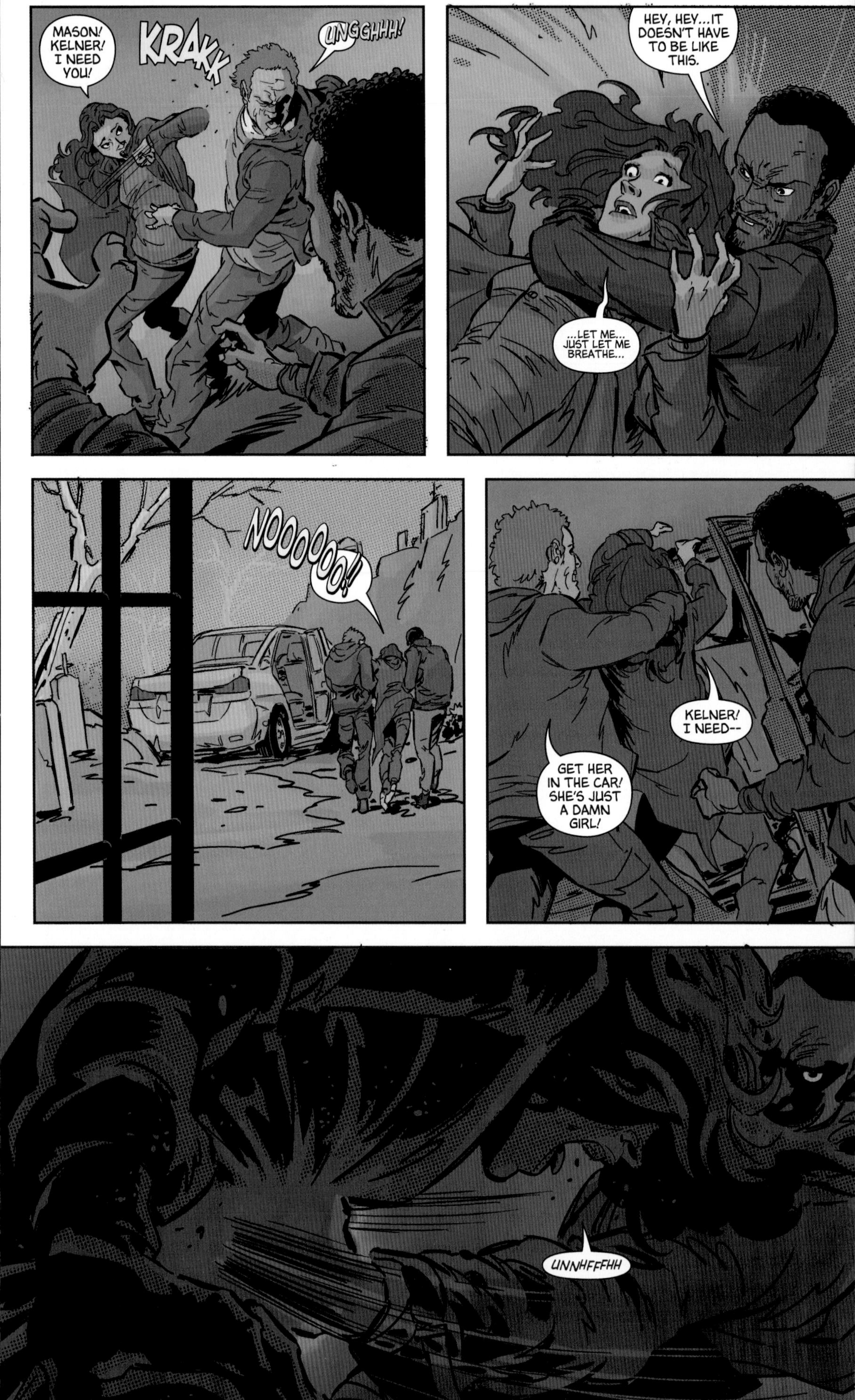
MASON! KELNER! I NEED YOU!
KRAKK
UNGGHHH!
HEY, HEY...IT DOESN'T HAVE TO BE LIKE THIS.
...LET ME... JUST LET ME BREATHE...
NOOOOOO!!
KELNER! I NEED--
GET HER IN THE CAR! SHE'S JUST A DAMN GIRL!
UNNHFFFHH

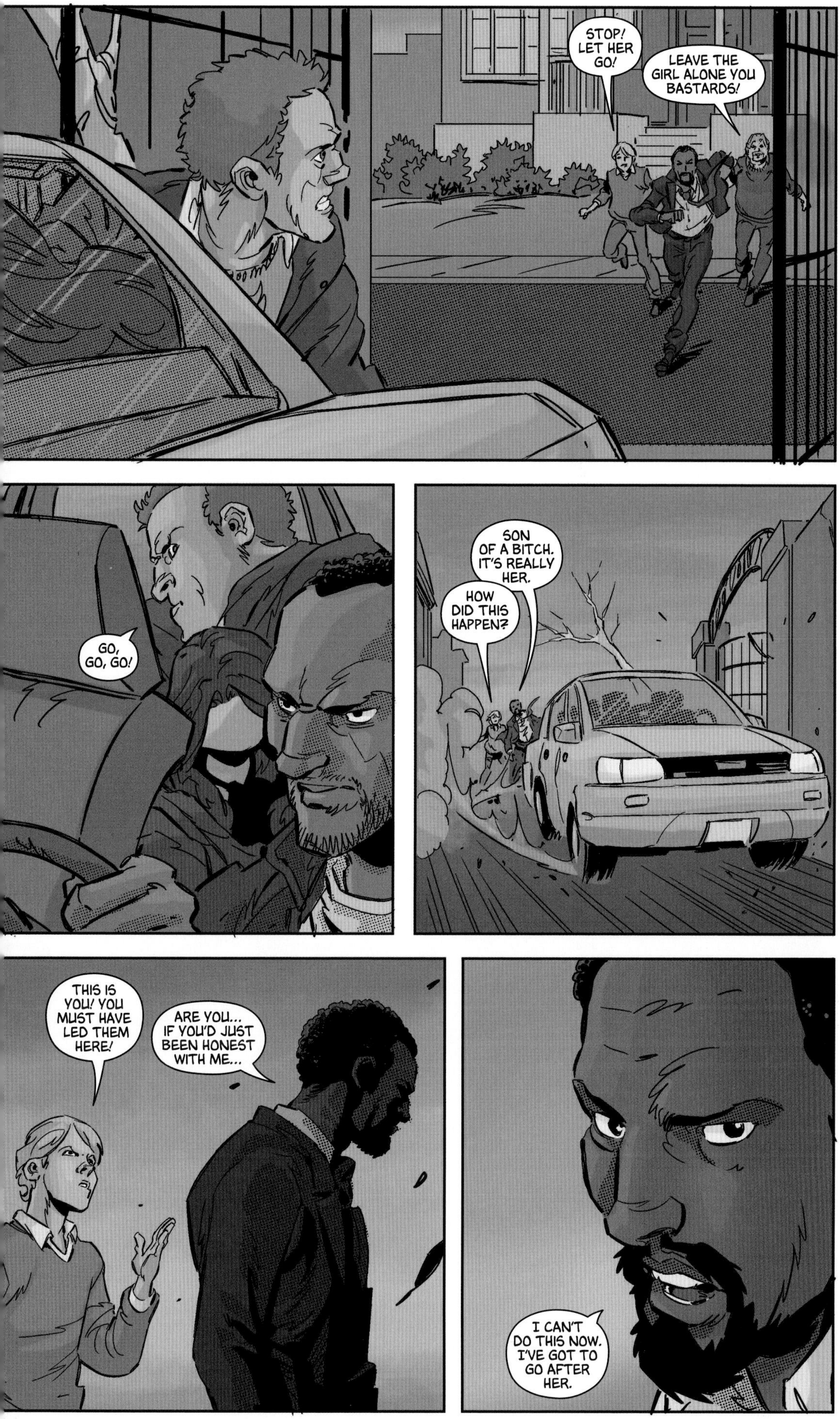
STOP! LET HER GO!
LEAVE THE GIRL ALONE YOU BASTARDS!
GO, GO, GO!
SON OF A BITCH. IT'S REALLY HER.
HOW DID THIS HAPPEN?
THIS IS YOU! YOU MUST HAVE LED THEM HERE!
ARE YOU... IF YOU'D JUST BEEN HONEST WITH ME...
I CAN'T DO THIS NOW. I'VE GOT TO GO AFTER HER.

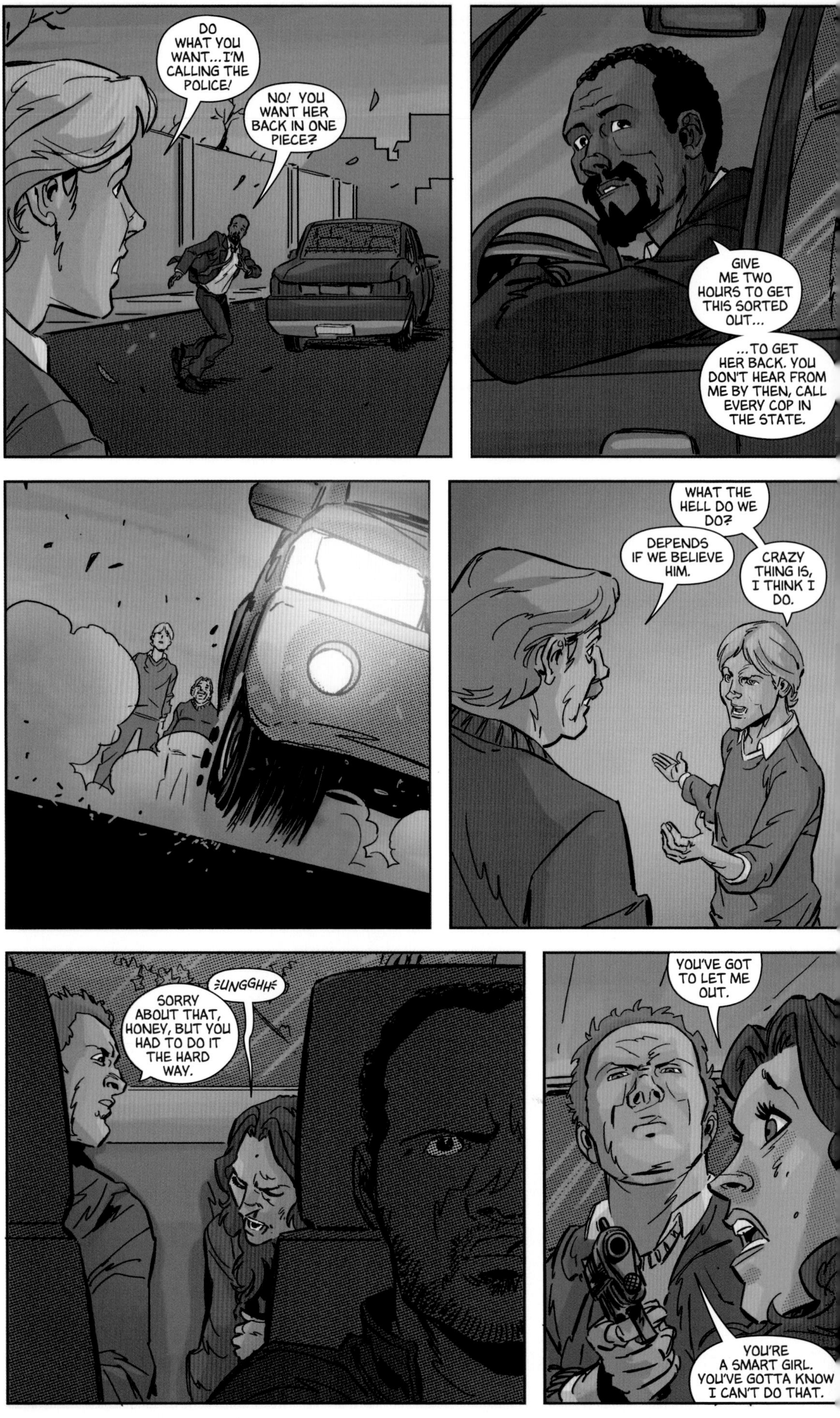
DO WHAT YOU WANT...I'M CALLING THE POLICE!
NO! YOU WANT HER BACK IN ONE PIECE?
GIVE ME TWO HOURS TO GET THIS SORTED OUT...
...TO GET HER BACK. YOU DON'T HEAR FROM ME BY THEN, CALL EVERY COP IN THE STATE.
WHAT THE HELL DO WE DO?
DEPENDS IF WE BELIEVE HIM.
CRAZY THING IS, I THINK I DO.
SORRY ABOUT THAT, HONEY, BUT YOU HAD TO DO IT THE HARD WAY.
UNGGHH
YOU'VE GOT TO LET ME OUT.
YOU'RE A SMART GIRL. YOU'VE GOTTA KNOW I CAN'T DO THAT.

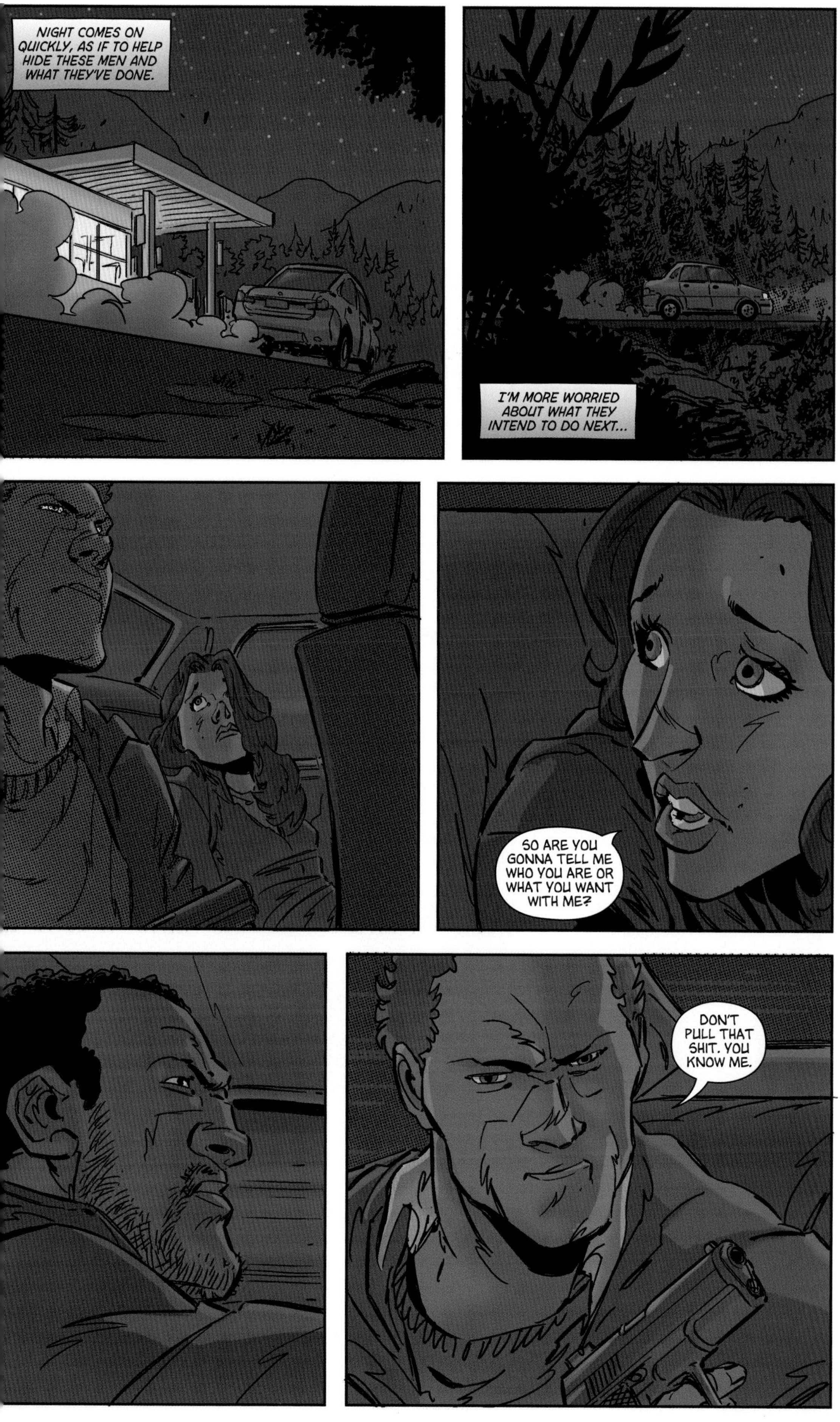
NIGHT COMES ON QUICKLY, AS IF TO HELP HIDE THESE MEN AND WHAT THEY'VE DONE.
I'M MORE WORRIED ABOUT WHAT THEY INTEND TO DO NEXT...
SO ARE YOU GONNA TELL ME WHO YOU ARE OR WHAT YOU WANT WITH ME?
DON'T PULL THAT SHIT. YOU KNOW ME.

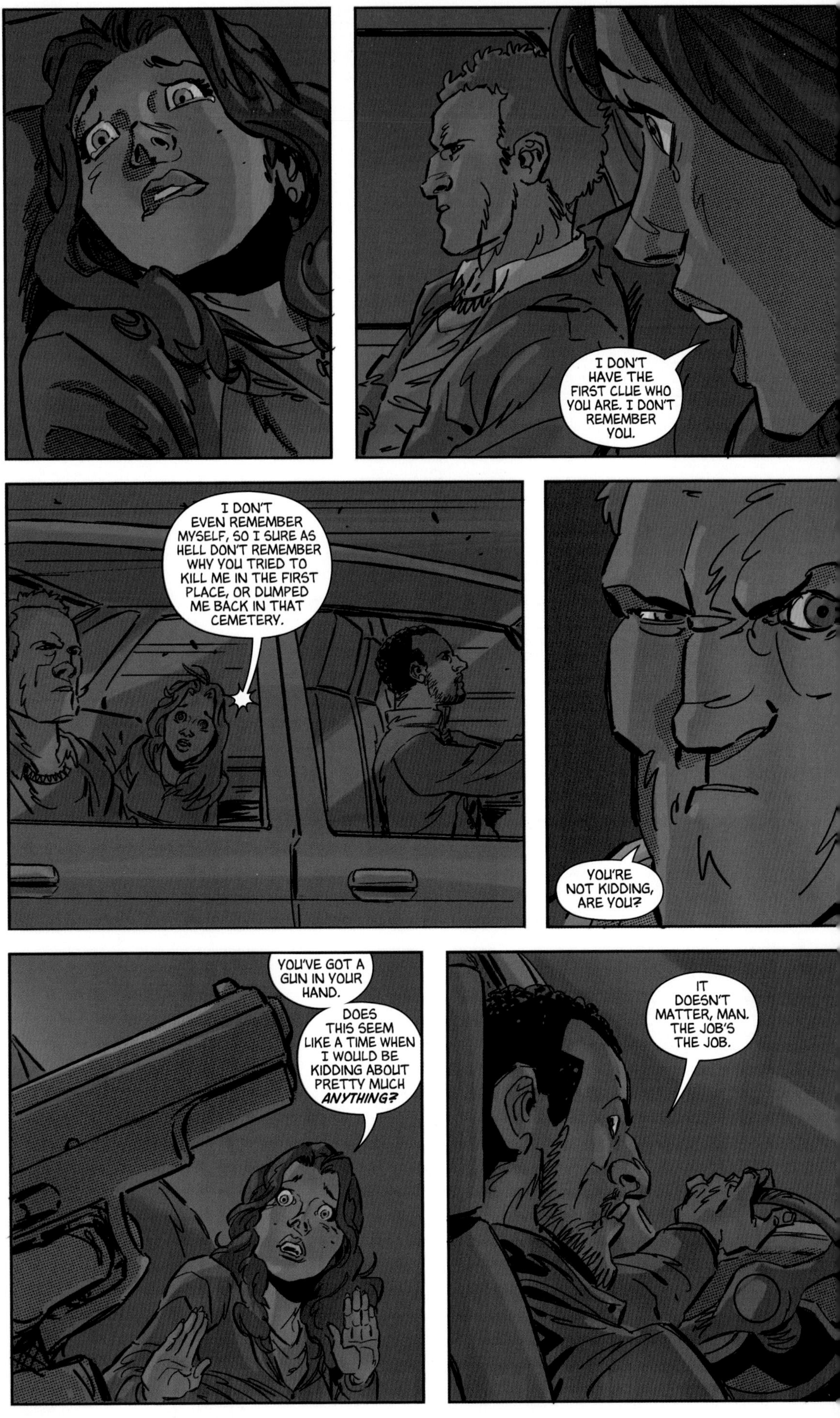
I DON'T HAVE THE FIRST CLUE WHO YOU ARE. I DON'T REMEMBER YOU.
I DON'T EVEN REMEMBER MYSELF, SO I SURE AS HELL DON'T REMEMBER WHY YOU TRIED TO KILL ME IN THE FIRST PLACE, OR DUMPED ME BACK IN THAT CEMETERY.
YOU'RE NOT KIDDING, ARE YOU?
YOU'VE GOT A GUN IN YOUR HAND.
DOES THIS SEEM LIKE A TIME WHEN I WOULD BE KIDDING ABOUT PRETTY MUCH *ANYTHING?*
IT DOESN'T MATTER, MAN. THE JOB'S THE JOB.

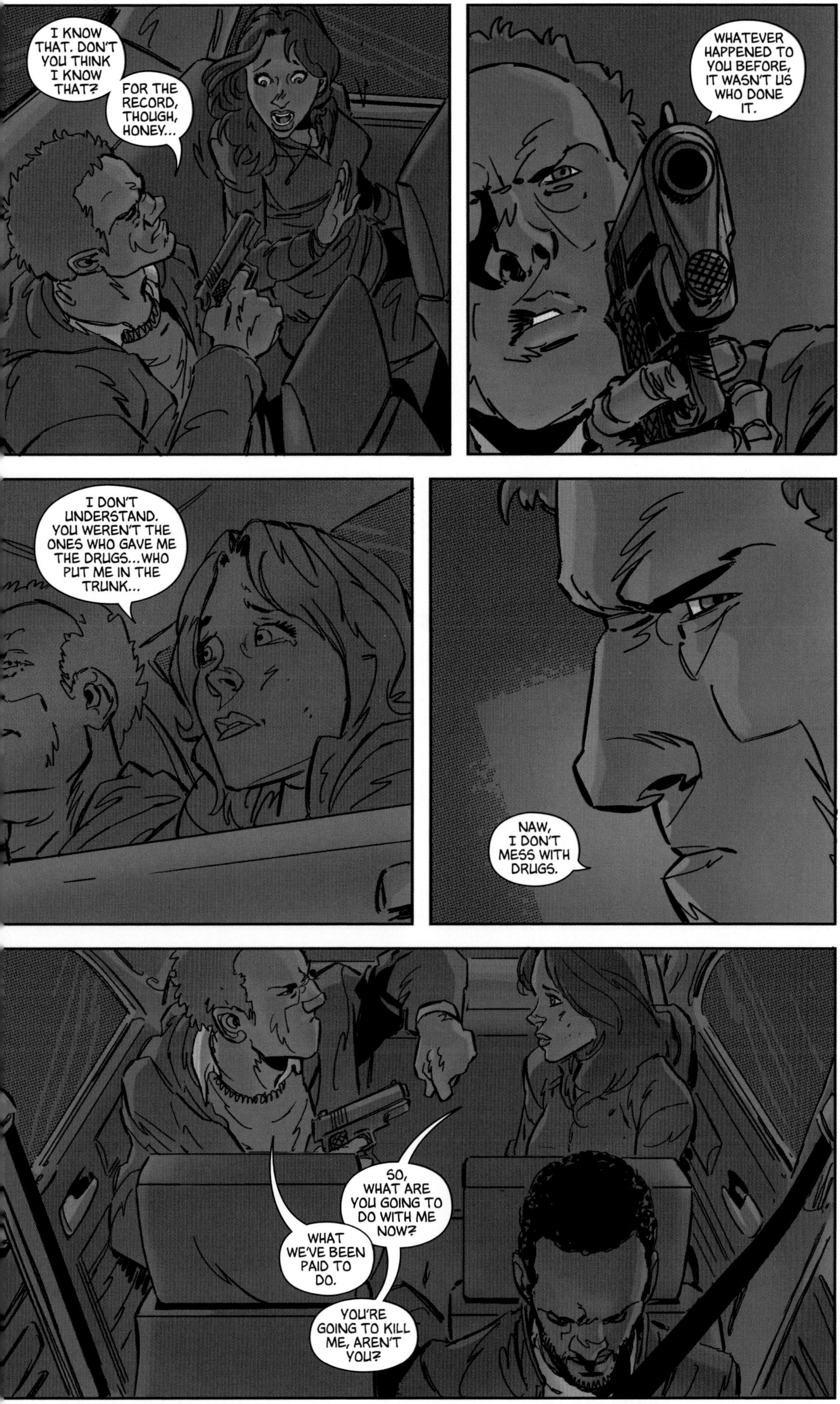
I KNOW THAT. DON'T YOU THINK I KNOW THAT?
FOR THE RECORD, THOUGH, HONEY...
WHATEVER HAPPENED TO YOU BEFORE, IT WASN'T US WHO DONE IT.
I DON'T UNDERSTAND. YOU WEREN'T THE ONES WHO GAVE ME THE DRUGS...WHO PUT ME IN THE TRUNK...
NAW, I DON'T MESS WITH DRUGS.
SO, WHAT ARE YOU GOING TO DO WITH ME NOW?
WHAT WE'VE BEEN PAID TO DO.
YOU'RE GOING TO KILL ME, AREN'T YOU?

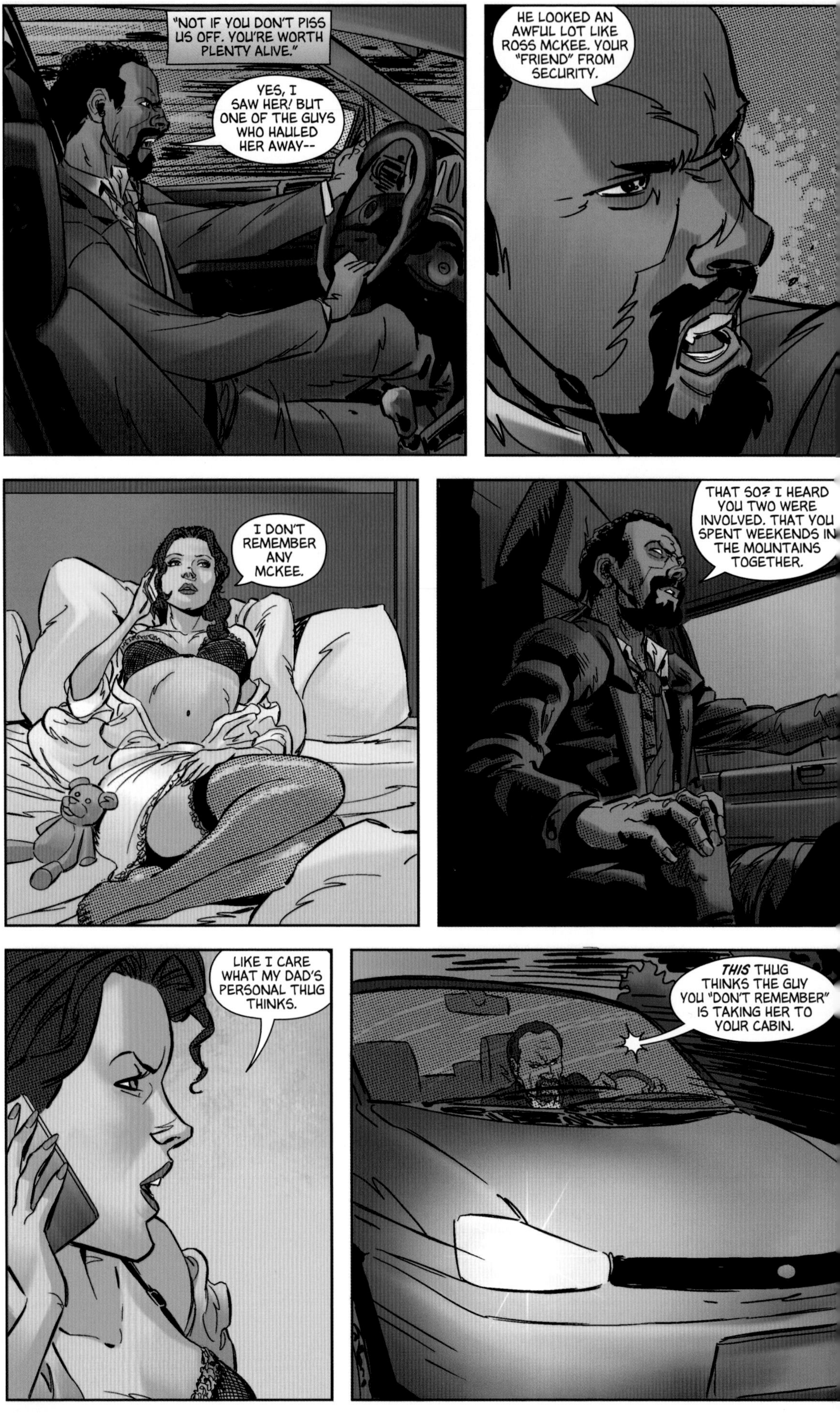
"NOT IF YOU DON'T PISS US OFF. YOU'RE WORTH PLENTY ALIVE."
YES, I SAW HER! BUT ONE OF THE GUYS WHO HAULED HER AWAY--
HE LOOKED AN AWFUL LOT LIKE ROSS MCKEE. YOUR "FRIEND" FROM SECURITY.
I DON'T REMEMBER ANY MCKEE.
THAT SO? I HEARD YOU TWO WERE INVOLVED. THAT YOU SPENT WEEKENDS IN THE MOUNTAINS TOGETHER.
LIKE I CARE WHAT MY DAD'S PERSONAL THUG THINKS.
THIS THUG THINKS THE GUY YOU "DON'T REMEMBER" IS TAKING HER TO YOUR CABIN.

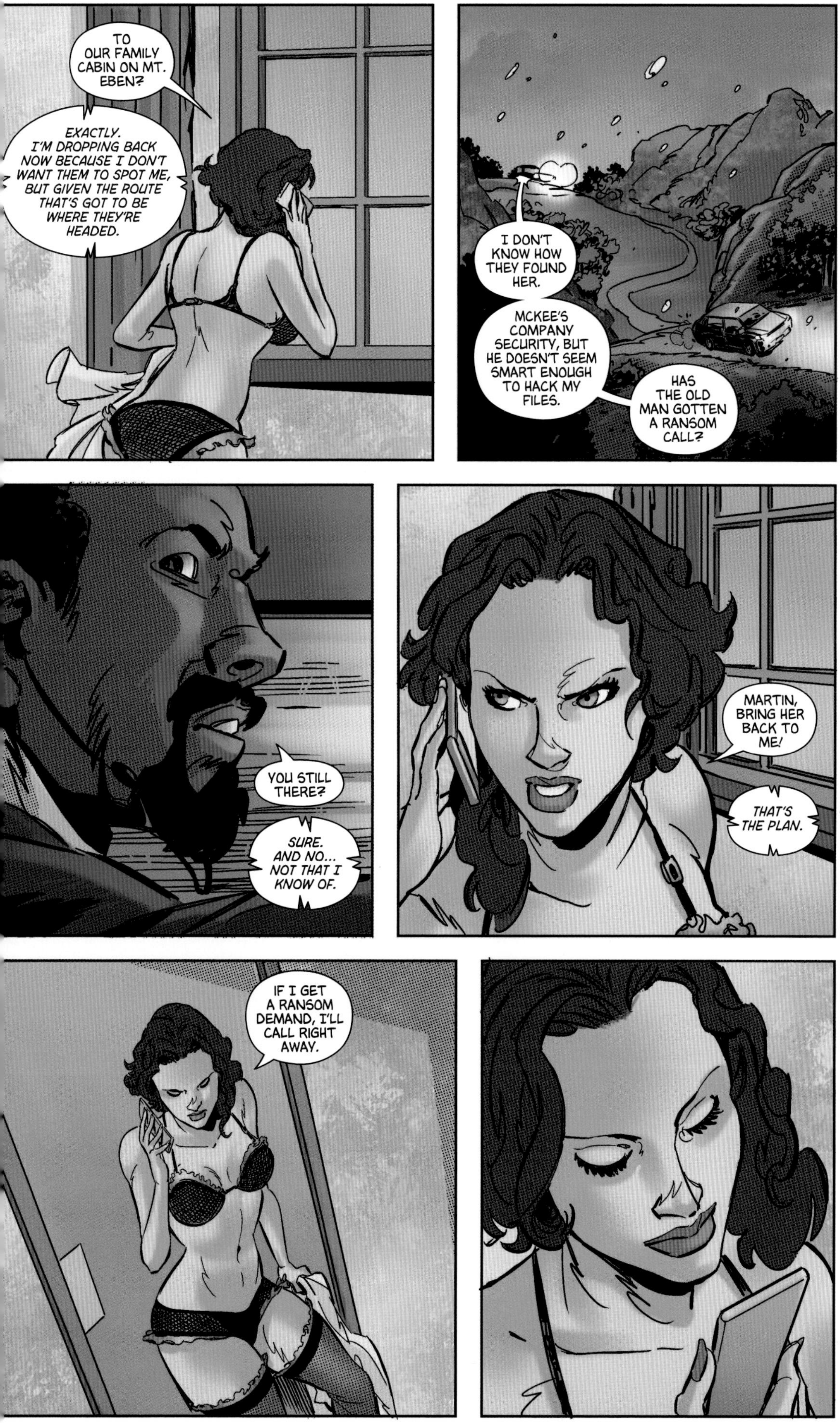
TO OUR FAMILY CABIN ON MT. EBEN?
EXACTLY. I'M DROPPING BACK NOW BECAUSE I DON'T WANT THEM TO SPOT ME, BUT GIVEN THE ROUTE THAT'S GOT TO BE WHERE THEY'RE HEADED.
I DON'T KNOW HOW THEY FOUND HER.
MCKEE'S COMPANY SECURITY, BUT HE DOESN'T SEEM SMART ENOUGH TO HACK MY FILES.
HAS THE OLD MAN GOTTEN A RANSOM CALL?
YOU STILL THERE?
SURE. AND NO... NOT THAT I KNOW OF.
MARTIN, BRING HER BACK TO ME!
THAT'S THE PLAN.
IF I GET A RANSOM DEMAND, I'LL CALL RIGHT AWAY.

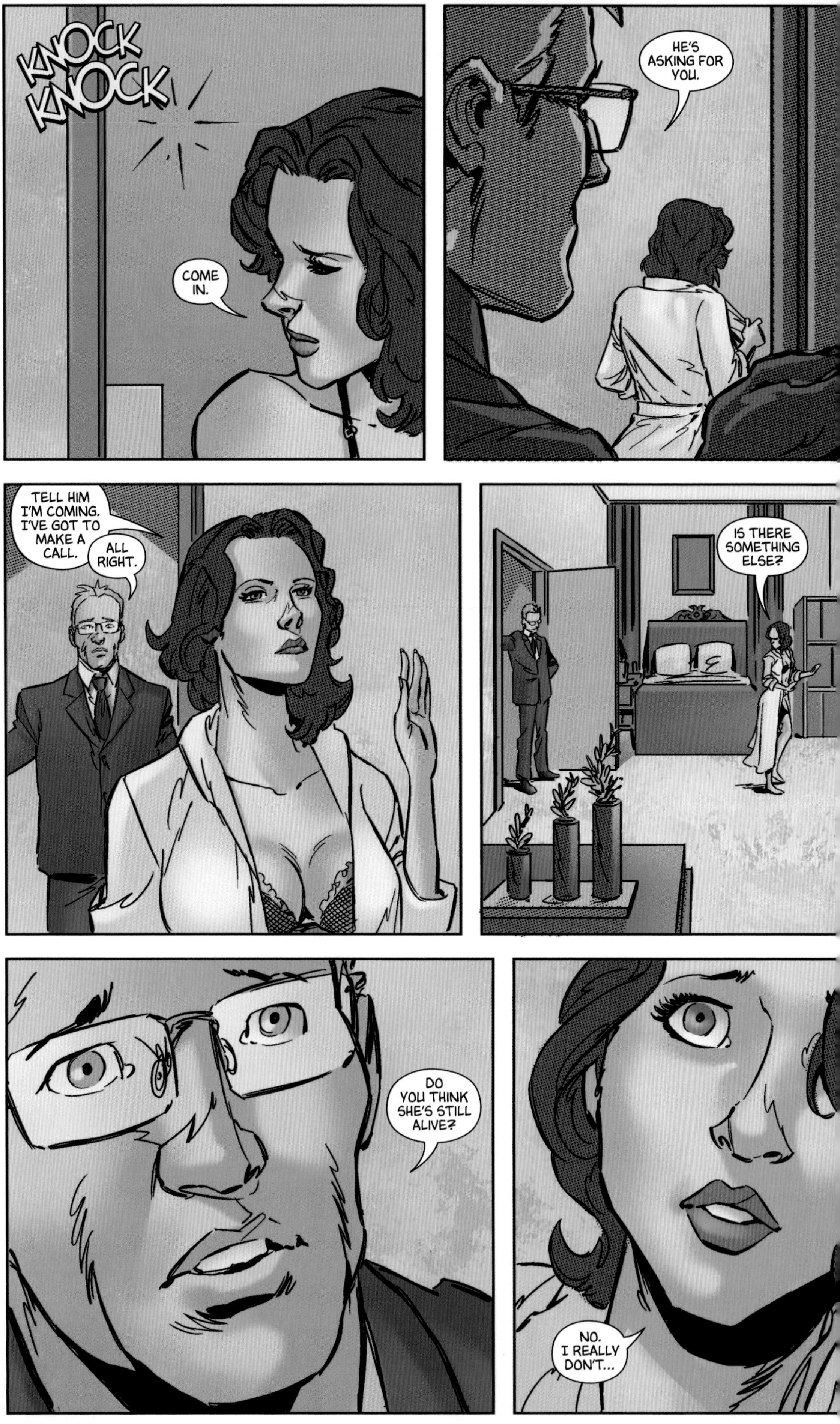
KNOCK KNOCK
COME IN.
HE'S ASKING FOR YOU.
TELL HIM I'M COMING. I'VE GOT TO MAKE A CALL.
ALL RIGHT.
IS THERE SOMETHING ELSE?
DO YOU THINK SHE'S STILL ALIVE?
NO. I REALLY DON'T...

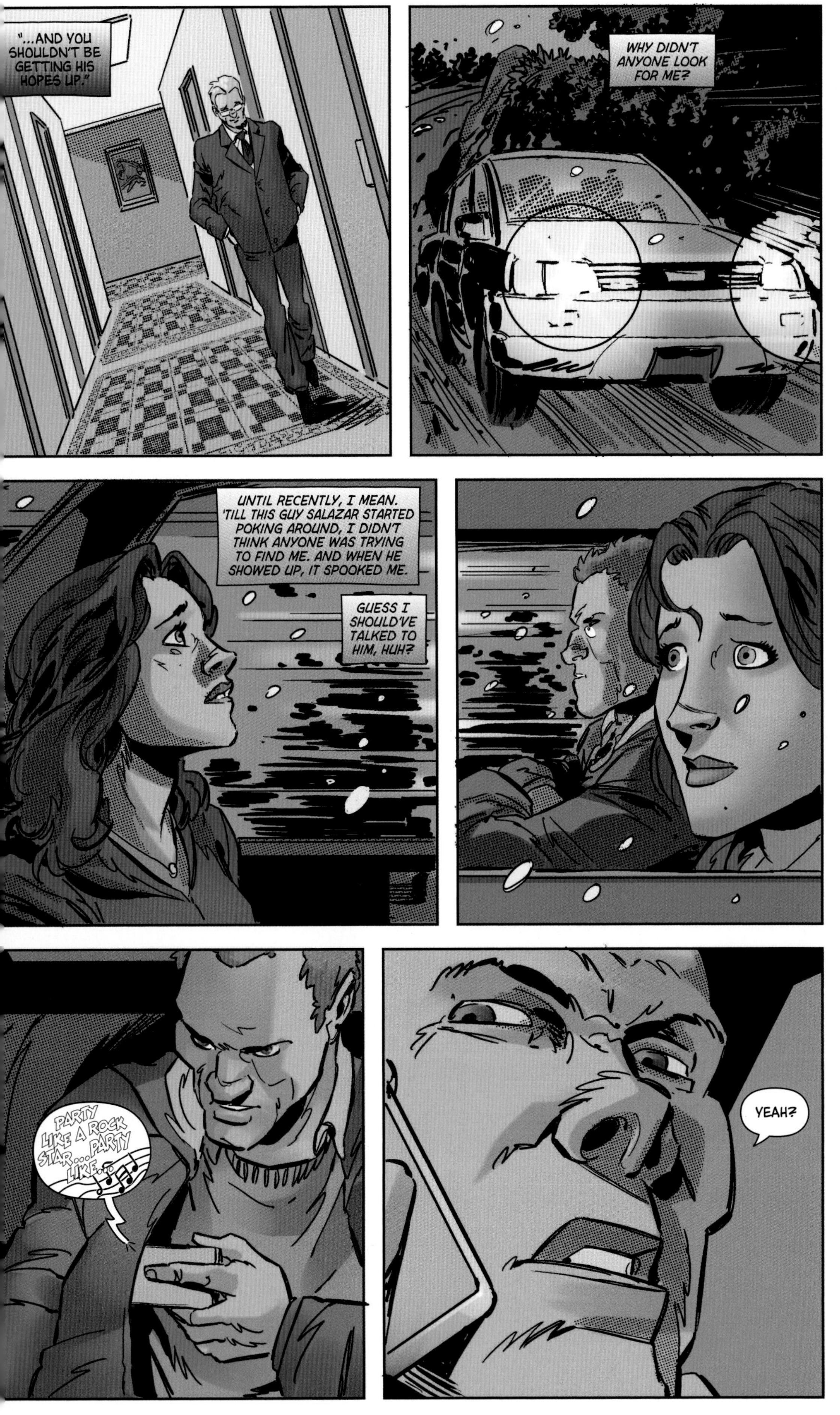
"...AND YOU SHOULDN'T BE GETTING HIS HOPES UP."
WHY DIDN'T ANYONE LOOK FOR ME?
UNTIL RECENTLY, I MEAN. 'TILL THIS GUY SALAZAR STARTED POKING AROUND, I DIDN'T THINK ANYONE WAS TRYING TO FIND ME. AND WHEN HE SHOWED UP, IT SPOOKED ME.
GUESS I SHOULD'VE TALKED TO HIM, HUH?
PARTY LIKE A ROCK STAR...PARTY LIKE...
YEAH?

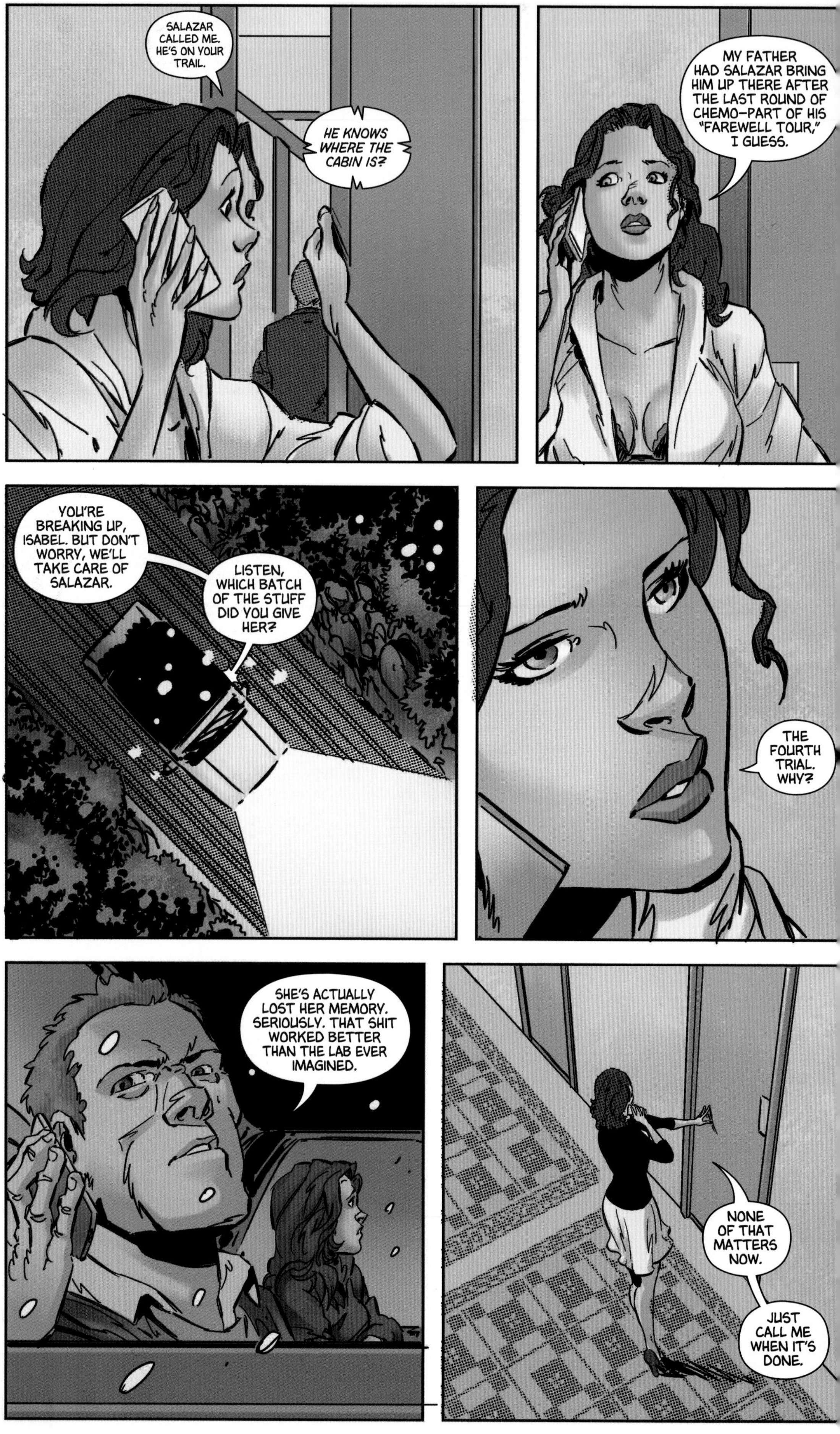
SALAZAR CALLED ME. HE'S ON YOUR TRAIL.
HE KNOWS WHERE THE CABIN IS?
MY FATHER HAD SALAZAR BRING HIM UP THERE AFTER THE LAST ROUND OF CHEMO—PART OF HIS "FAREWELL TOUR," I GUESS.
YOU'RE BREAKING UP, ISABEL. BUT DON'T WORRY, WE'LL TAKE CARE OF SALAZAR.
LISTEN, WHICH BATCH OF THE STUFF DID YOU GIVE HER?
THE FOURTH TRIAL. WHY?
SHE'S ACTUALLY LOST HER MEMORY. SERIOUSLY. THAT SHIT WORKED BETTER THAN THE LAB EVER IMAGINED.
NONE OF THAT MATTERS NOW.
JUST CALL ME WHEN IT'S DONE.

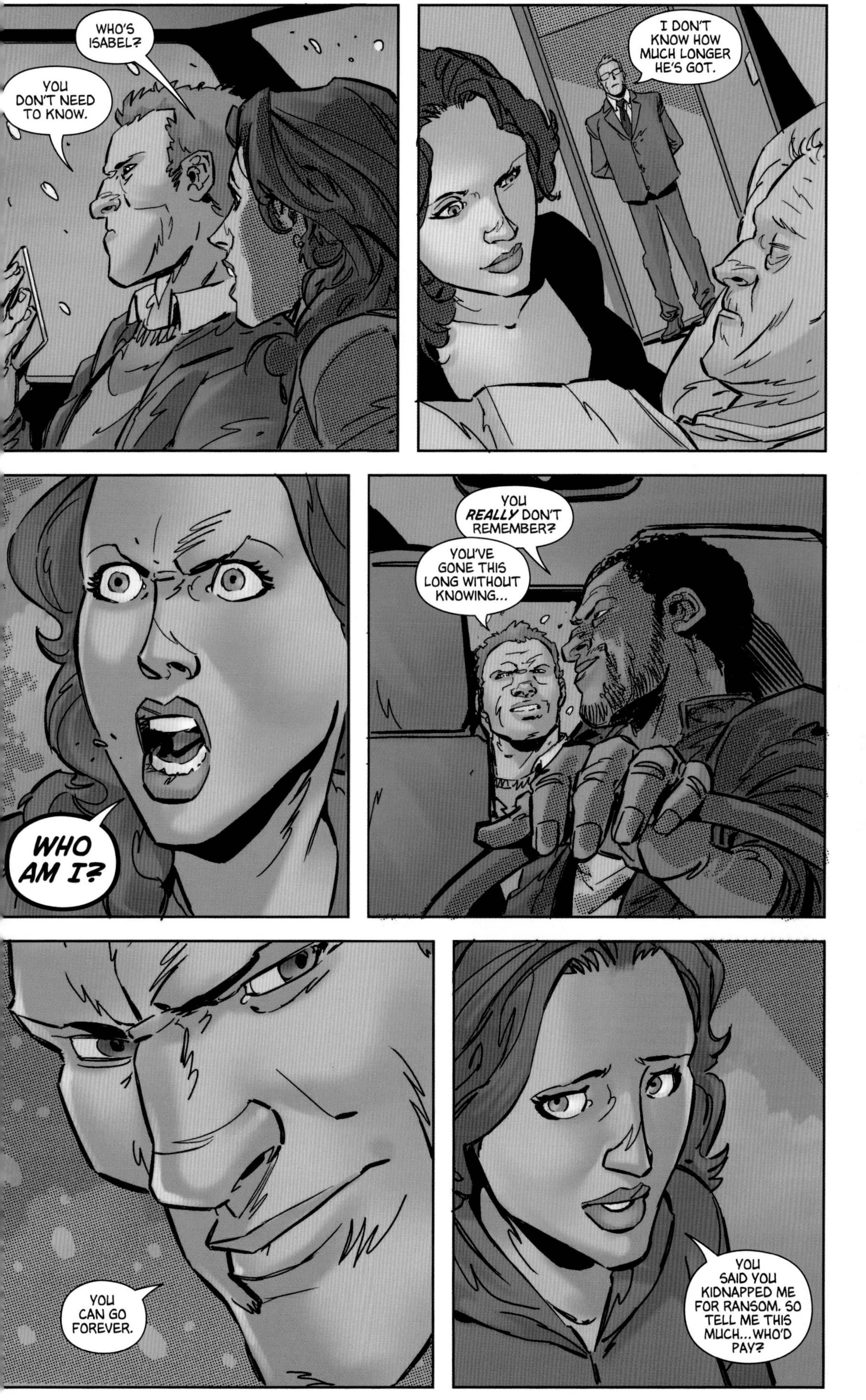
WHO'S ISABEL?
YOU DON'T NEED TO KNOW.
I DON'T KNOW HOW MUCH LONGER HE'S GOT.
WHO AM I?
YOU *REALLY* DON'T REMEMBER?
YOU'VE GONE THIS LONG WITHOUT KNOWING...
YOU CAN GO FOREVER.
YOU SAID YOU KIDNAPPED ME FOR RANSOM. SO TELL ME THIS MUCH...WHO'D PAY?

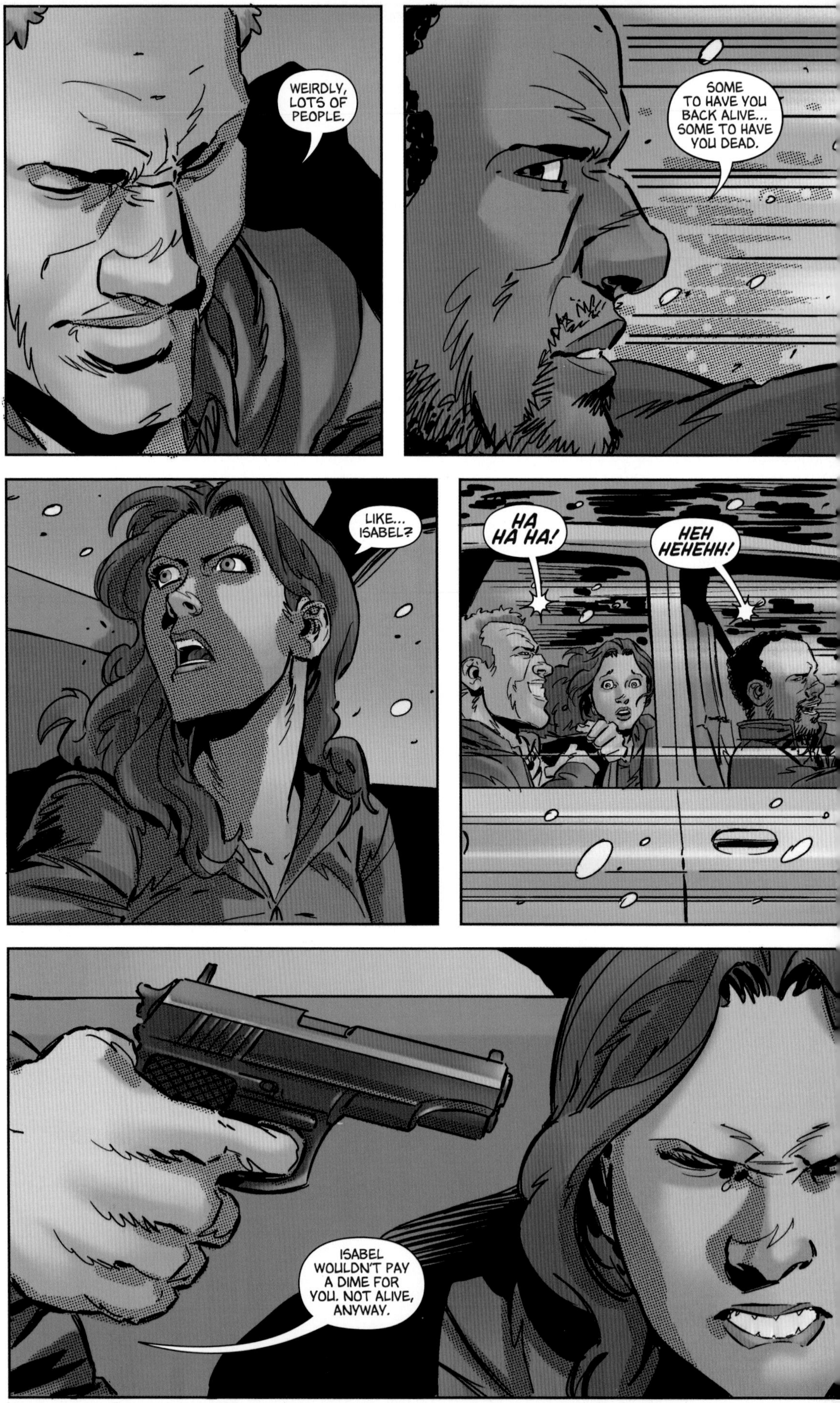
WEIRDLY, LOTS OF PEOPLE.
SOME TO HAVE YOU BACK ALIVE... SOME TO HAVE YOU DEAD.
LIKE... ISABEL?
HA HA HA!
HEH HEHEHH!
ISABEL WOULDN'T PAY A DIME FOR YOU. NOT ALIVE, ANYWAY.

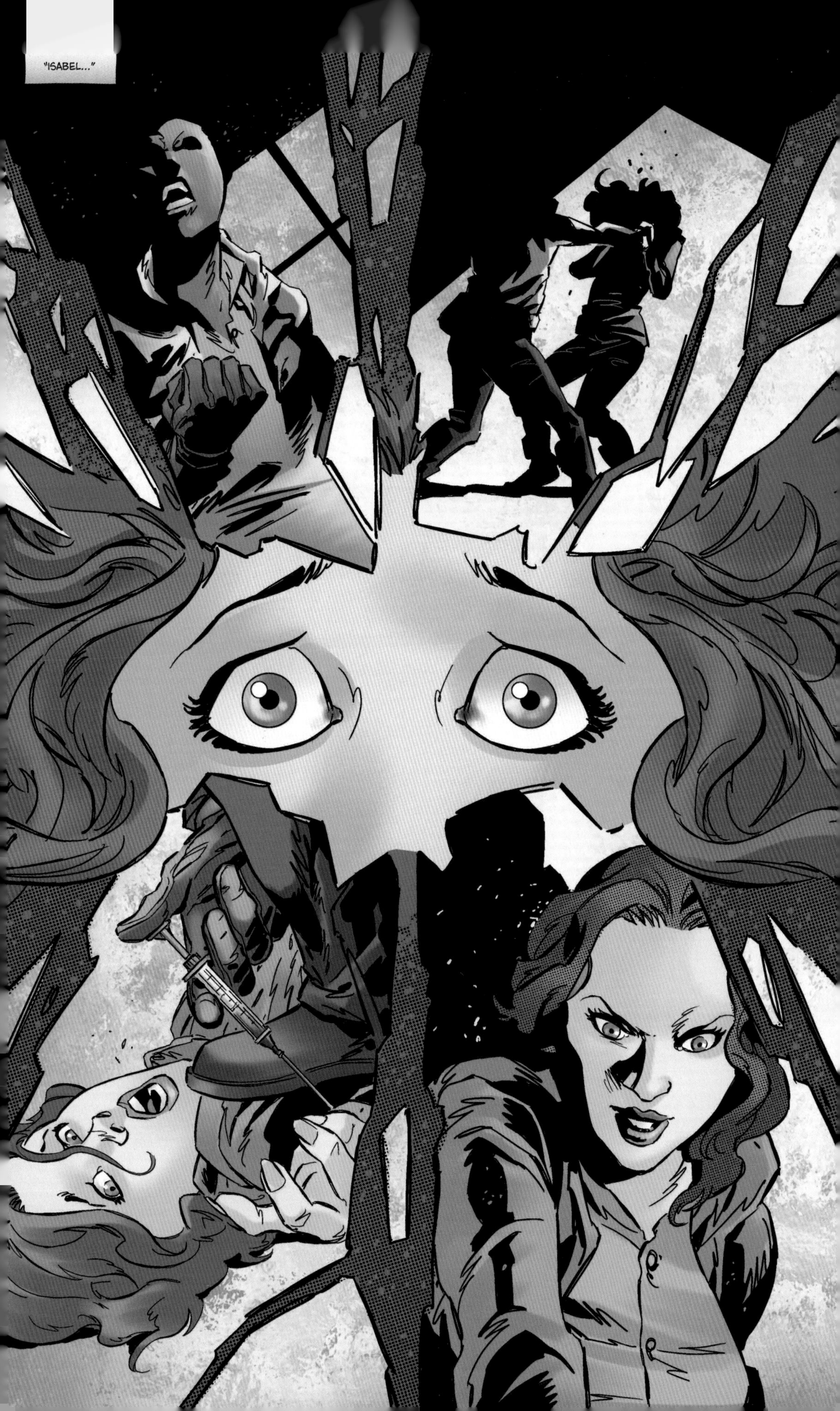
"ISABEL..."

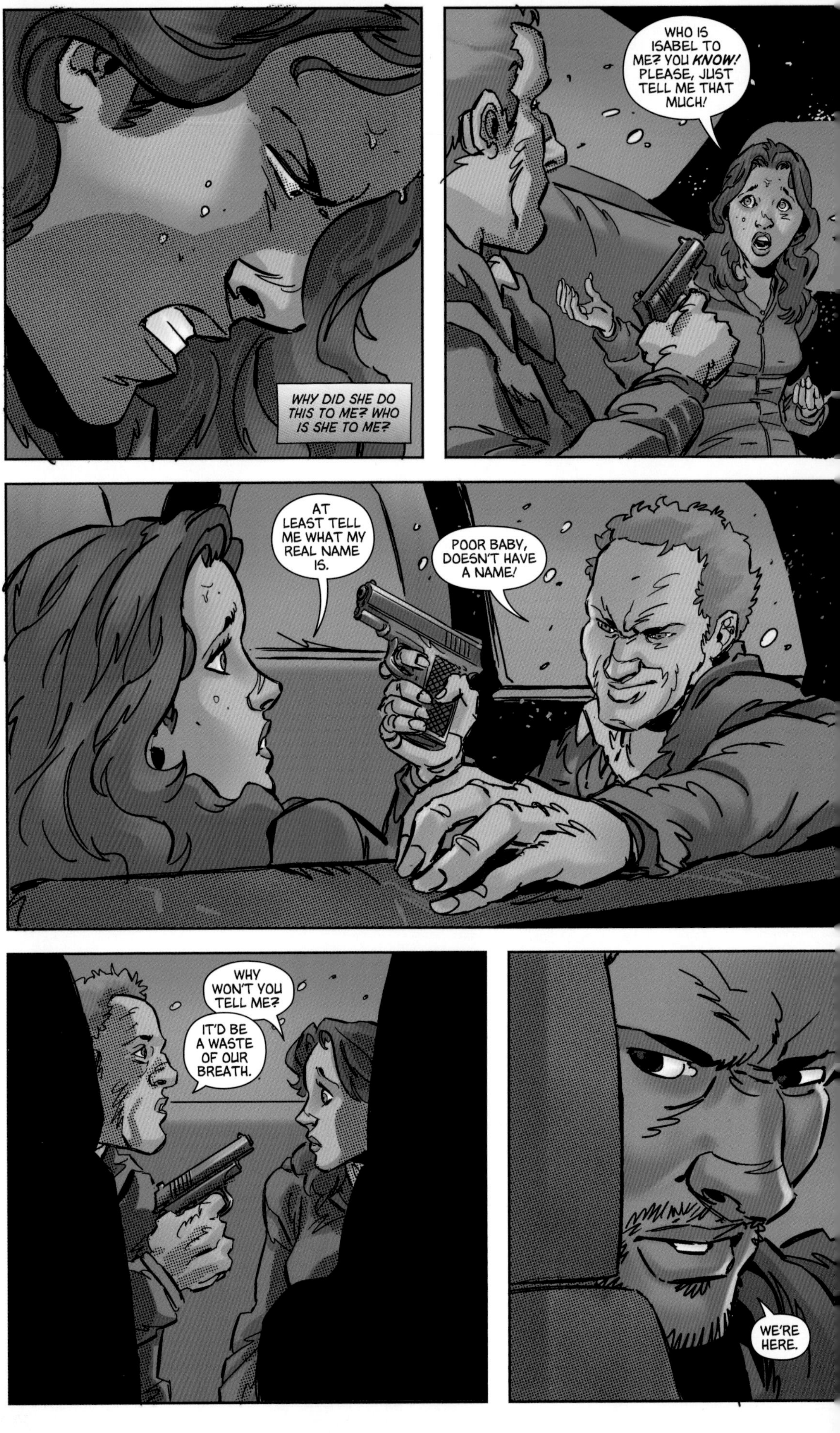
WHY DID SHE DO THIS TO ME? WHO IS SHE TO ME?
WHO IS ISABEL TO ME? YOU *KNOW!* PLEASE, JUST TELL ME THAT MUCH!
AT LEAST TELL ME WHAT MY REAL NAME IS.
POOR BABY, DOESN'T HAVE A NAME!
WHY WON'T YOU TELL ME?
IT'D BE A WASTE OF OUR BREATH.
WE'RE HERE.

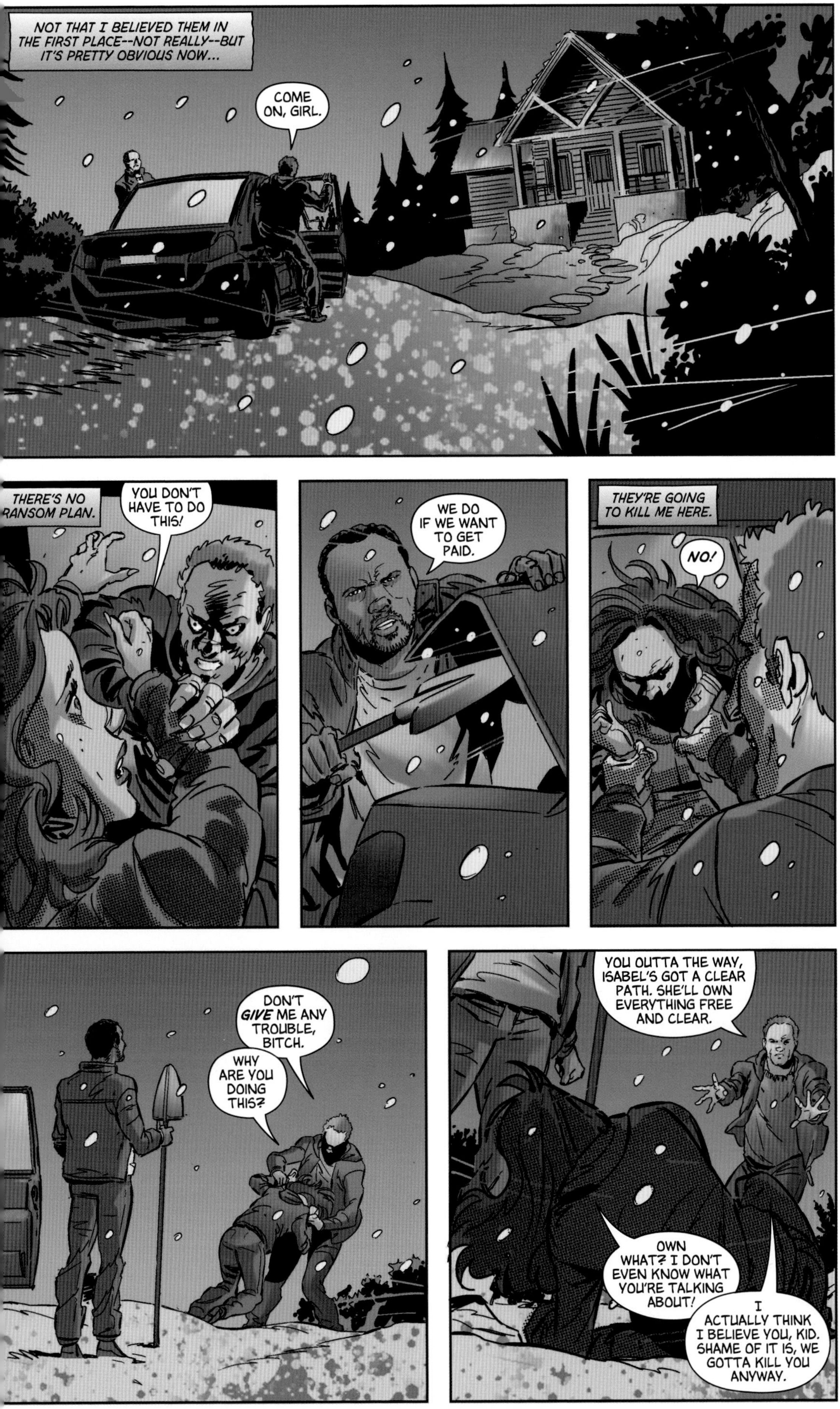
NOT THAT I BELIEVED THEM IN THE FIRST PLACE--NOT REALLY--BUT IT'S PRETTY OBVIOUS NOW...
COME ON, GIRL.
THERE'S NO RANSOM PLAN.
YOU DON'T HAVE TO DO THIS!
WE DO IF WE WANT TO GET PAID.
THEY'RE GOING TO KILL ME HERE.
NO!
DON'T GIVE ME ANY TROUBLE, BITCH.
WHY ARE YOU DOING THIS?
YOU OUTTA THE WAY, ISABEL'S GOT A CLEAR PATH. SHE'LL OWN EVERYTHING FREE AND CLEAR.
OWN WHAT? I DON'T EVEN KNOW WHAT YOU'RE TALKING ABOUT!
I ACTUALLY THINK I BELIEVE YOU, KID. SHAME OF IT IS, WE GOTTA KILL YOU ANYWAY.

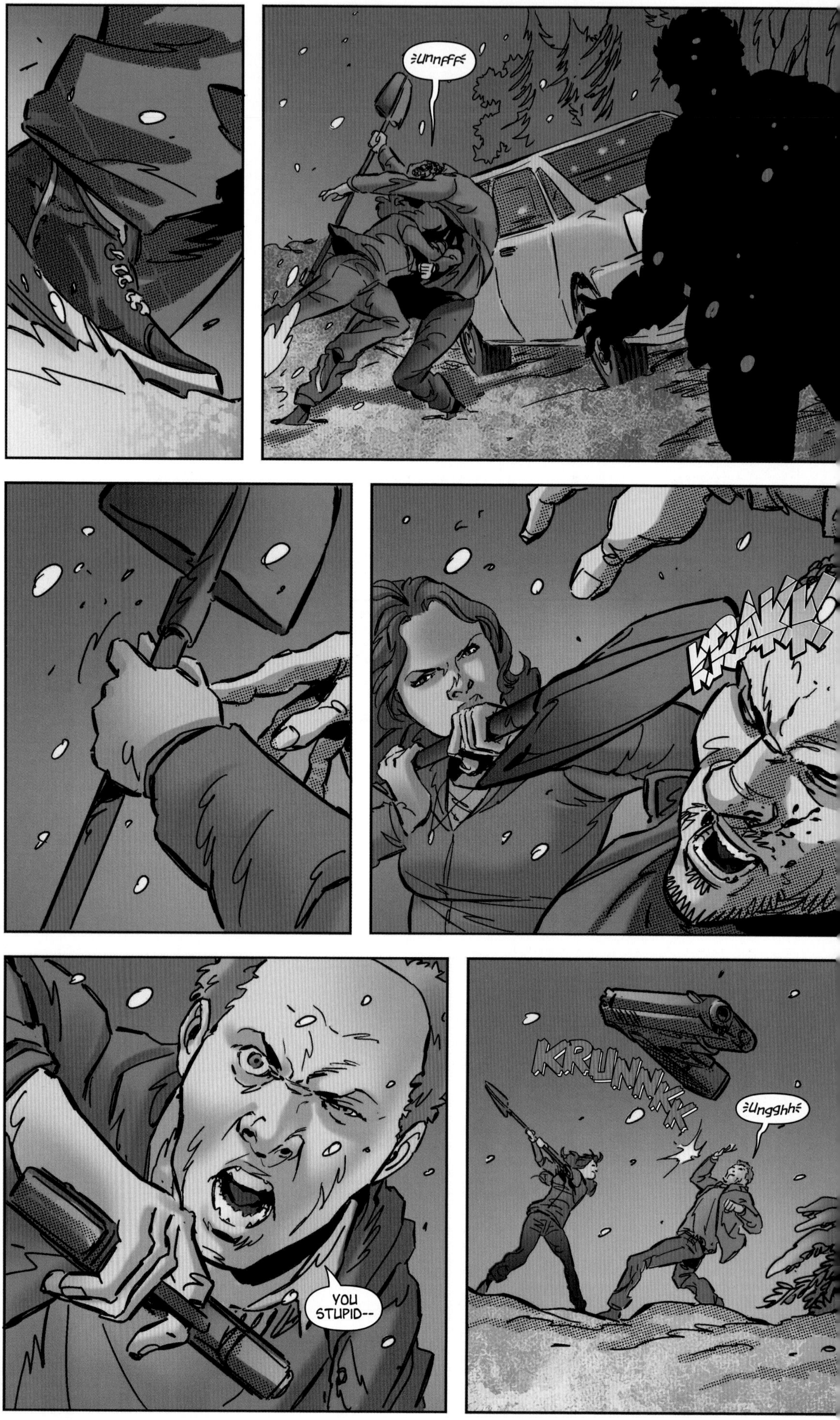
Unnfff
KRAKK!
YOU STUPID--
KRUNNKK
Ungghh

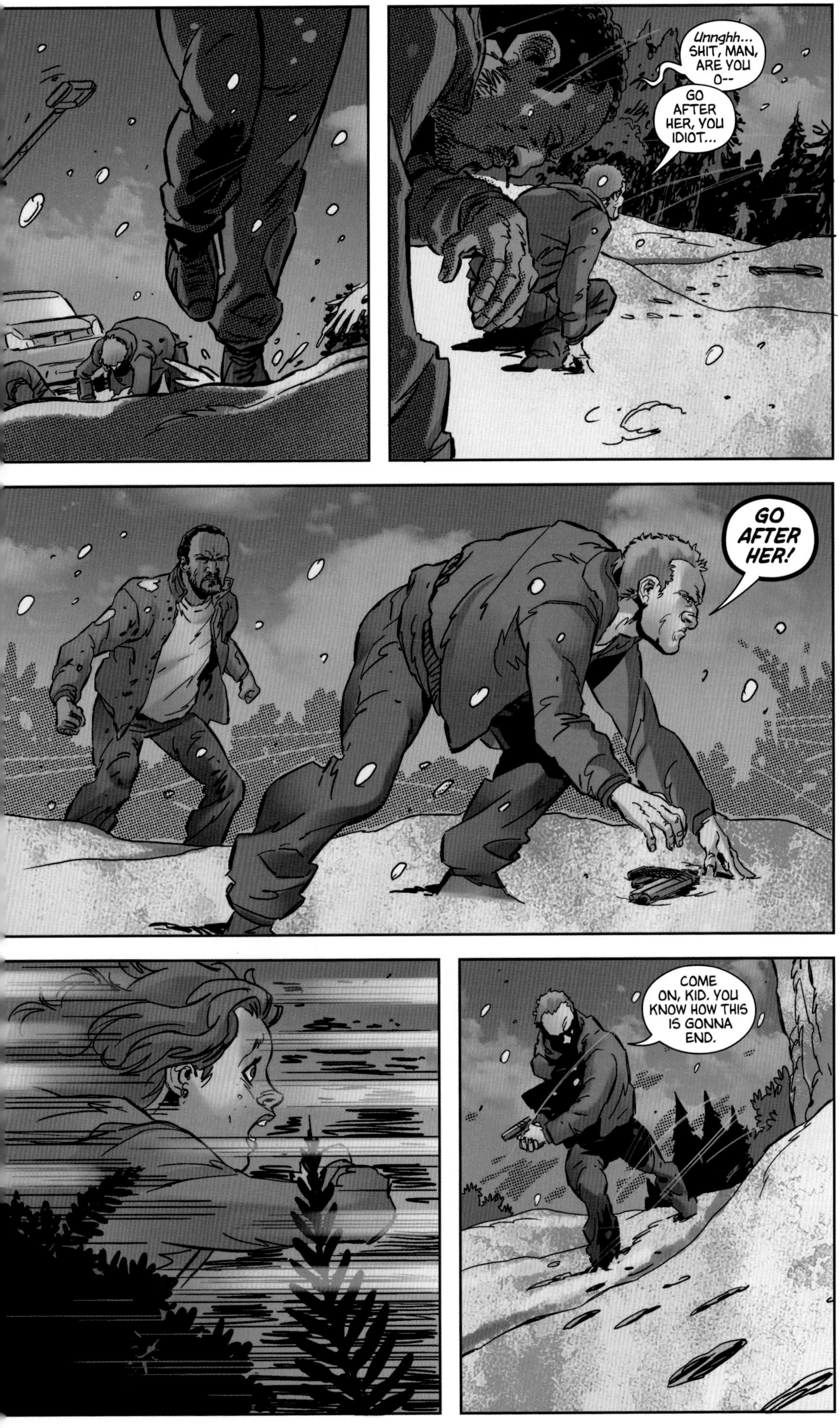
Unnghh... SHIT, MAN, ARE YOU O--
GO AFTER HER, YOU IDIOT...
GO AFTER HER!
COME ON, KID. YOU KNOW HOW THIS IS GONNA END.

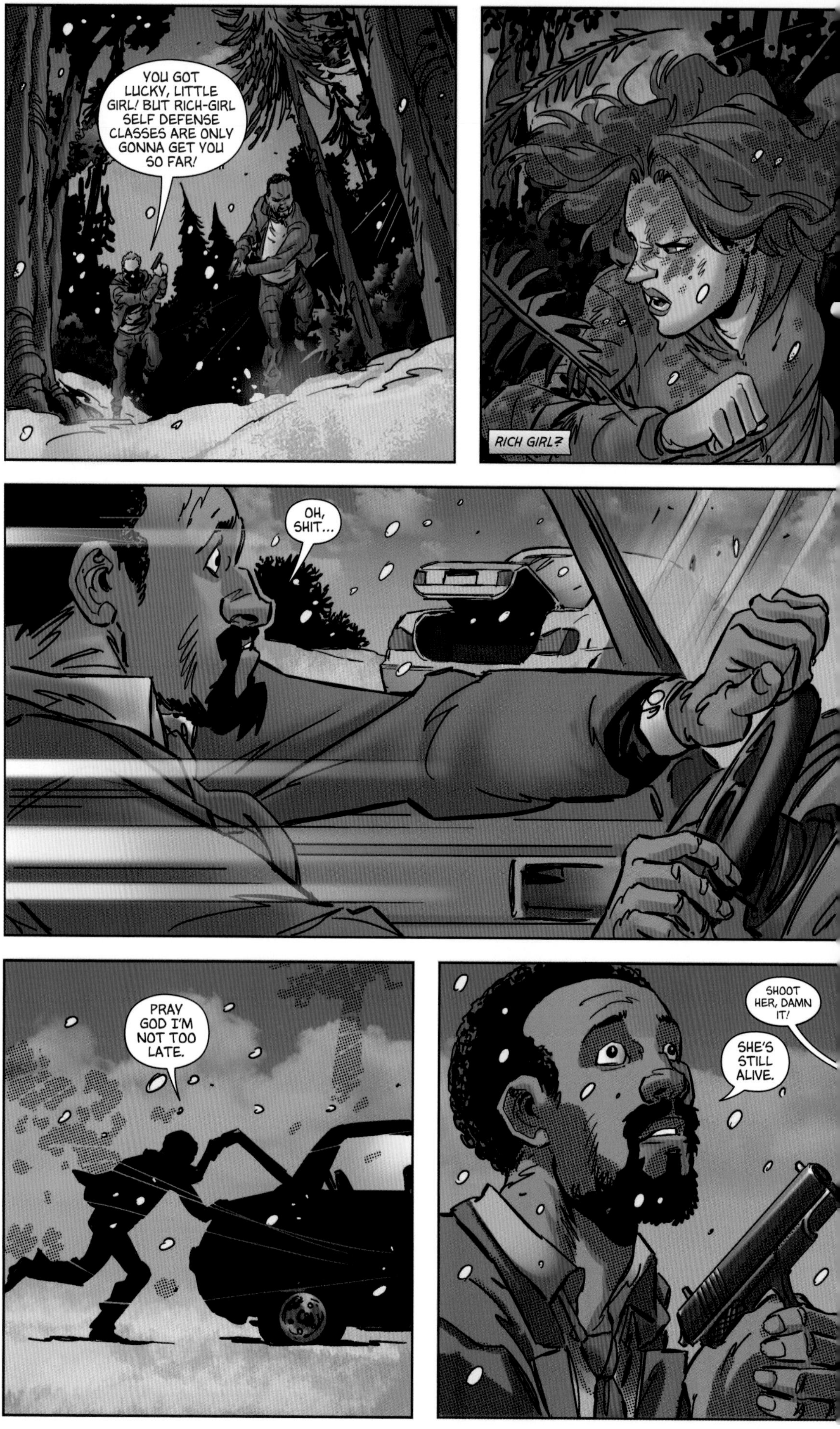
YOU GOT LUCKY, LITTLE GIRL! BUT RICH-GIRL SELF DEFENSE CLASSES ARE ONLY GONNA GET YOU SO FAR!
RICH GIRL?
OH, SHIT...
PRAY GOD I'M NOT TOO LATE.
SHOOT HER, DAMN IT!
SHE'S STILL ALIVE.

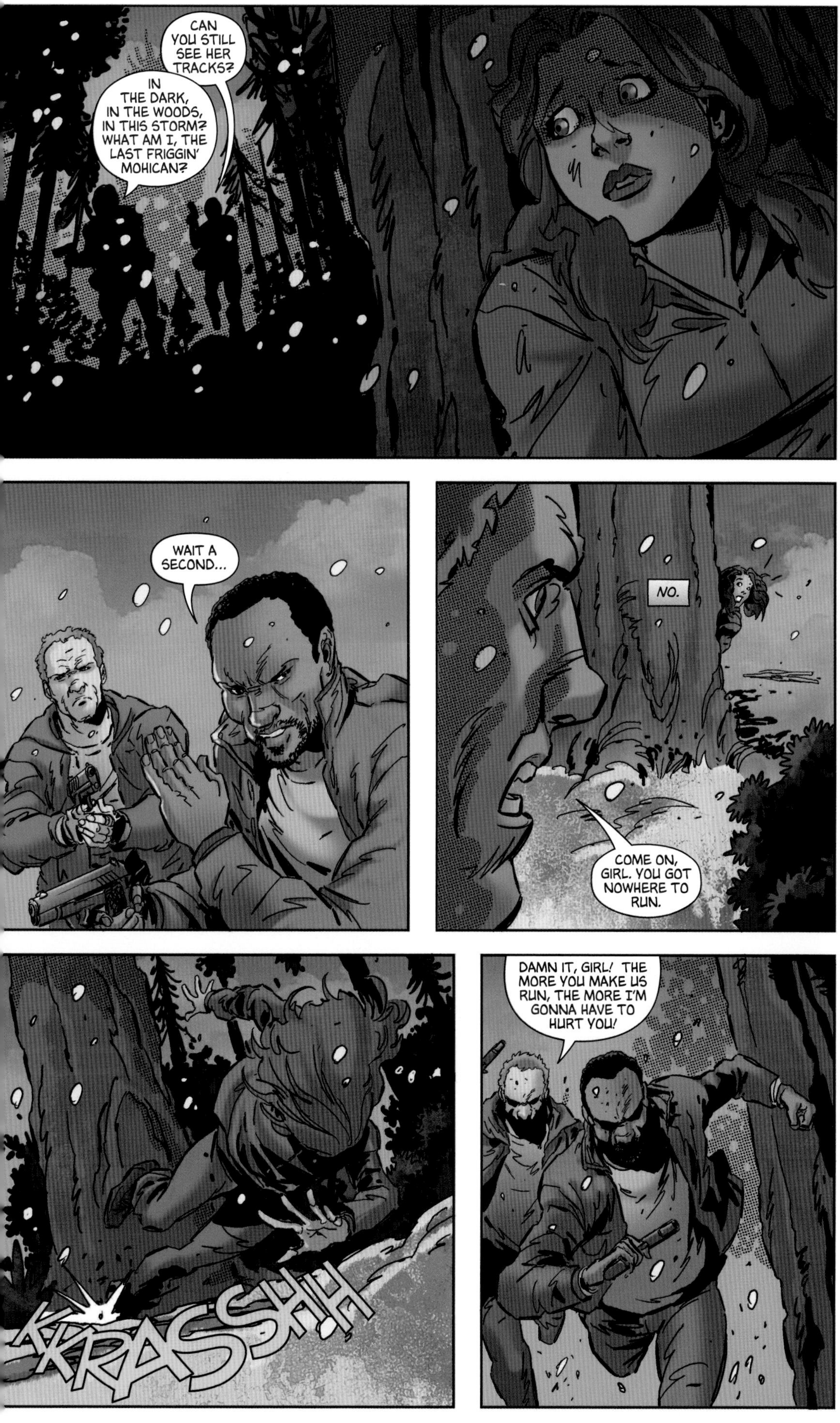
CAN YOU STILL SEE HER TRACKS?
IN THE DARK, IN THE WOODS, IN THIS STORM? WHAT AM I, THE LAST FRIGGIN' MOHICAN?
WAIT A SECOND...
NO.
COME ON, GIRL. YOU GOT NOWHERE TO RUN.
KKRASSHH
DAMN IT, GIRL! THE MORE YOU MAKE US RUN, THE MORE I'M GONNA HAVE TO HURT YOU!

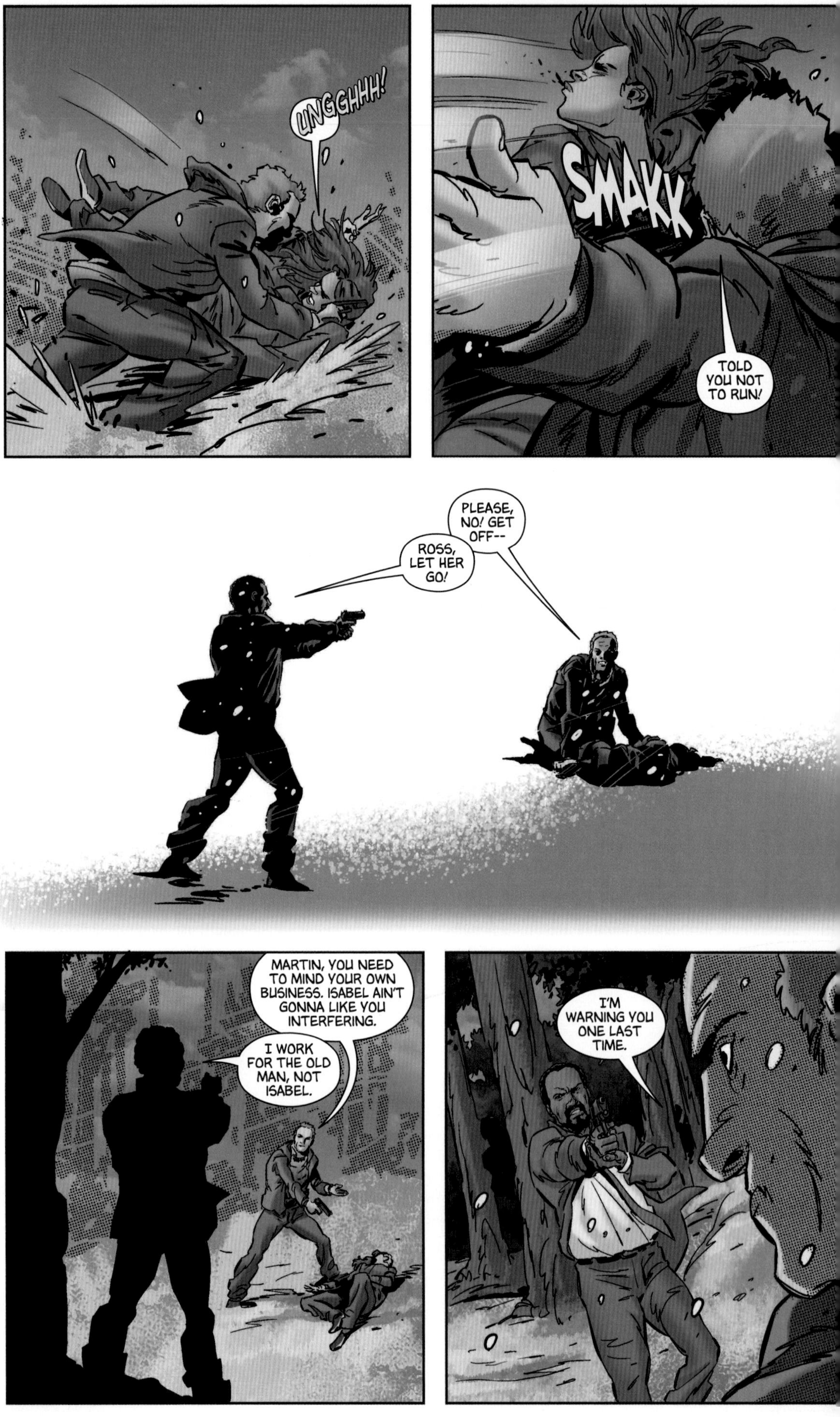
UNGGHHH!
SMAKK
TOLD YOU NOT TO RUN!
ROSS, LET HER GO!
PLEASE, NO! GET OFF--
MARTIN, YOU NEED TO MIND YOUR OWN BUSINESS. ISABEL AIN'T GONNA LIKE YOU INTERFERING.
I WORK FOR THE OLD MAN, NOT ISABEL.
I'M WARNING YOU ONE LAST TIME.

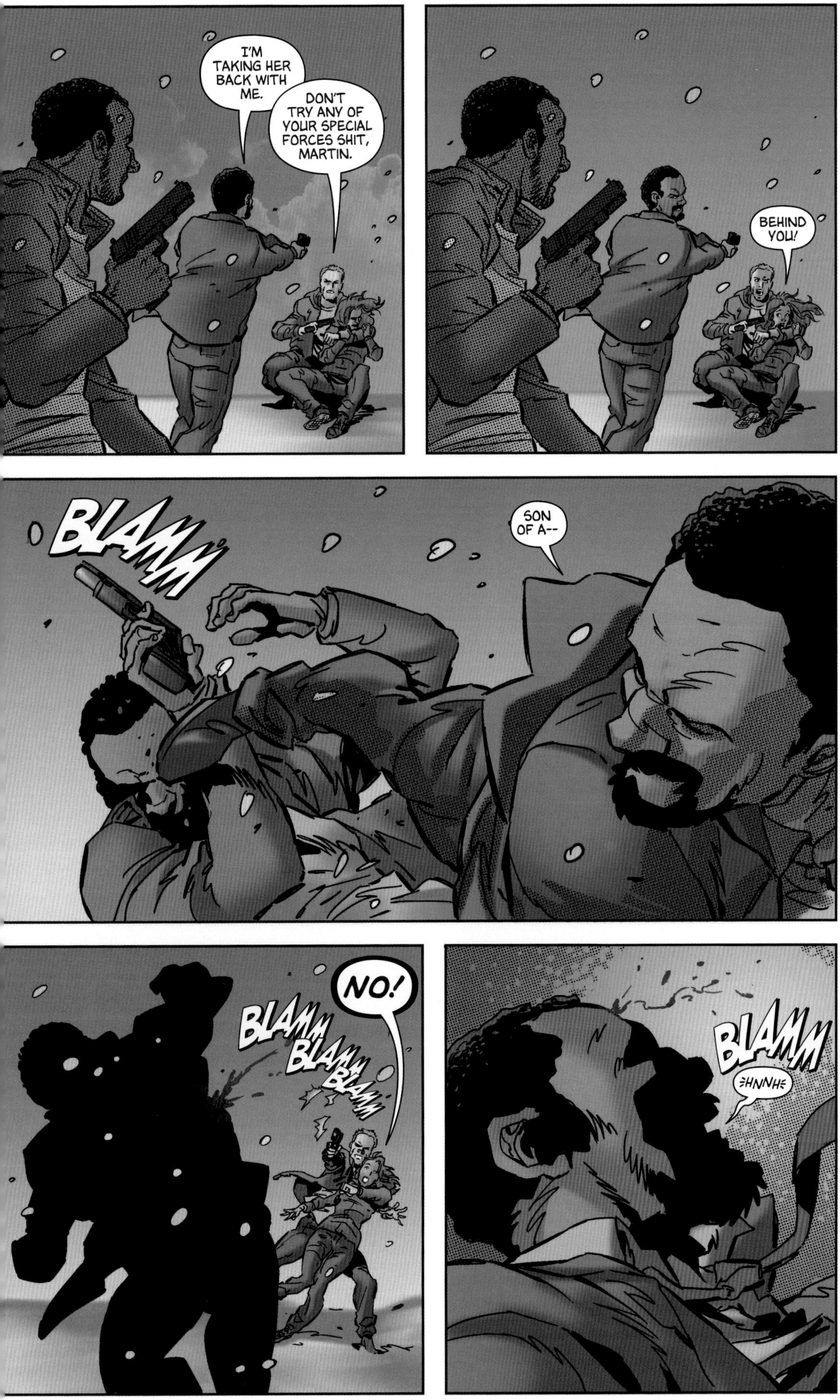
I'M TAKING HER BACK WITH ME.
DON'T TRY ANY OF YOUR SPECIAL FORCES SHIT, MARTIN.
BEHIND YOU!
BLAMM
SON OF A--
NO!
BLAMM BLAMM BLAMM
BLAMM
HNNH

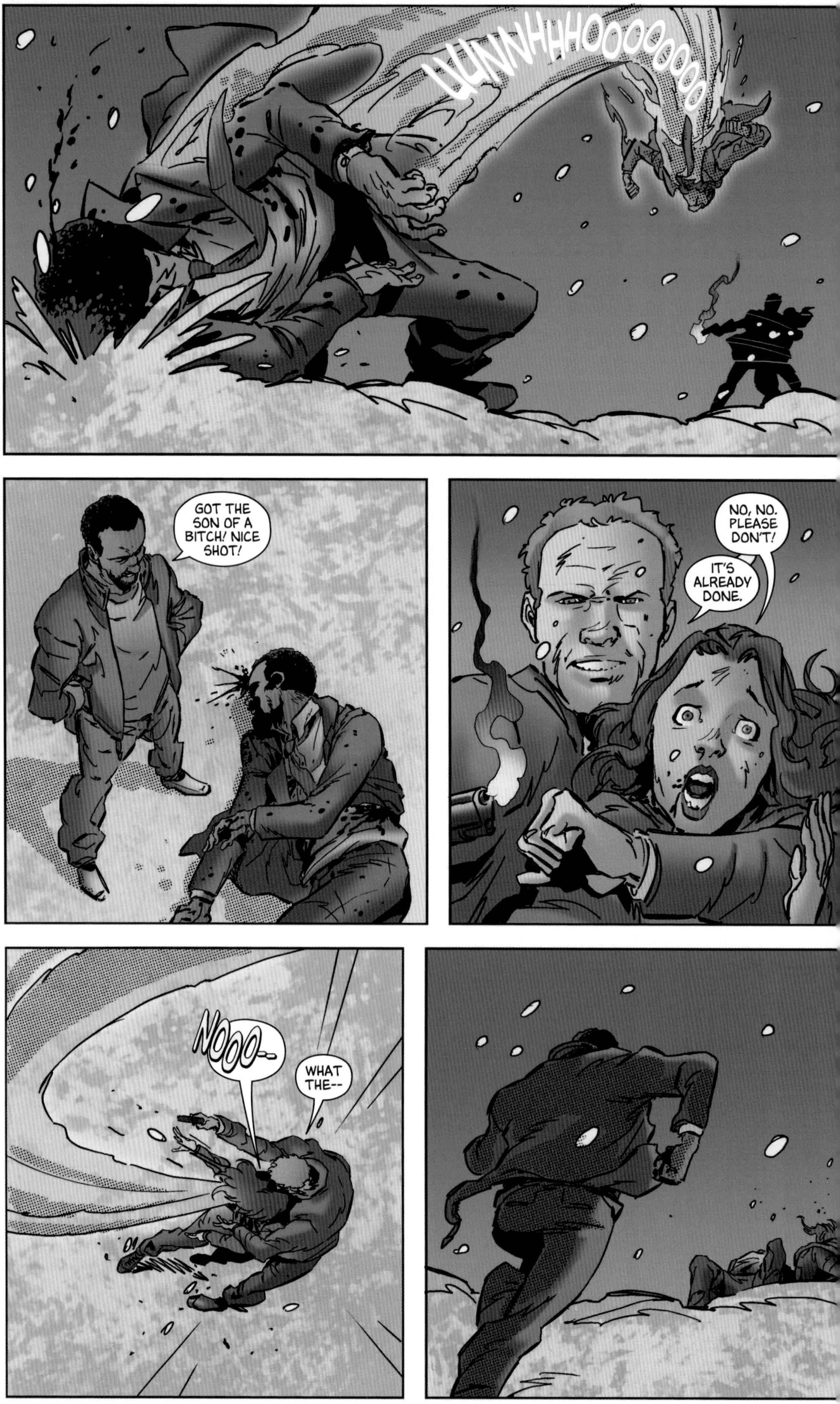
UUNNHHHOOOOOOOO
GOT THE SON OF A BITCH! NICE SHOT!
NO, NO. PLEASE DON'T!
IT'S ALREADY DONE.
NOOO--
WHAT THE--

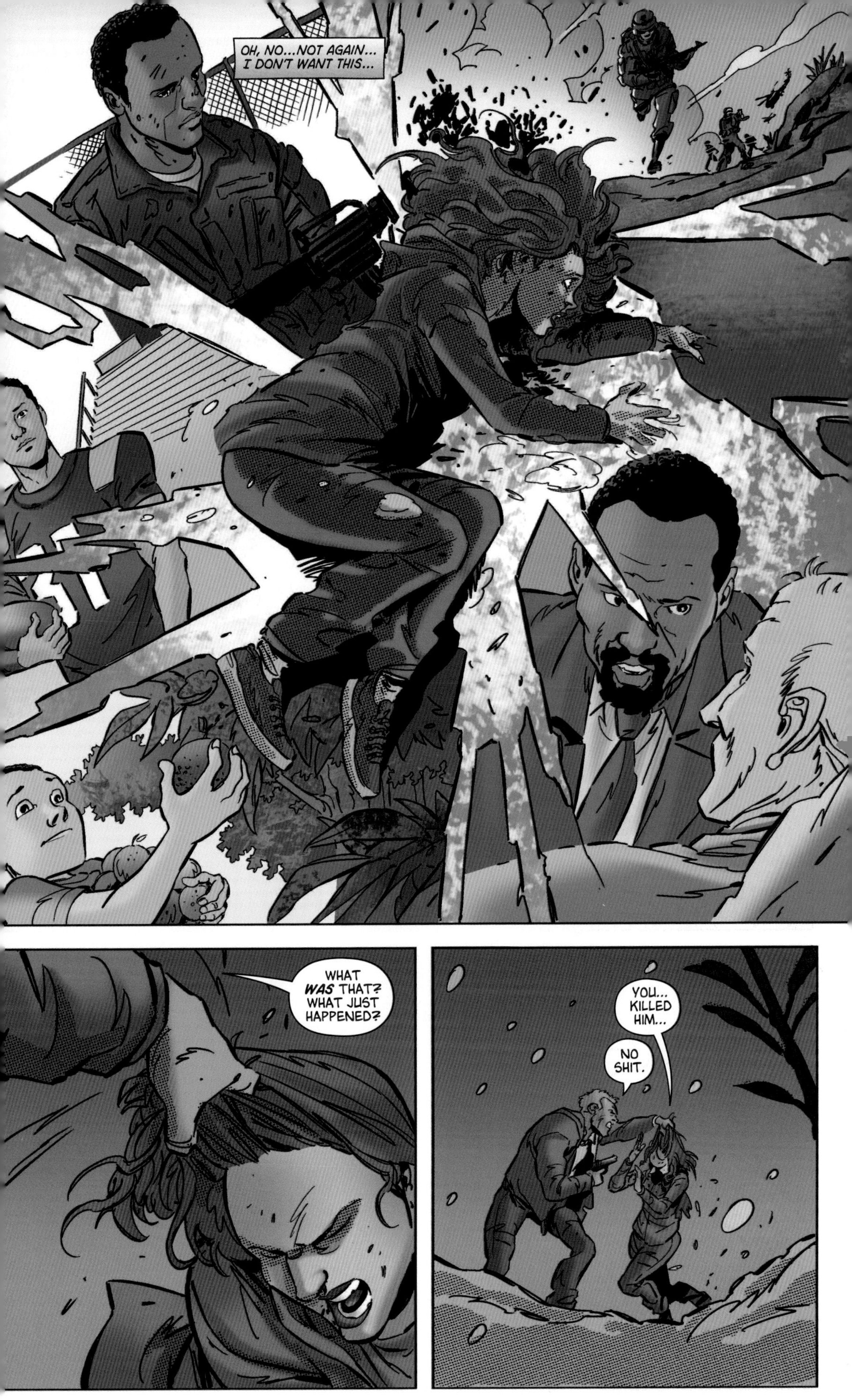
OH, NO...NOT AGAIN...
I DON'T WANT THIS...
WHAT WAS THAT? WHAT JUST HAPPENED?
YOU... KILLED HIM...
NO SHIT.

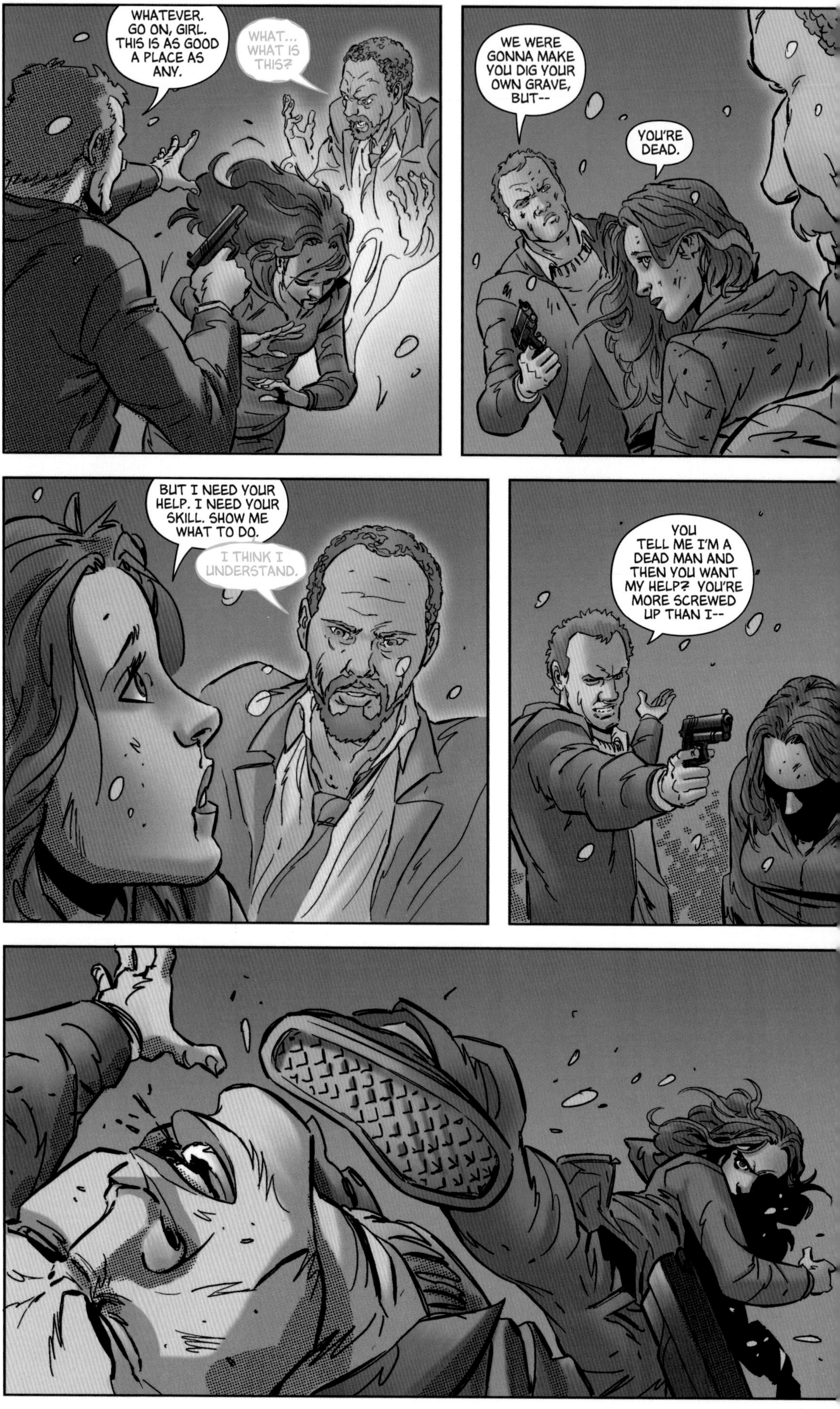
WHATEVER. GO ON, GIRL. THIS IS AS GOOD A PLACE AS ANY.
WHAT... WHAT IS THIS?
WE WERE GONNA MAKE YOU DIG YOUR OWN GRAVE, BUT--
YOU'RE DEAD.
BUT I NEED YOUR HELP. I NEED YOUR SKILL. SHOW ME WHAT TO DO.
I THINK I UNDERSTAND.
YOU TELL ME I'M A DEAD MAN AND THEN YOU WANT MY HELP? YOU'RE MORE SCREWED UP THAN I--

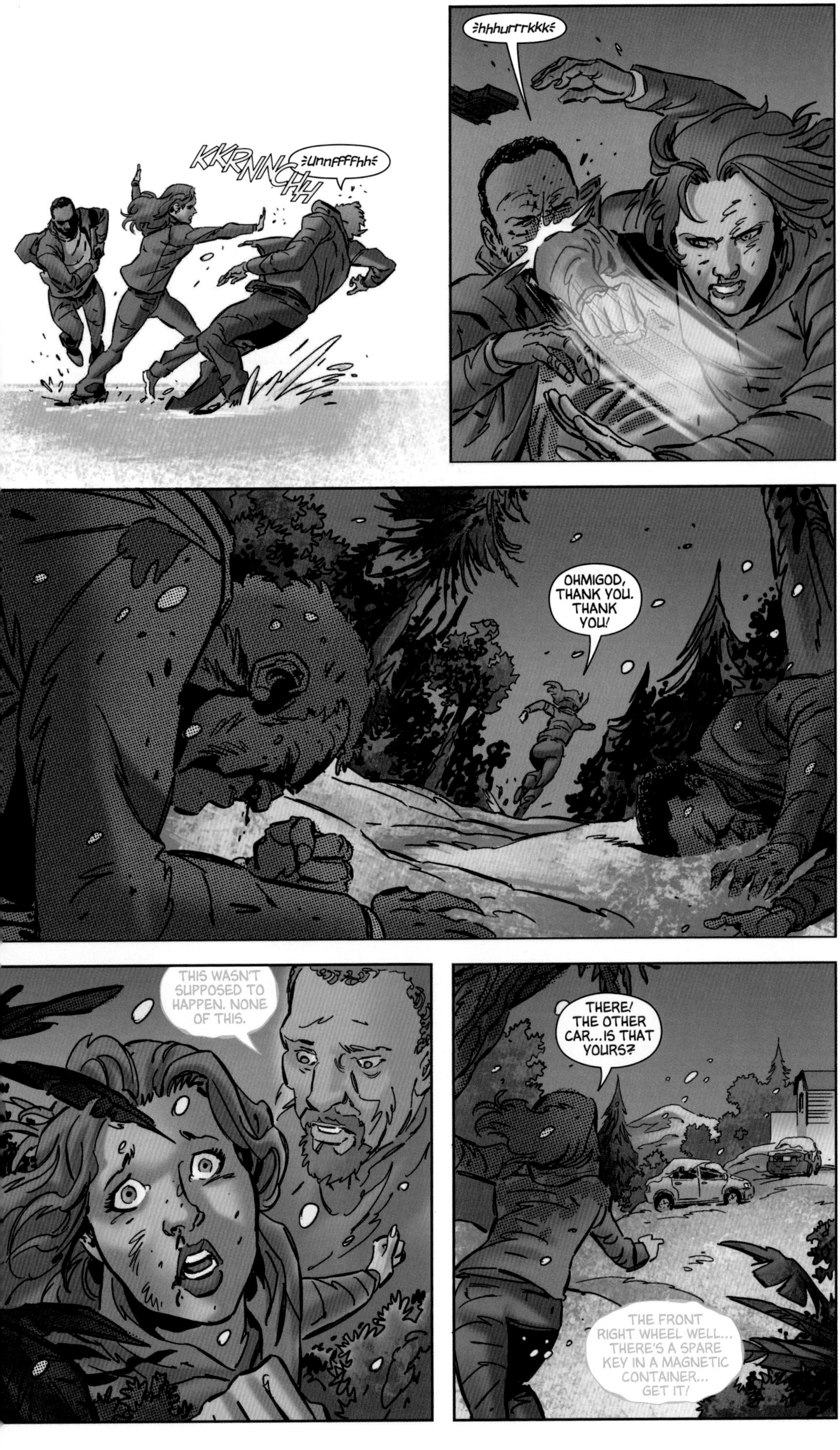
KKRNNCHH
UNNFFFHH
hhhurrrkkk
OHMIGOD, THANK YOU. THANK YOU!
THIS WASN'T SUPPOSED TO HAPPEN. NONE OF THIS.
THERE! THE OTHER CAR...IS THAT YOURS?
THE FRONT RIGHT WHEEL WELL... THERE'S A SPARE KEY IN A MAGNETIC CONTAINER... GET IT!

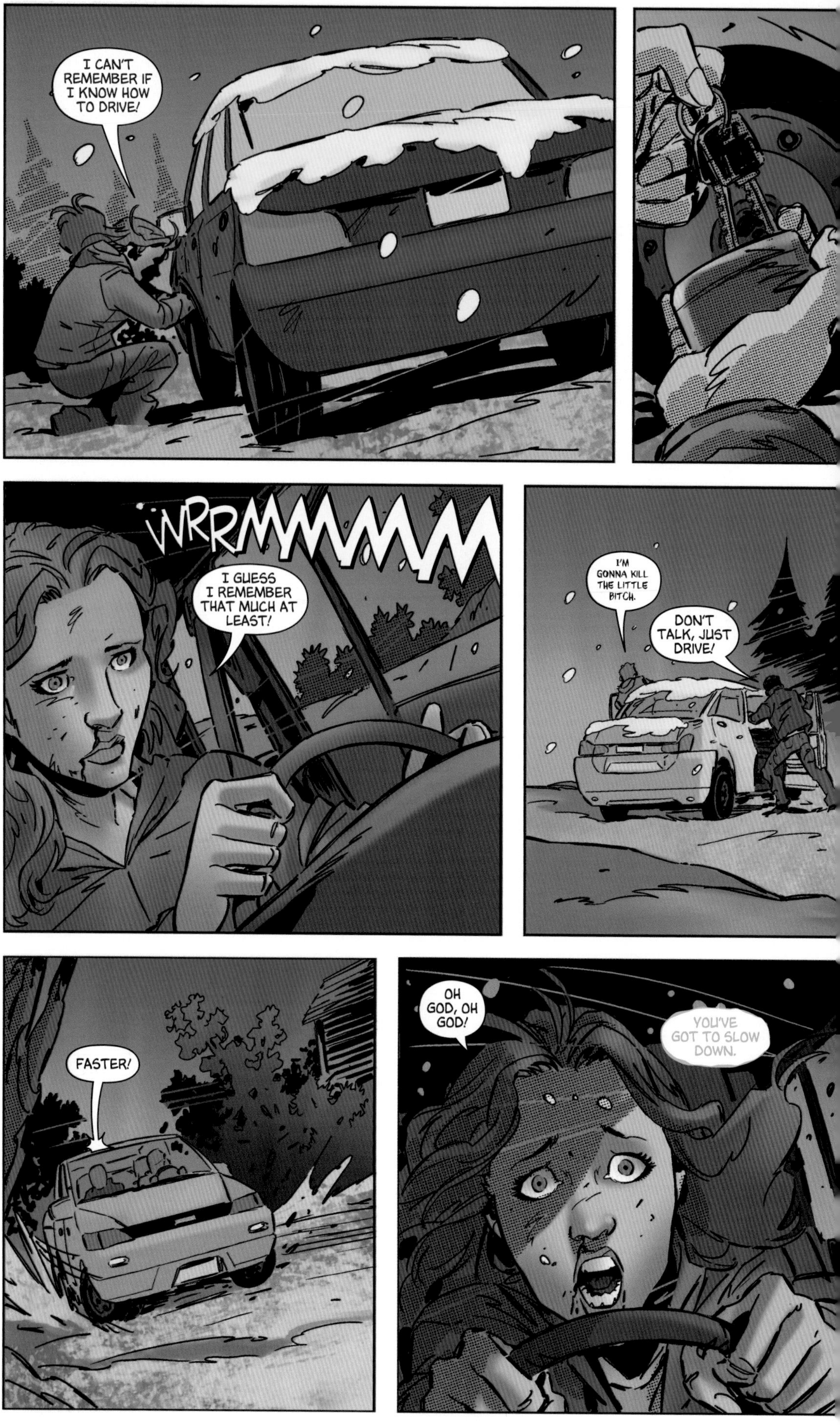
I CAN'T REMEMBER IF I KNOW HOW TO DRIVE!
WRRMMMMMM
I GUESS I REMEMBER THAT MUCH AT LEAST!
I'M GONNA KILL THE LITTLE BITCH.
DON'T TALK, JUST DRIVE!
FASTER!
OH GOD, OH GOD!
YOU'VE GOT TO SLOW DOWN.

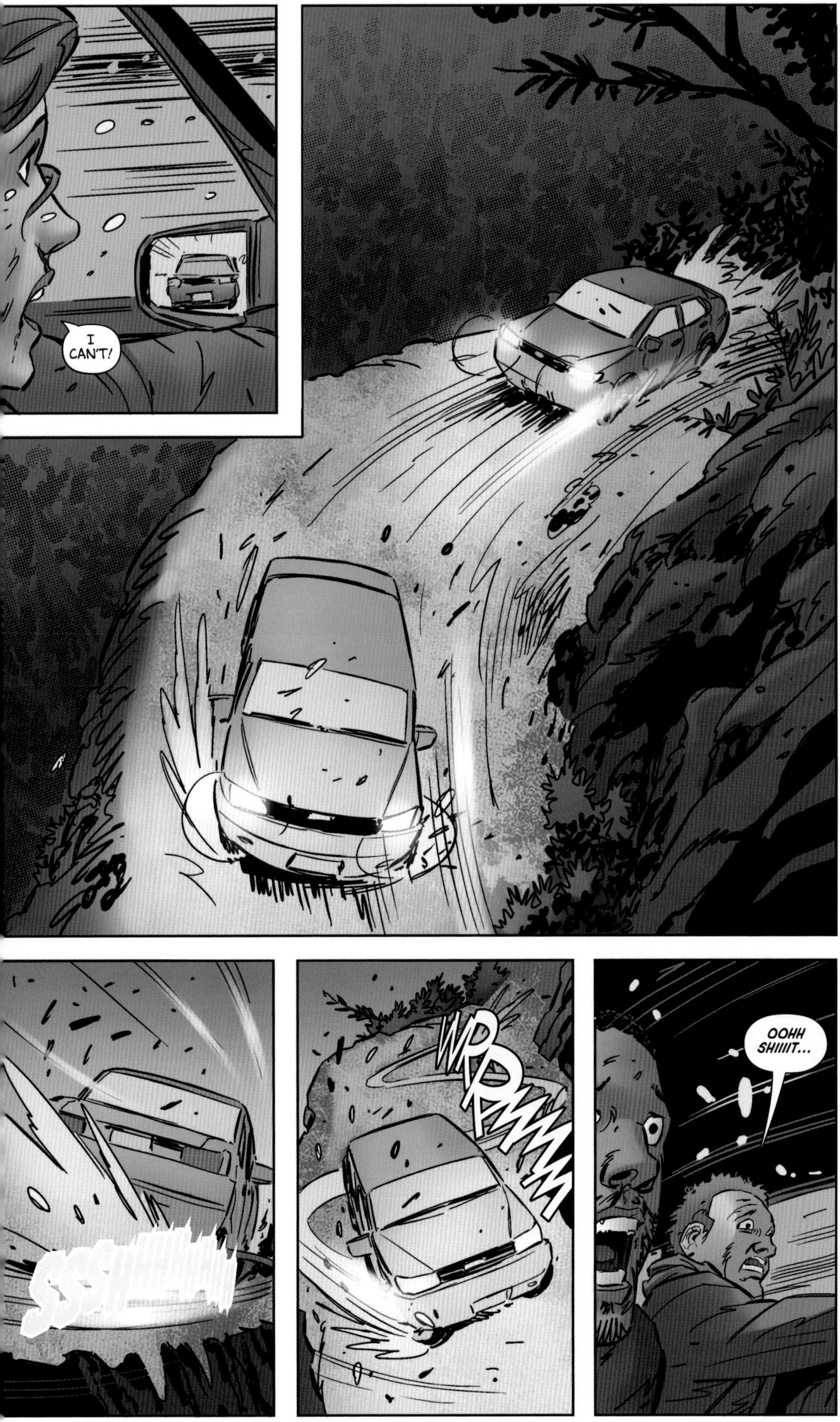
I CAN'T!
OOHH SHIIIT...

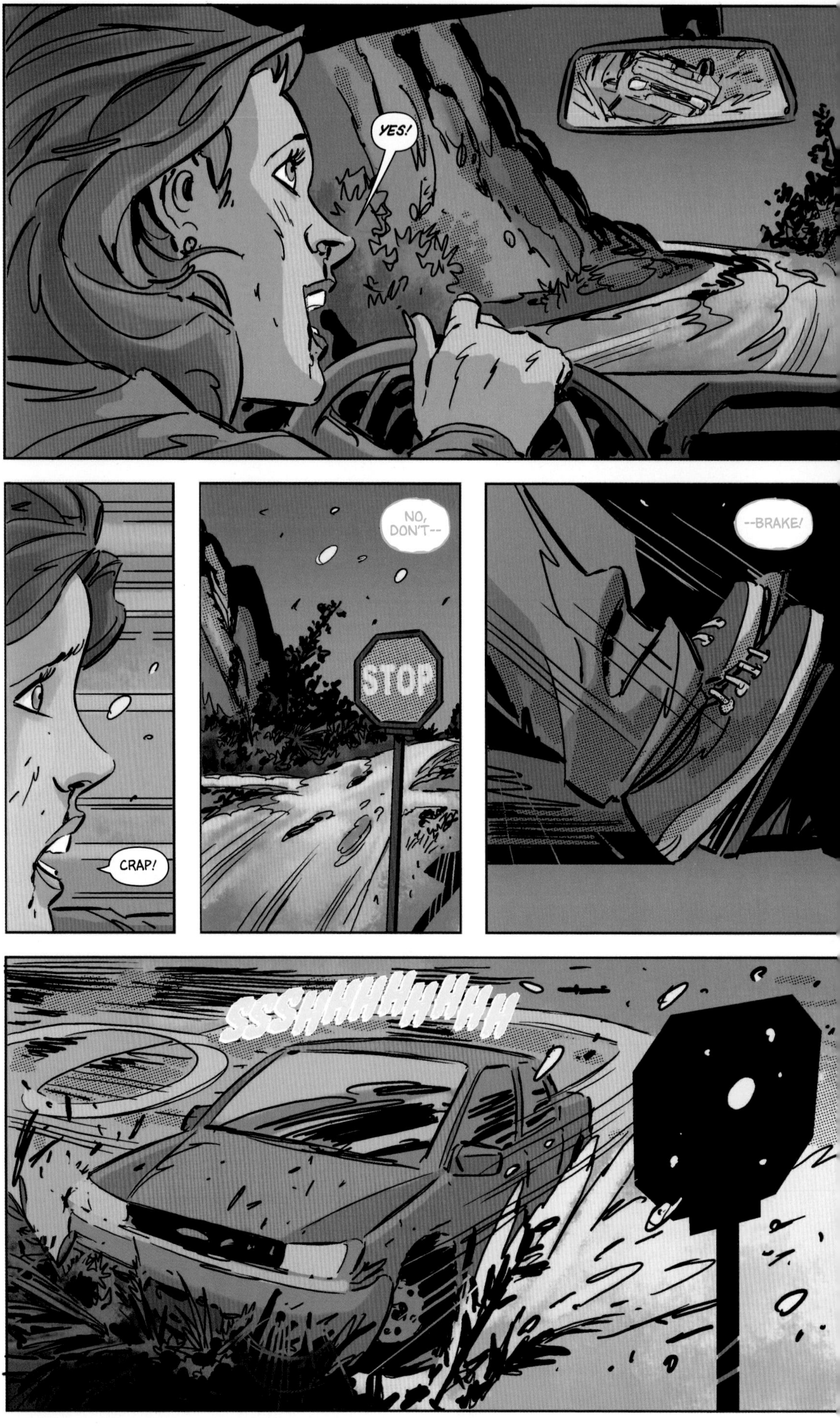
YES!
CRAP!
NO, DON'T--
STOP
--BRAKE!
SSSHHHHHHHHH

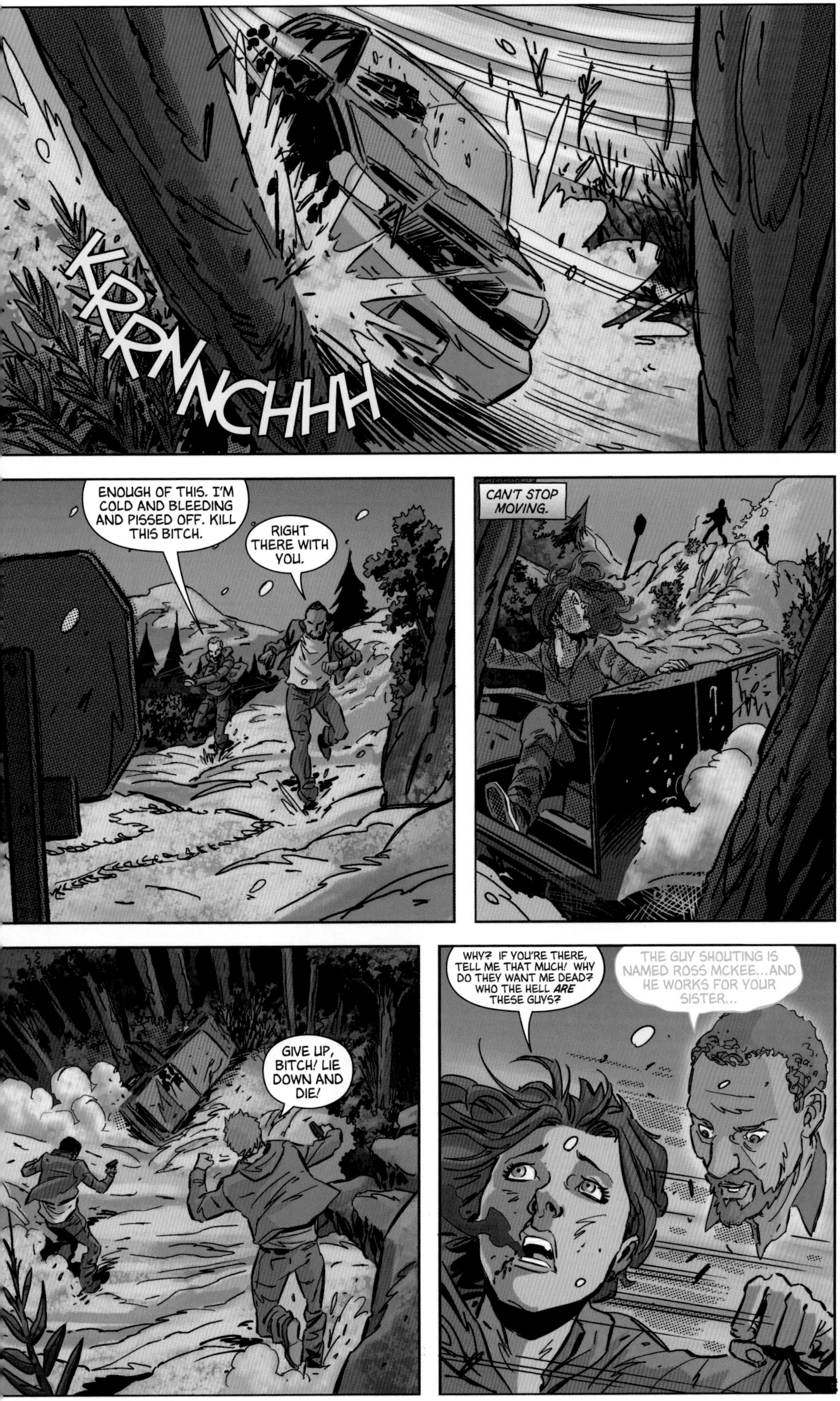
KRRNNCHHH
ENOUGH OF THIS. I'M COLD AND BLEEDING AND PISSED OFF. KILL THIS BITCH.
RIGHT THERE WITH YOU.
CAN'T STOP MOVING.
GIVE UP, BITCH! LIE DOWN AND DIE!
WHY? IF YOU'RE THERE, TELL ME THAT MUCH! WHY DO THEY WANT ME DEAD? WHO THE HELL ARE THESE GUYS?
THE GUY SHOUTING IS NAMED ROSS MCKEE...AND HE WORKS FOR YOUR SISTER...

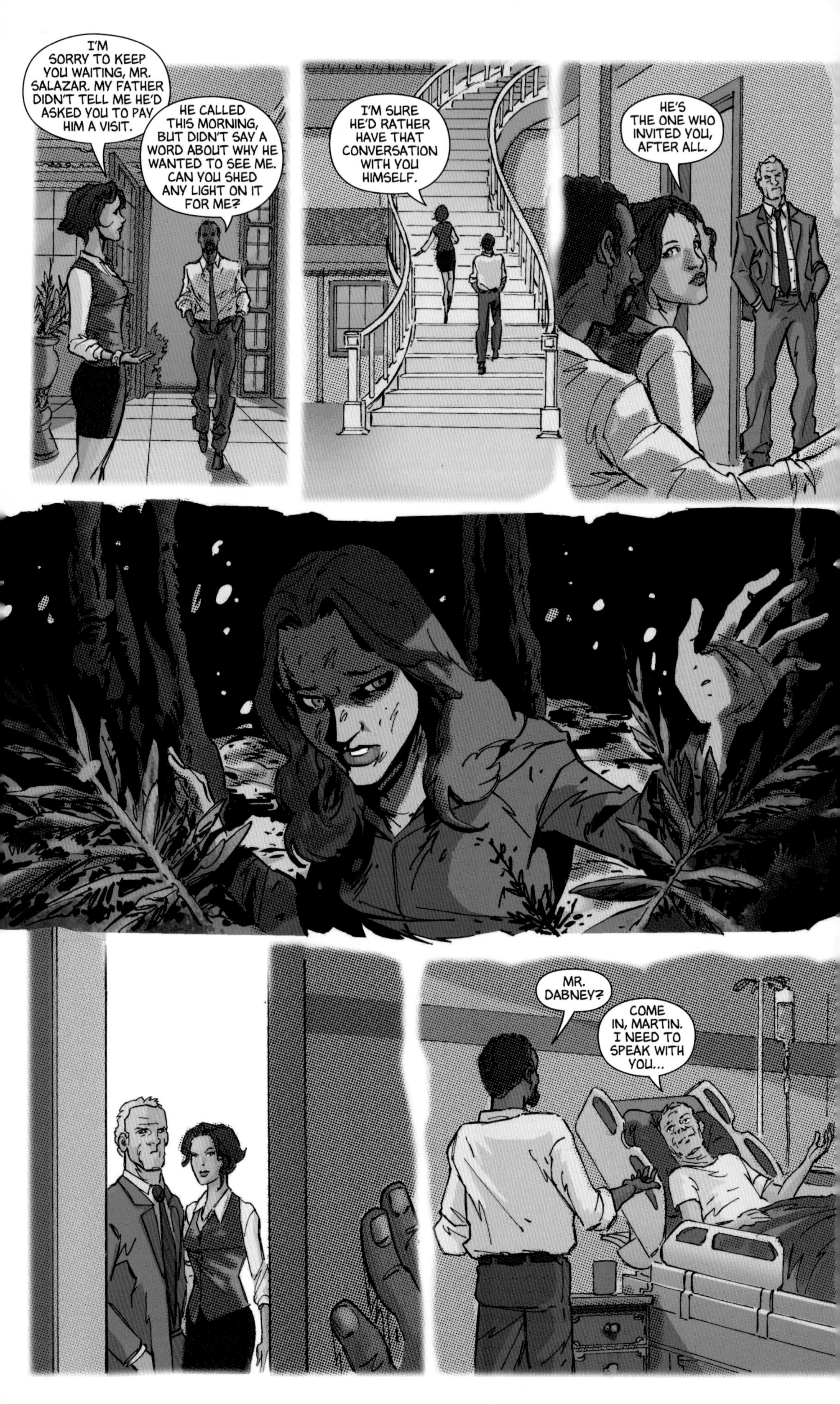
I'M SORRY TO KEEP YOU WAITING, MR. SALAZAR. MY FATHER DIDN'T TELL ME HE'D ASKED YOU TO PAY HIM A VISIT.
HE CALLED THIS MORNING, BUT DIDN'T SAY A WORD ABOUT WHY HE WANTED TO SEE ME. CAN YOU SHED ANY LIGHT ON IT FOR ME?
I'M SURE HE'D RATHER HAVE THAT CONVERSATION WITH YOU HIMSELF.
HE'S THE ONE WHO INVITED YOU, AFTER ALL.
MR. DABNEY?
COME IN, MARTIN. I NEED TO SPEAK WITH YOU...

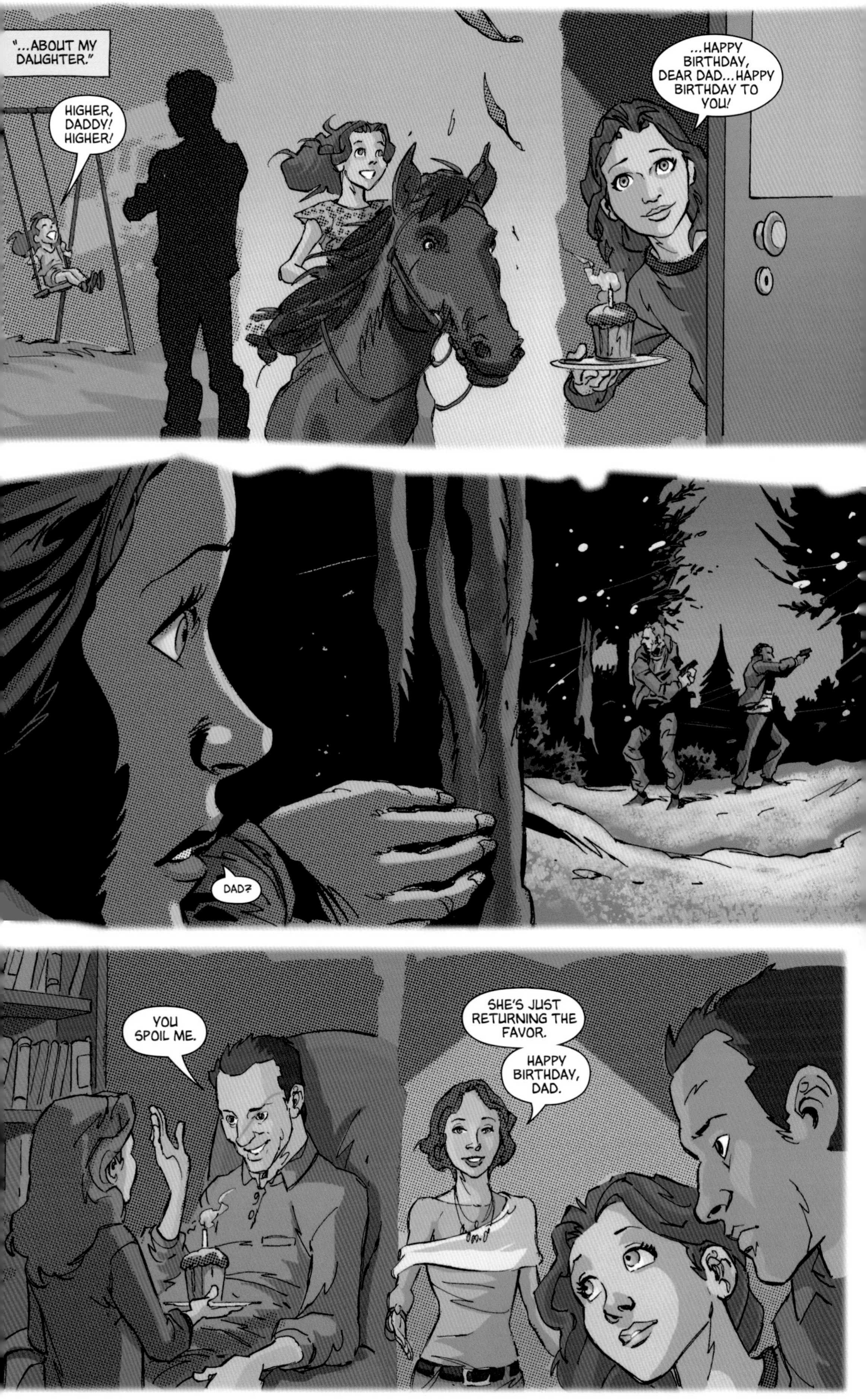
"...ABOUT MY DAUGHTER."
HIGHER, DADDY! HIGHER!
...HAPPY BIRTHDAY, DEAR DAD...HAPPY BIRTHDAY TO YOU!
DAD?
YOU SPOIL ME.
SHE'S JUST RETURNING THE FAVOR.
HAPPY BIRTHDAY, DAD.

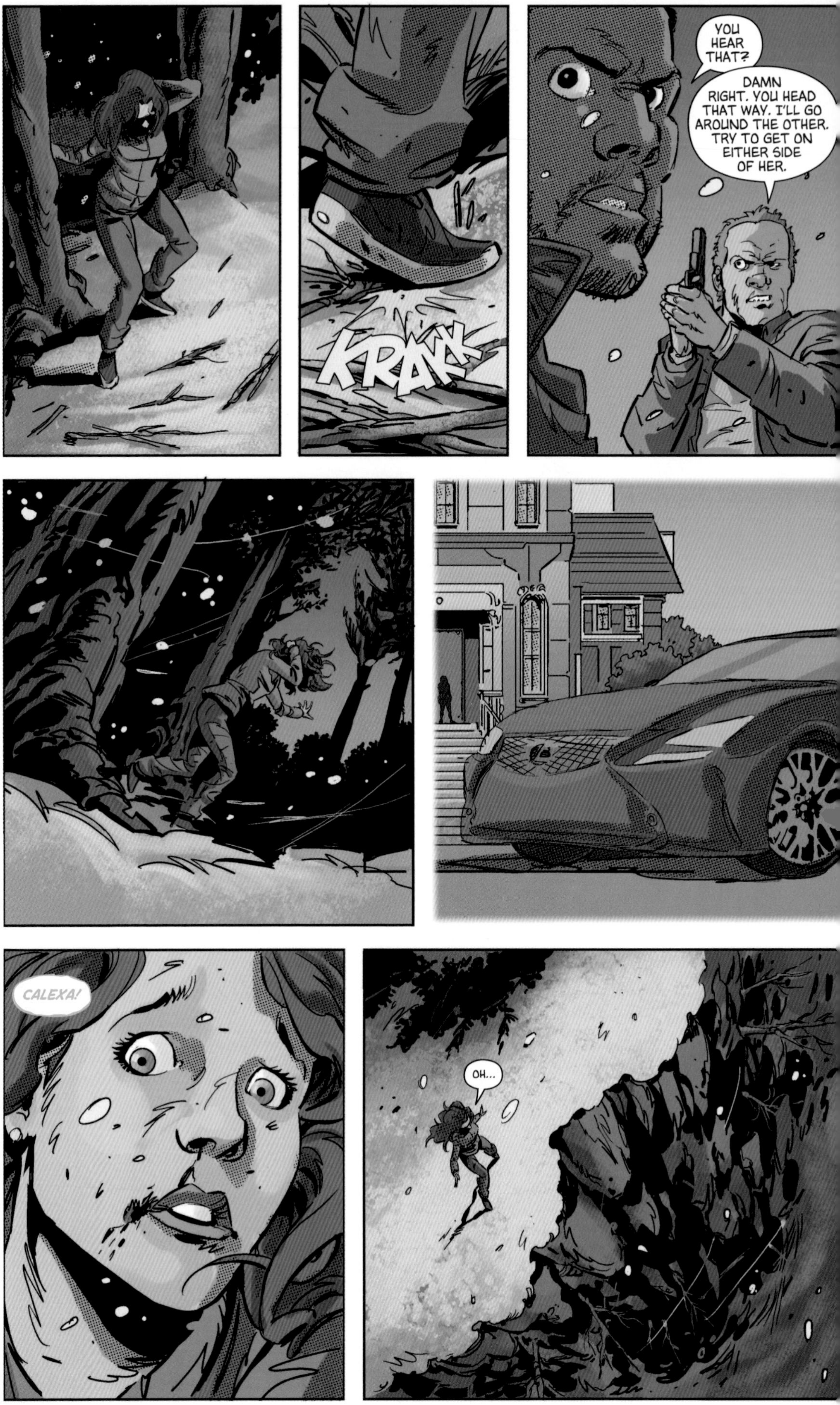
KRAKK
YOU HEAR THAT?
DAMN RIGHT. YOU HEAD THAT WAY. I'LL GO AROUND THE OTHER. TRY TO GET ON EITHER SIDE OF HER.
CALEXA!
OH...

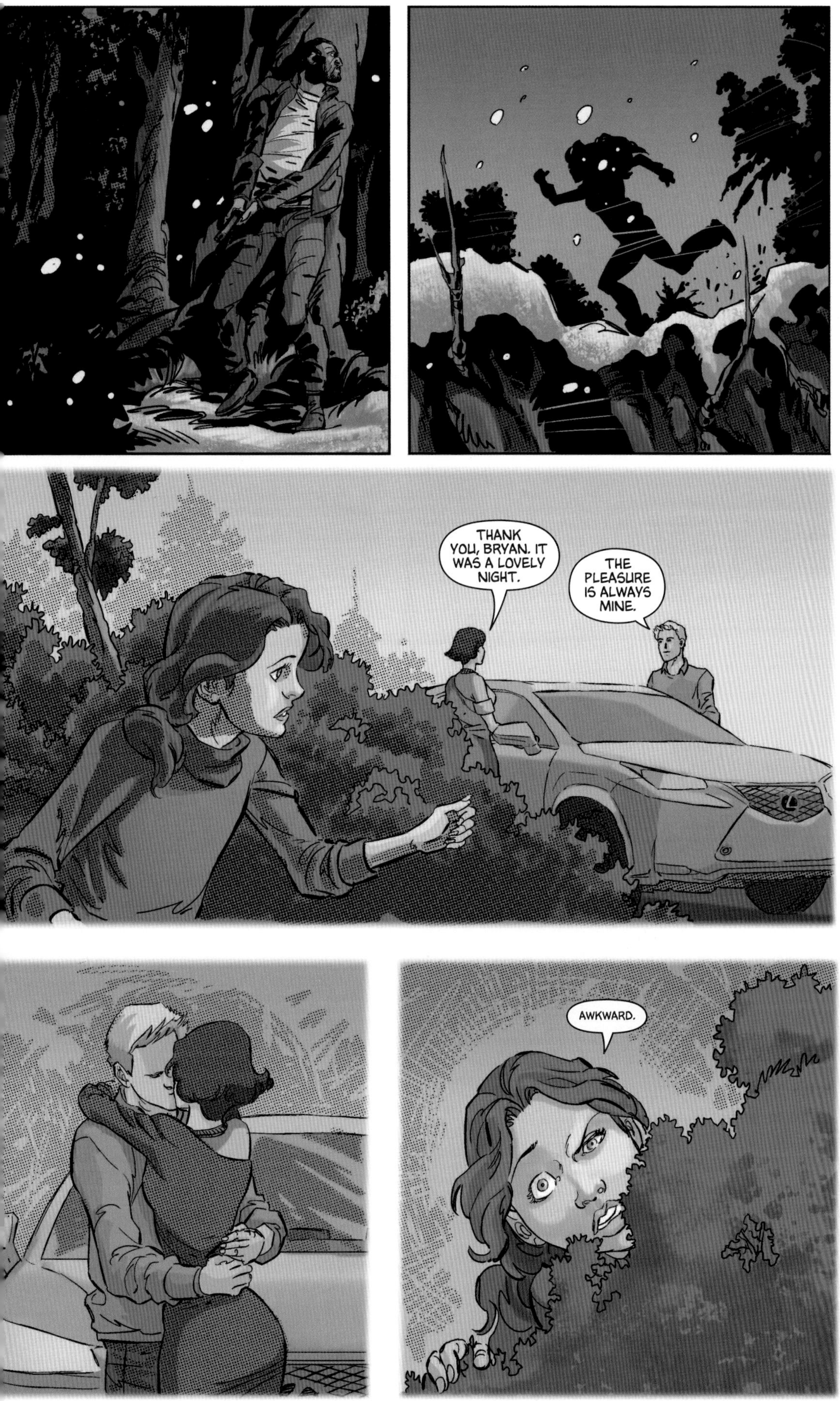
THANK YOU, BRYAN. IT WAS A LOVELY NIGHT.
THE PLEASURE IS ALWAYS MINE.
AWKWARD.

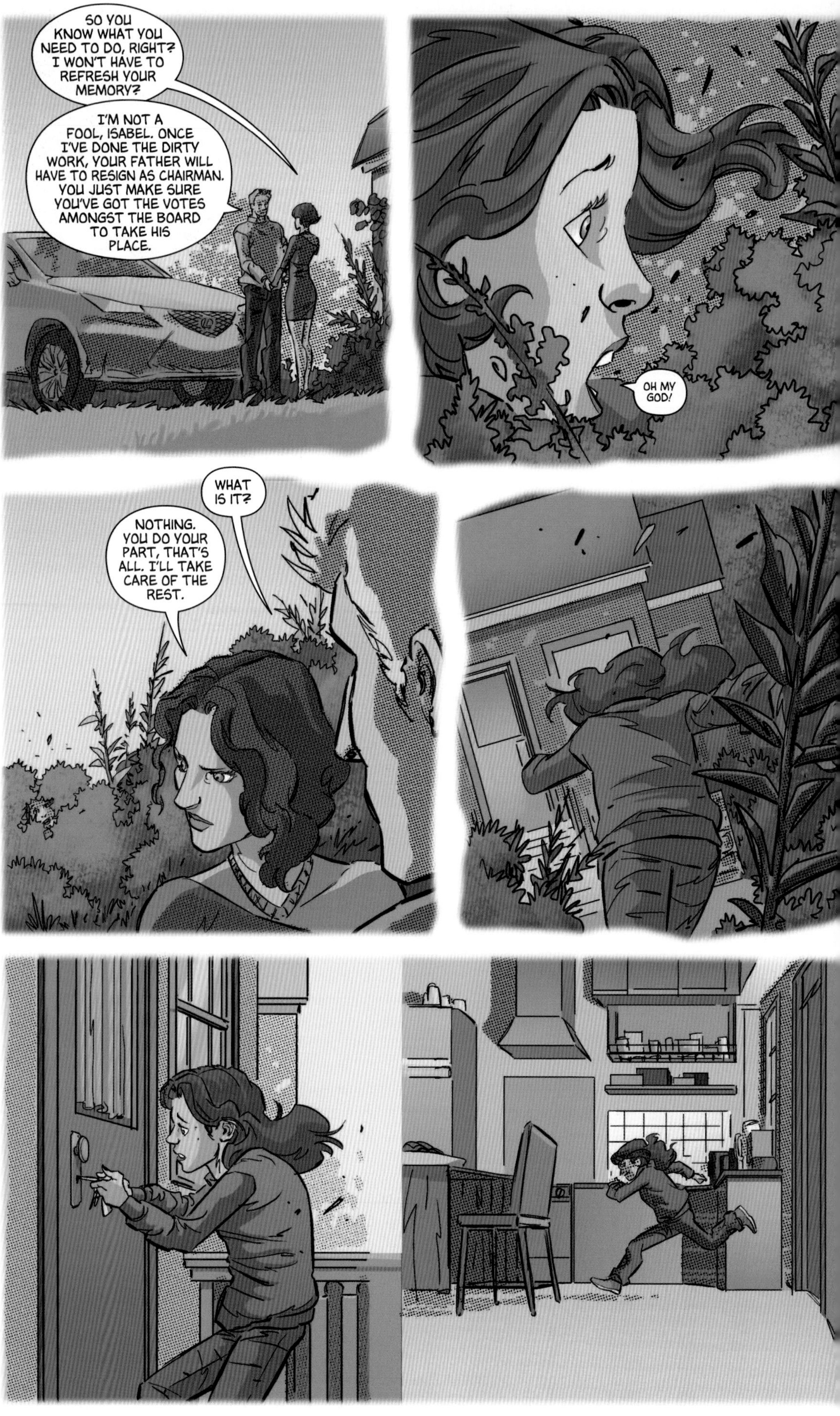
SO YOU KNOW WHAT YOU NEED TO DO, RIGHT? I WON'T HAVE TO REFRESH YOUR MEMORY?
I'M NOT A FOOL, ISABEL. ONCE I'VE DONE THE DIRTY WORK, YOUR FATHER WILL HAVE TO RESIGN AS CHAIRMAN. YOU JUST MAKE SURE YOU'VE GOT THE VOTES AMONGST THE BOARD TO TAKE HIS PLACE.
OH MY GOD!
WHAT IS IT?
NOTHING. YOU DO YOUR PART, THAT'S ALL. I'LL TAKE CARE OF THE REST.

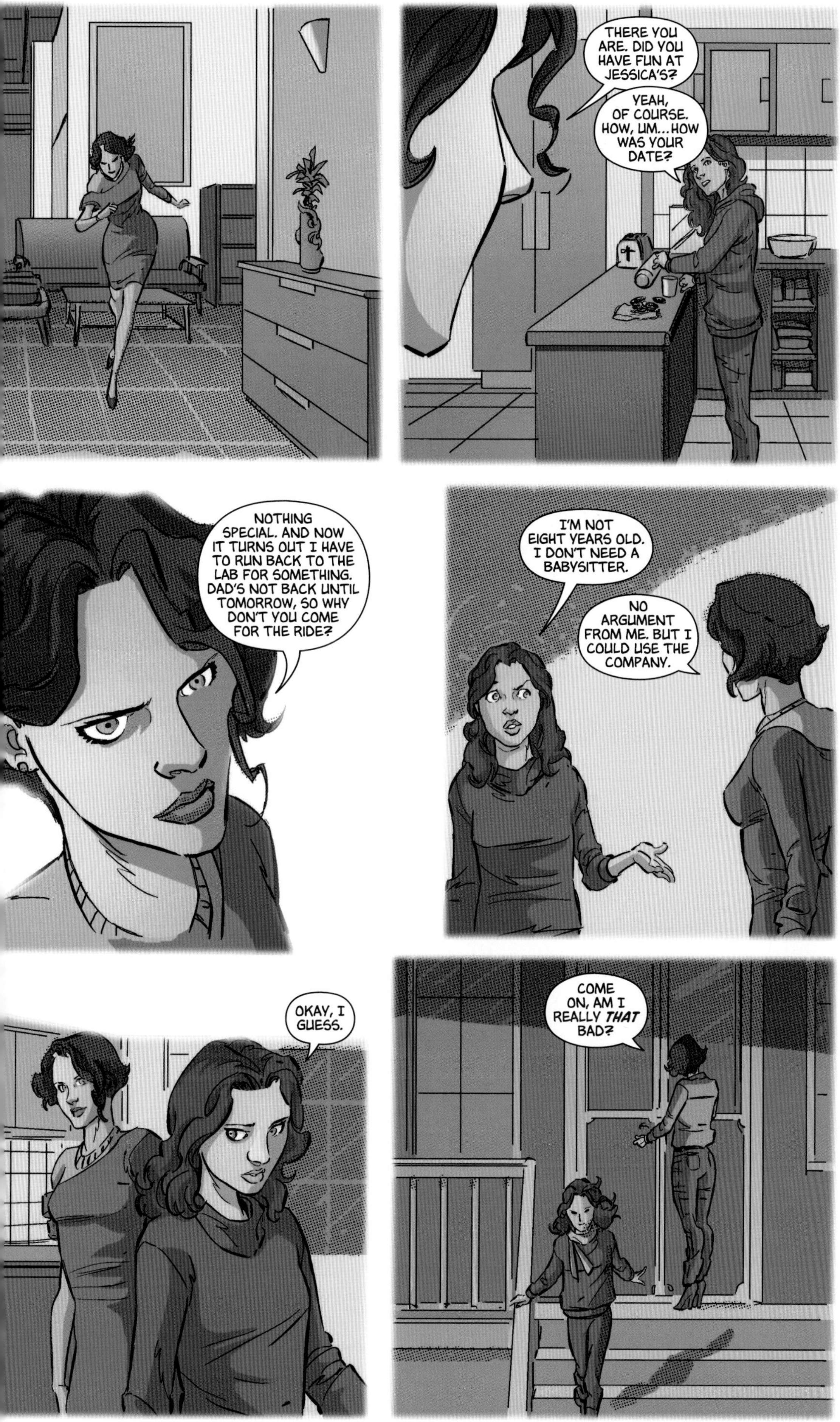
THERE YOU ARE. DID YOU HAVE FUN AT JESSICA'S?
YEAH, OF COURSE. HOW, UM...HOW WAS YOUR DATE?
NOTHING SPECIAL. AND NOW IT TURNS OUT I HAVE TO RUN BACK TO THE LAB FOR SOMETHING. DAD'S NOT BACK UNTIL TOMORROW, SO WHY DON'T YOU COME FOR THE RIDE?
I'M NOT EIGHT YEARS OLD. I DON'T NEED A BABYSITTER.
NO ARGUMENT FROM ME. BUT I COULD USE THE COMPANY.
OKAY, I GUESS.
COME ON, AM I REALLY *THAT* BAD?

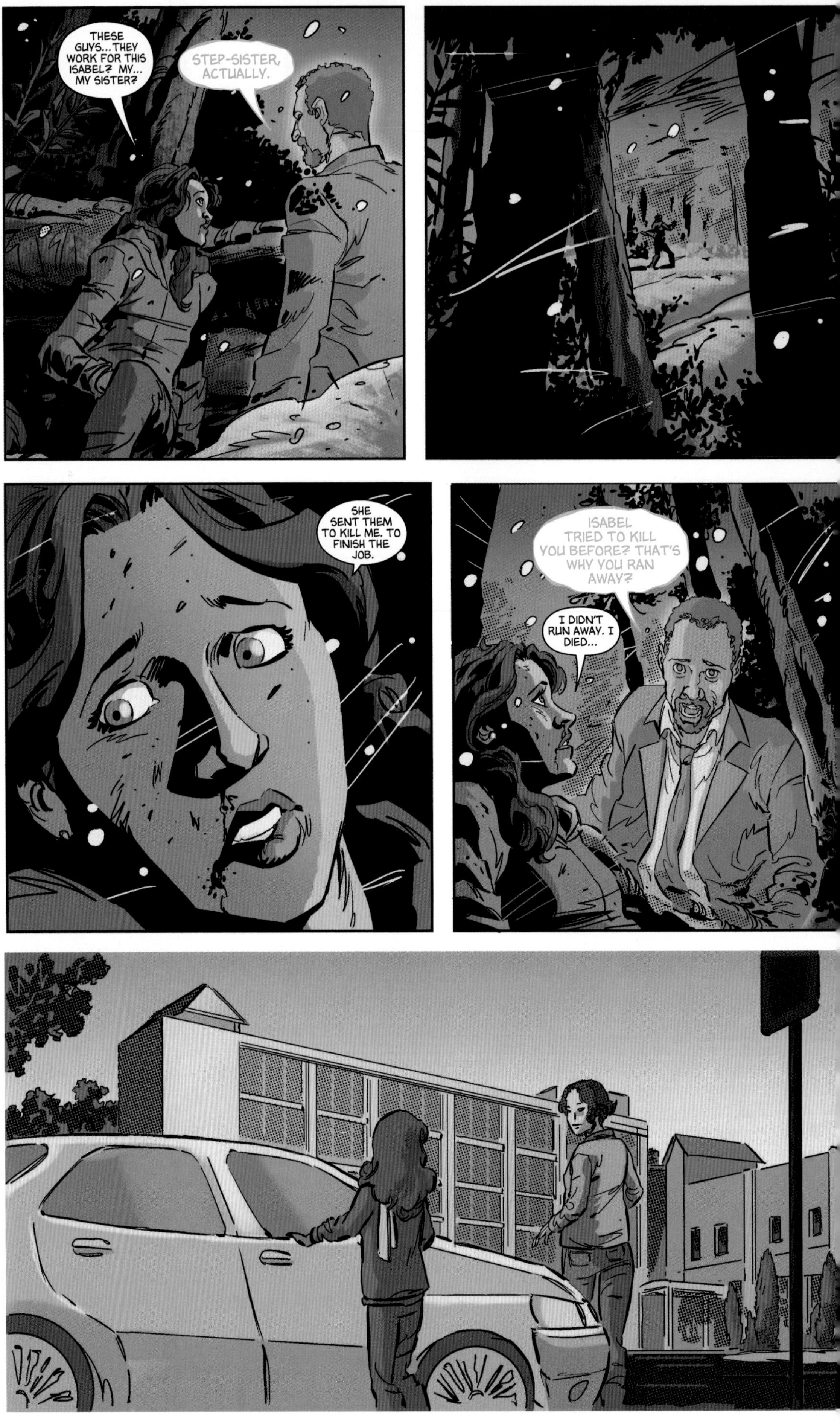
THESE GUYS... THEY WORK FOR THIS ISABEL? MY... MY SISTER?
STEP-SISTER, ACTUALLY.
SHE SENT THEM TO KILL ME. TO FINISH THE JOB.
ISABEL TRIED TO KILL YOU BEFORE? THAT'S WHY YOU RAN AWAY?
I DIDN'T RUN AWAY. I DIED...

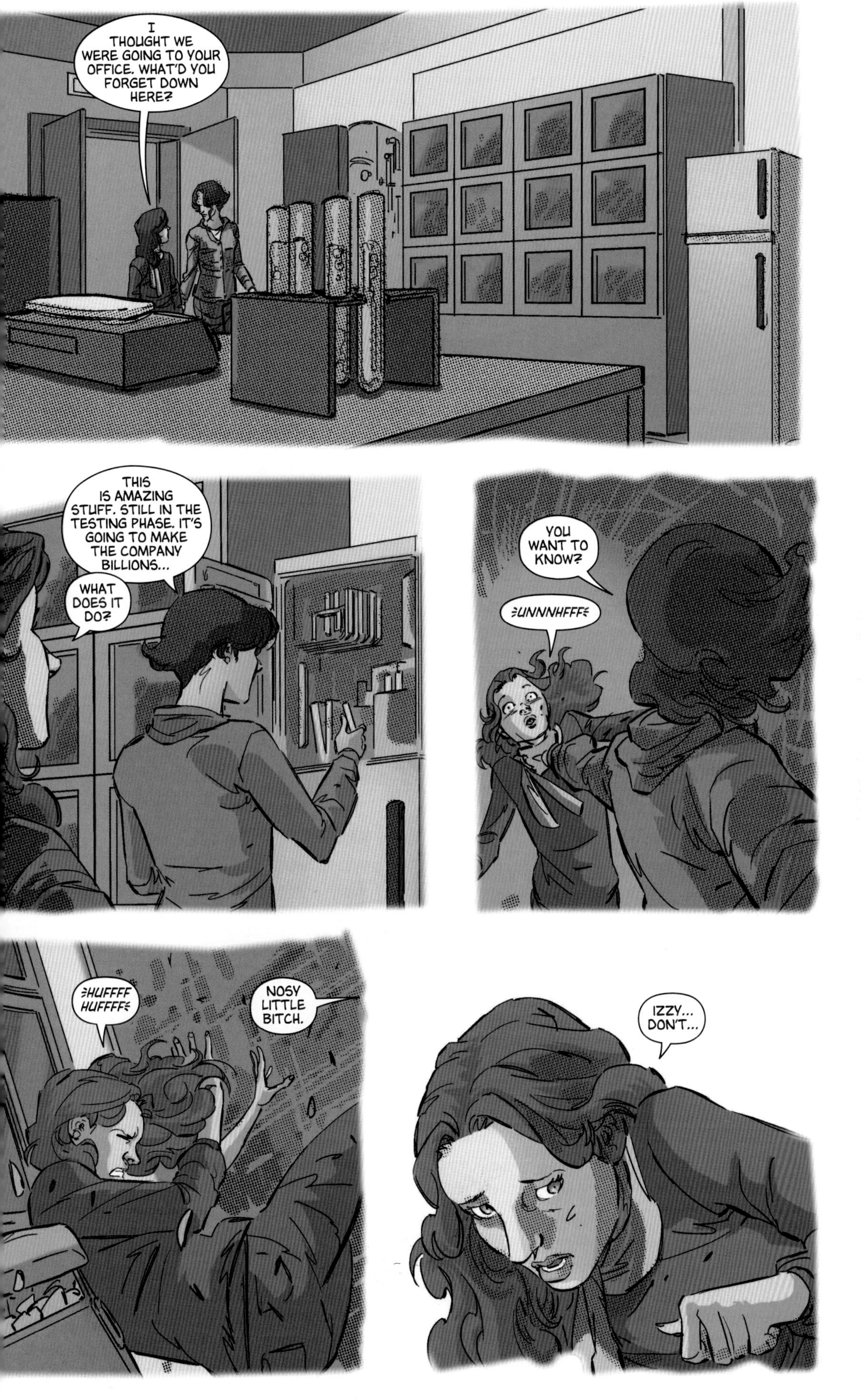
I THOUGHT WE WERE GOING TO YOUR OFFICE. WHAT'D YOU FORGET DOWN HERE?
THIS IS AMAZING STUFF. STILL IN THE TESTING PHASE. IT'S GOING TO MAKE THE COMPANY BILLIONS...
WHAT DOES IT DO?
YOU WANT TO KNOW?
UNNNHFFF
HUFFFF HUFFFF
NOSY LITTLE BITCH.
IZZY... DON'T...

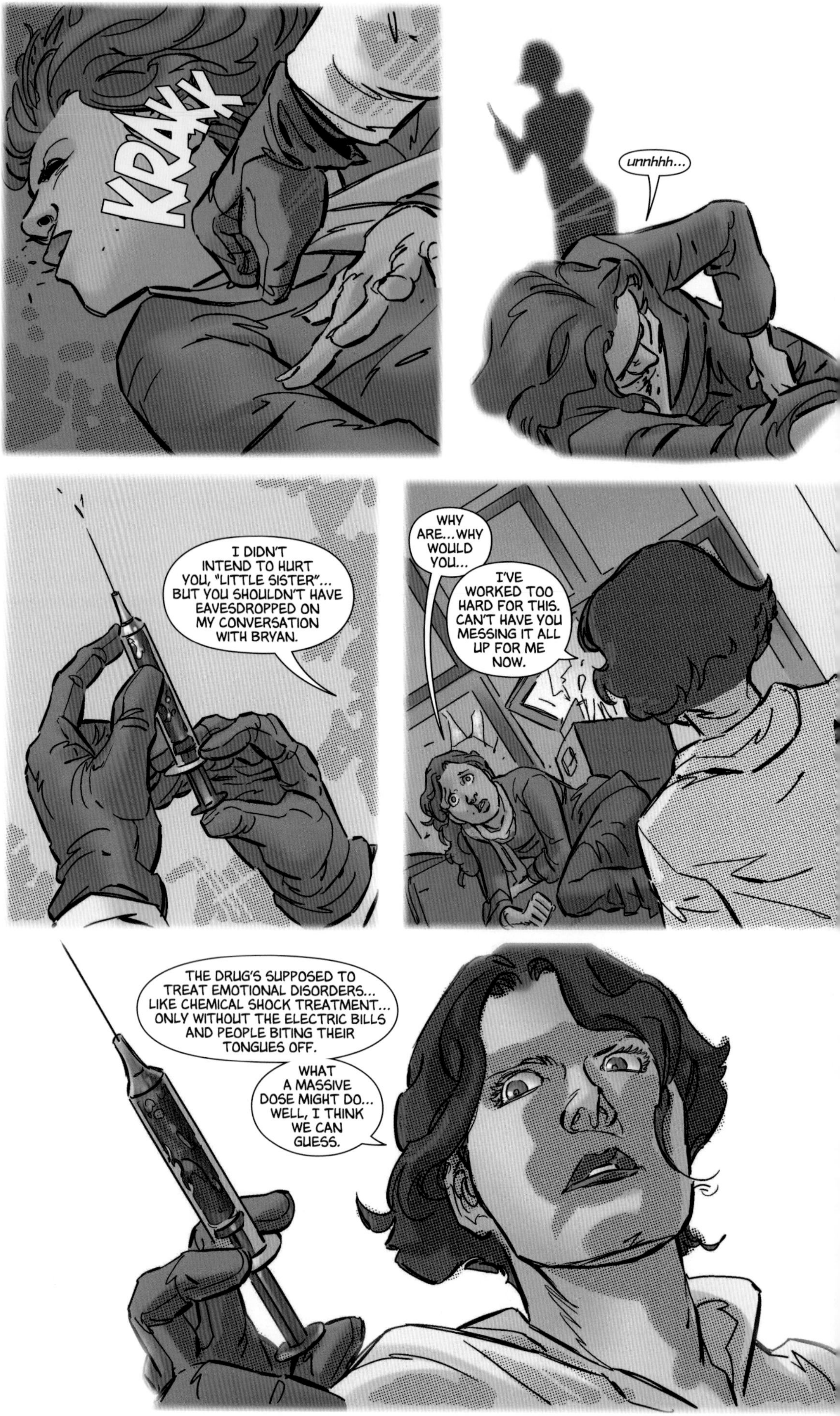
KRAKK
unnhhh...
I DIDN'T INTEND TO HURT YOU, "LITTLE SISTER"... BUT YOU SHOULDN'T HAVE EAVESDROPPED ON MY CONVERSATION WITH BRYAN.
WHY ARE...WHY WOULD YOU...
I'VE WORKED TOO HARD FOR THIS. CAN'T HAVE YOU MESSING IT ALL UP FOR ME NOW.
THE DRUG'S SUPPOSED TO TREAT EMOTIONAL DISORDERS... LIKE CHEMICAL SHOCK TREATMENT... ONLY WITHOUT THE ELECTRIC BILLS AND PEOPLE BITING THEIR TONGUES OFF.
WHAT A MASSIVE DOSE MIGHT DO... WELL, I THINK WE CAN GUESS.

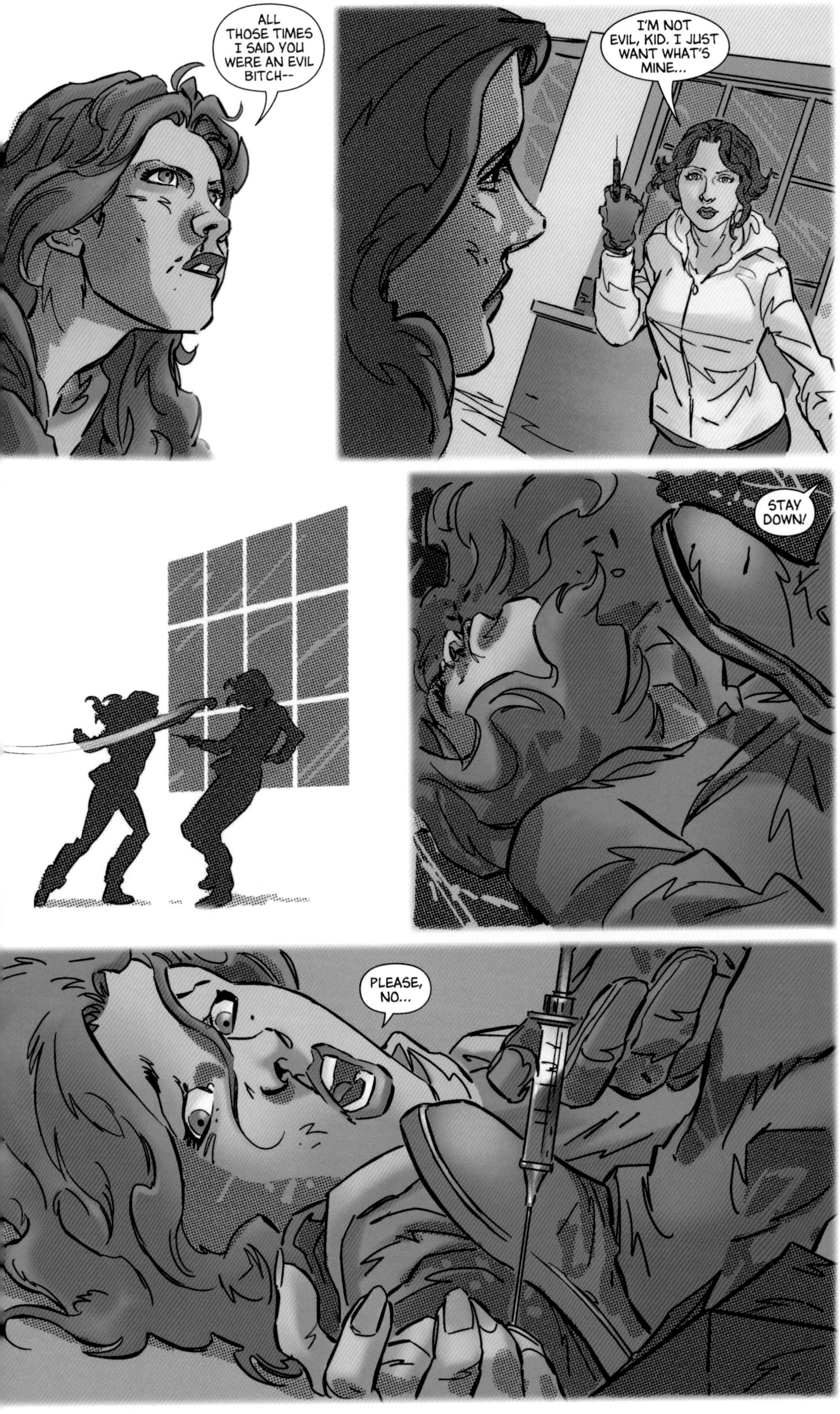
ALL THOSE TIMES I SAID YOU WERE AN EVIL BITCH--
I'M NOT EVIL, KID. I JUST WANT WHAT'S MINE...
STAY DOWN!
PLEASE, NO...

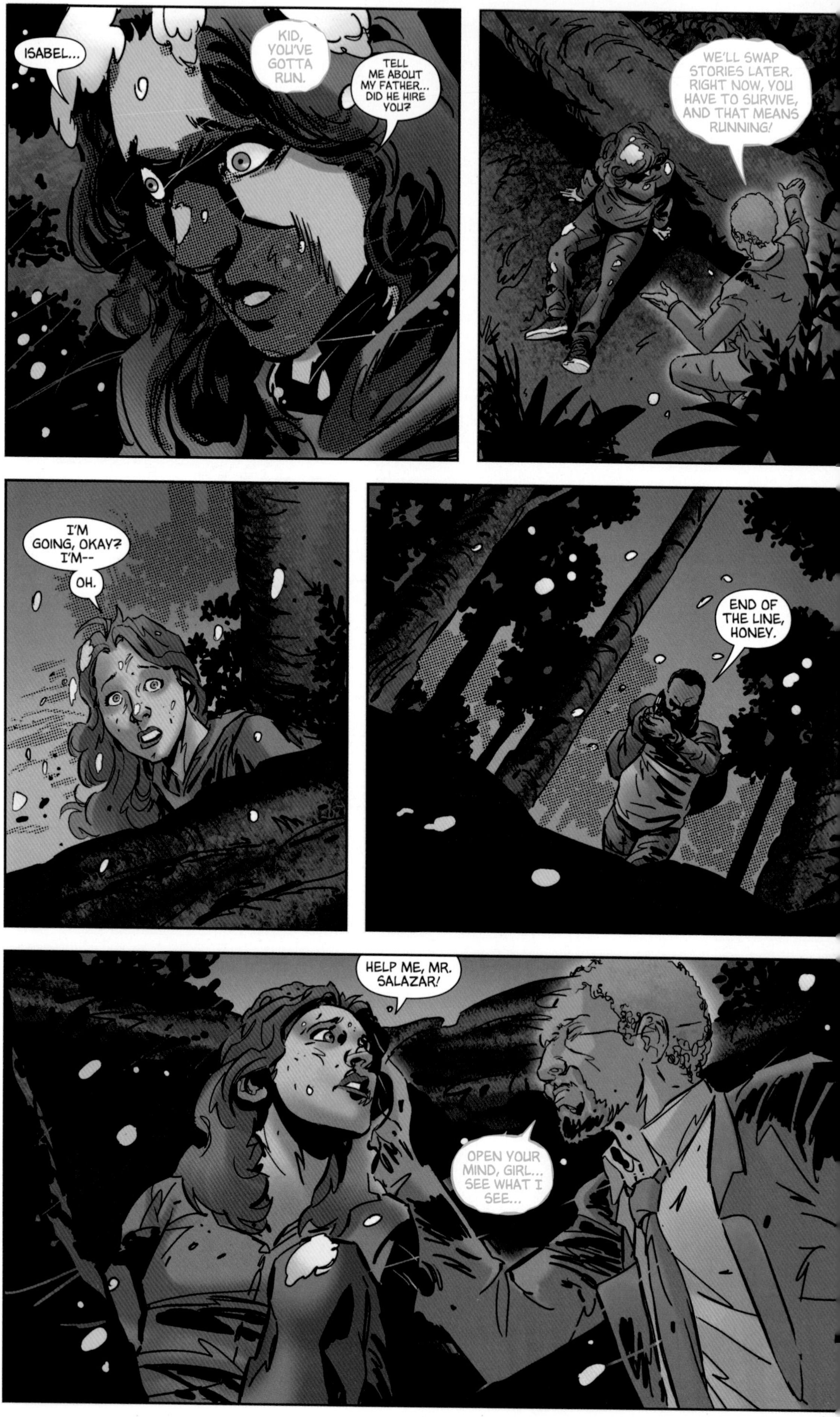
ISABEL...
KID, YOU'VE GOTTA RUN.
TELL ME ABOUT MY FATHER... DID HE HIRE YOU?
WE'LL SWAP STORIES LATER. RIGHT NOW, YOU HAVE TO SURVIVE, AND THAT MEANS RUNNING!
I'M GOING, OKAY? I'M--
OH.
END OF THE LINE, HONEY.
HELP ME, MR. SALAZAR!
OPEN YOUR MIND, GIRL... SEE WHAT I SEE...

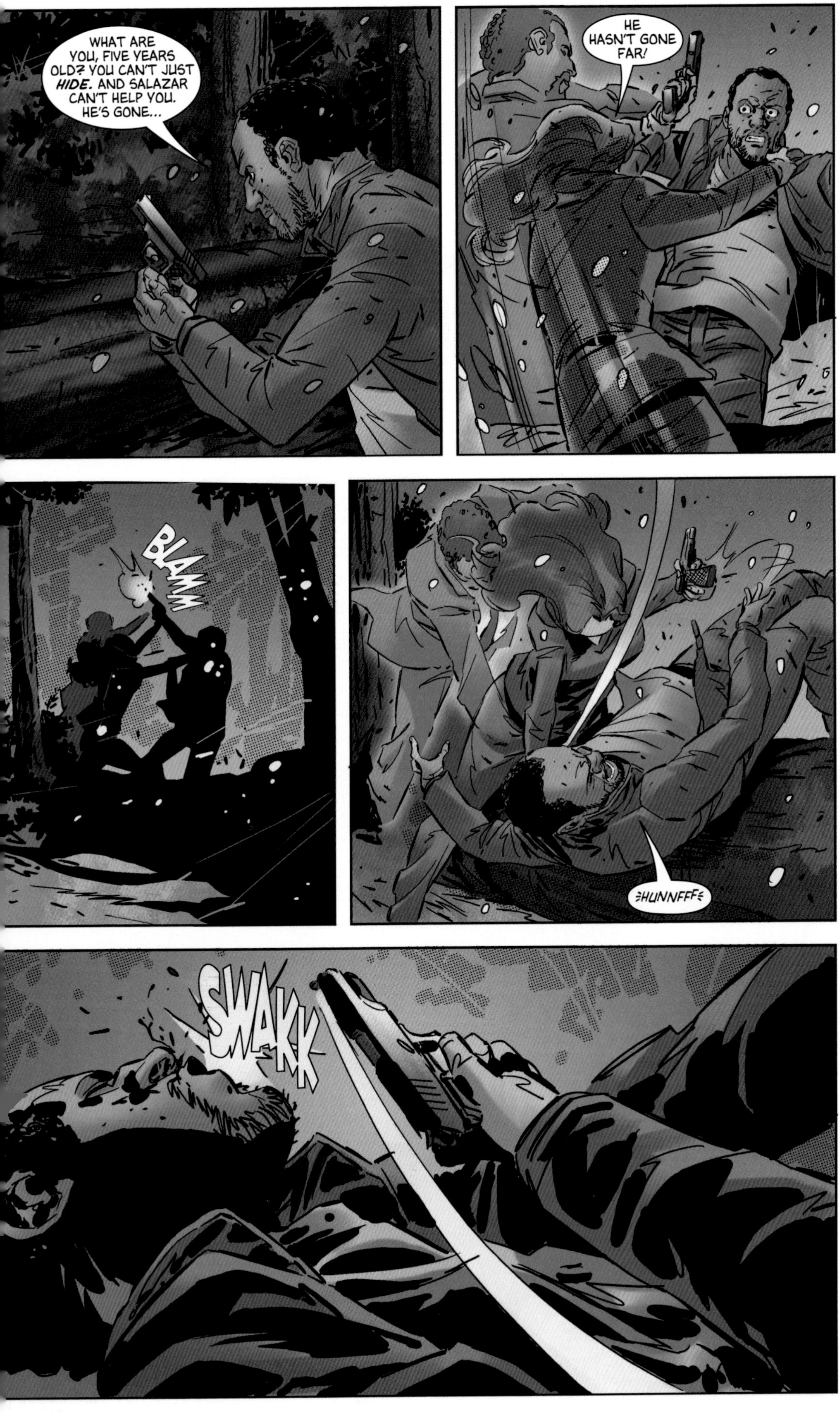
WHAT ARE YOU, FIVE YEARS OLD? YOU CAN'T JUST *HIDE*. AND SALAZAR CAN'T HELP YOU. HE'S GONE...
HE HASN'T GONE FAR!
BLAMM
HUNNFFF
SWAKK

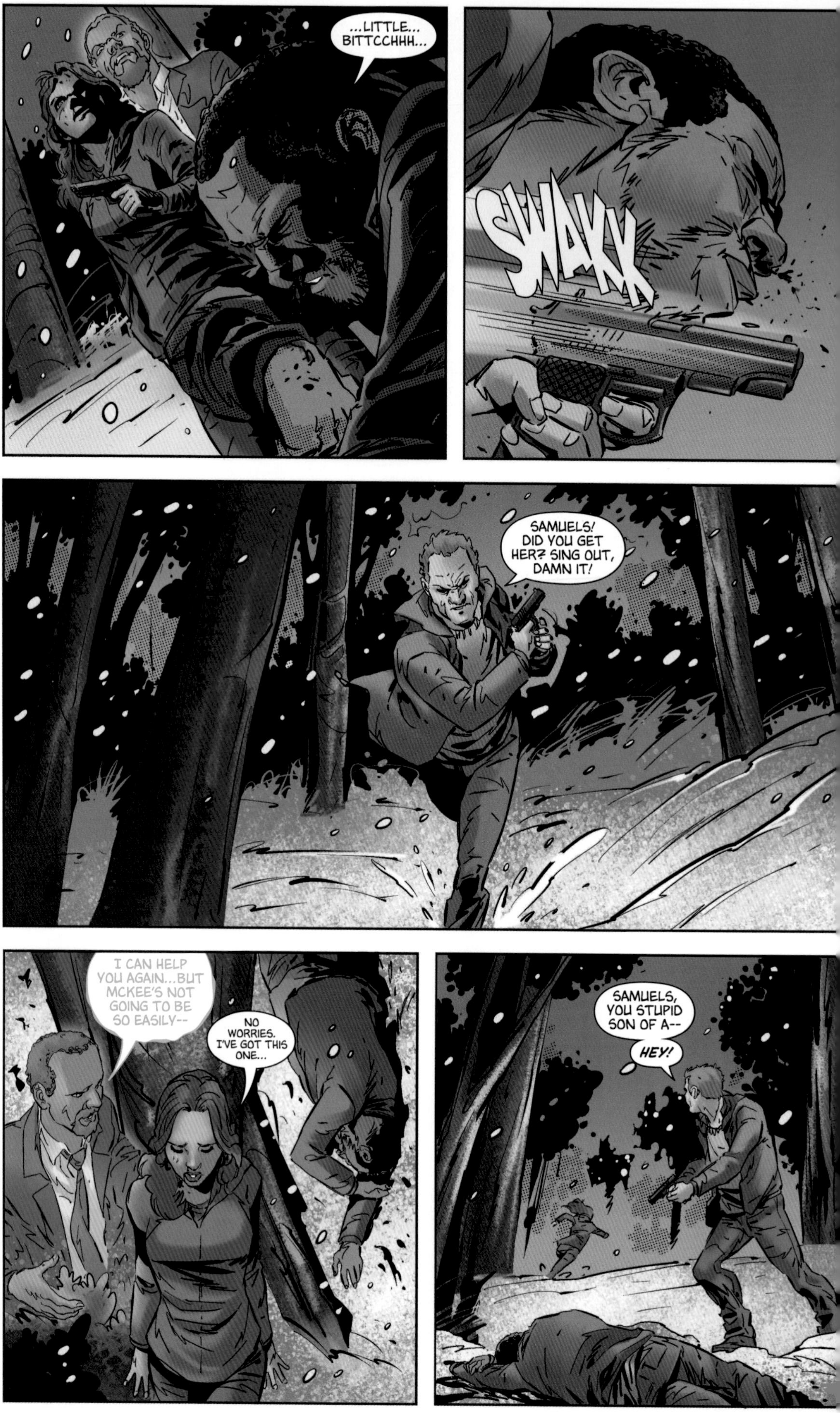
...LITTLE... BITTCCHHH...
SWAKK
SAMUELS! DID YOU GET HER? SING OUT, DAMN IT!
I CAN HELP YOU AGAIN...BUT MCKEE'S NOT GOING TO BE SO EASILY--
NO WORRIES. I'VE GOT THIS ONE...
SAMUELS, YOU STUPID SON OF A--
HEY!

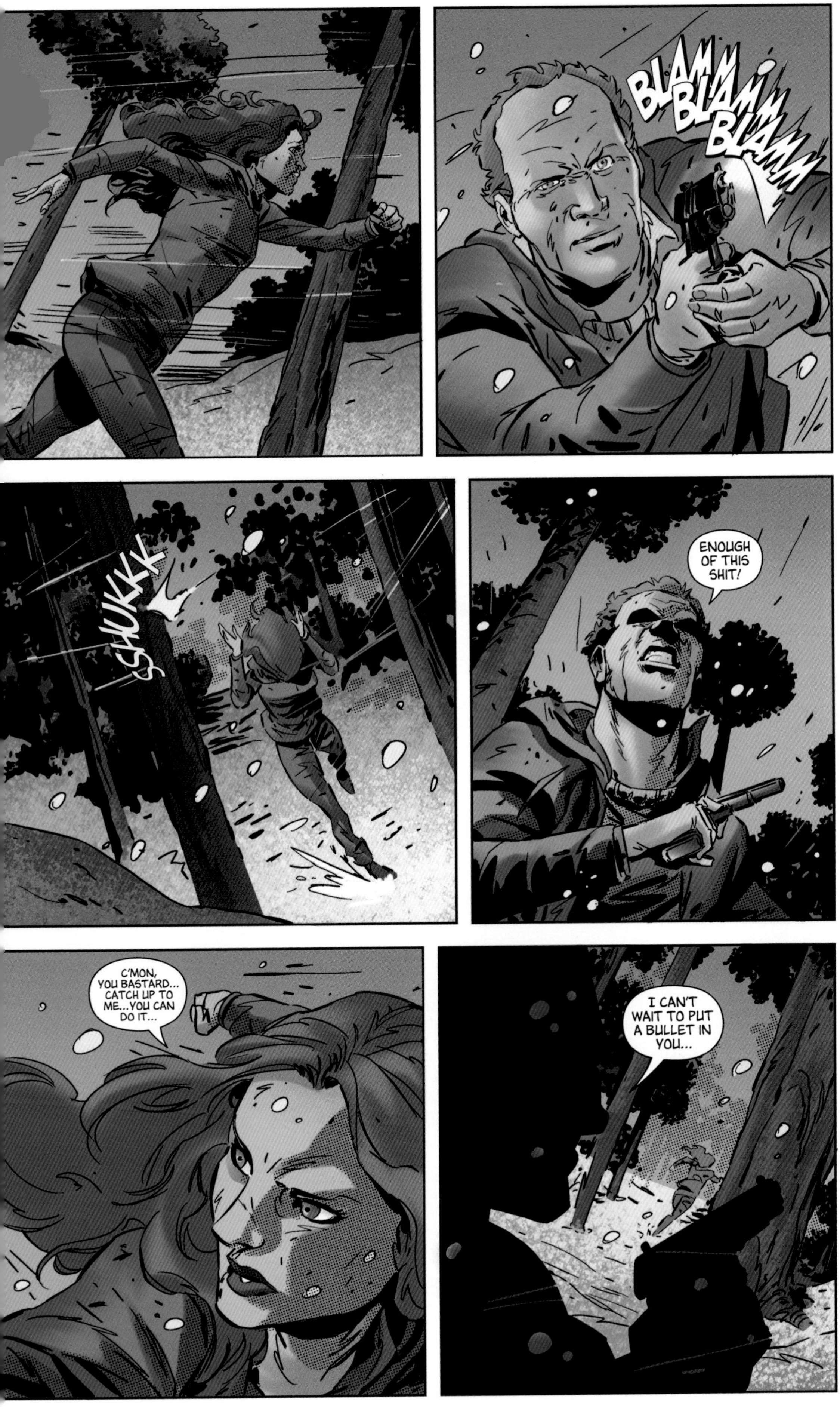
BLAMM
BLAMM
BLAMM
SHUKKK
ENOUGH OF THIS SHIT!
C'MON, YOU BASTARD... CATCH UP TO ME...YOU CAN DO IT...
I CAN'T WAIT TO PUT A BULLET IN YOU...

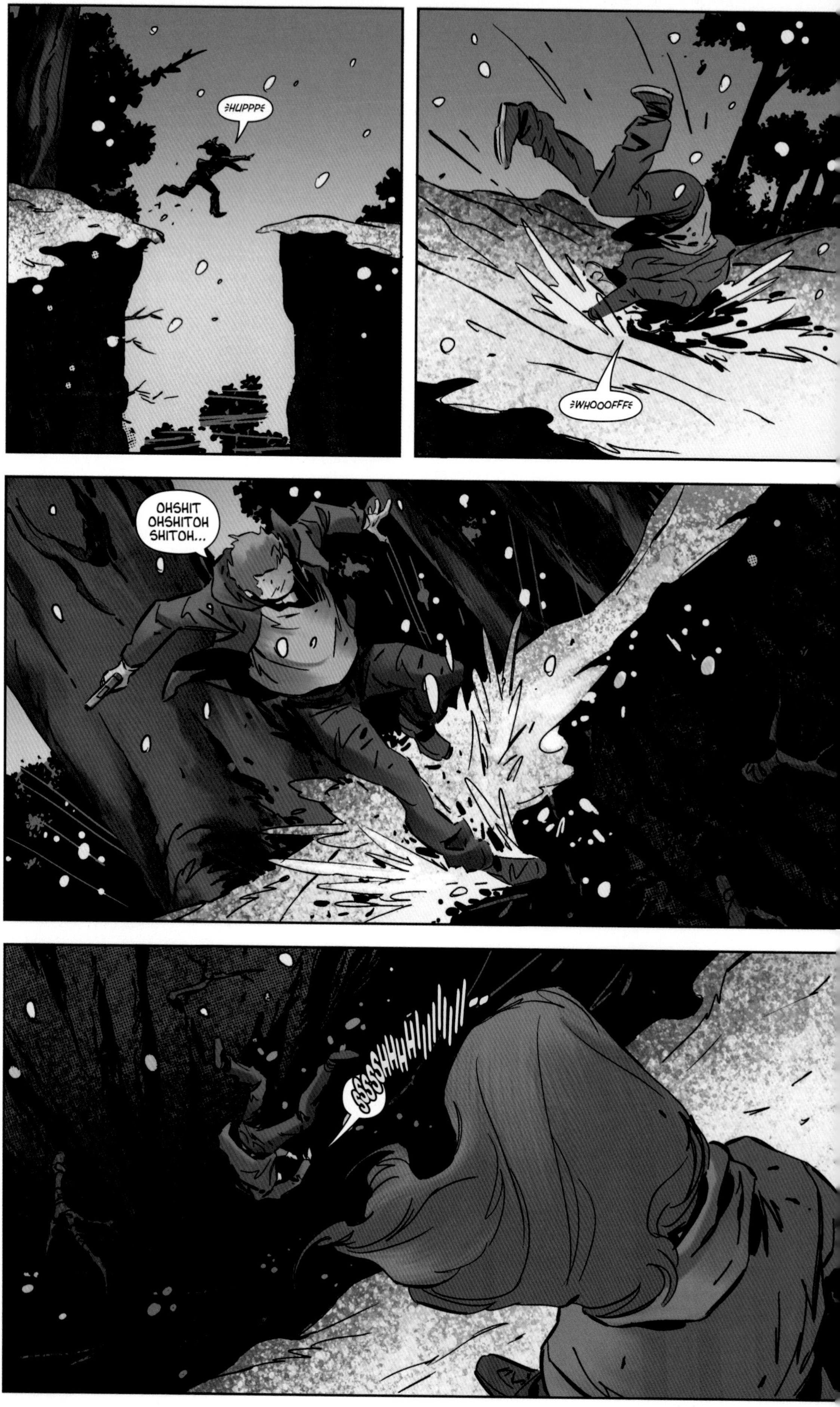
HUPPP
WHOOOFFF
OHSHIT OHSHITOH SHITOH...
SSSSSHHHHH

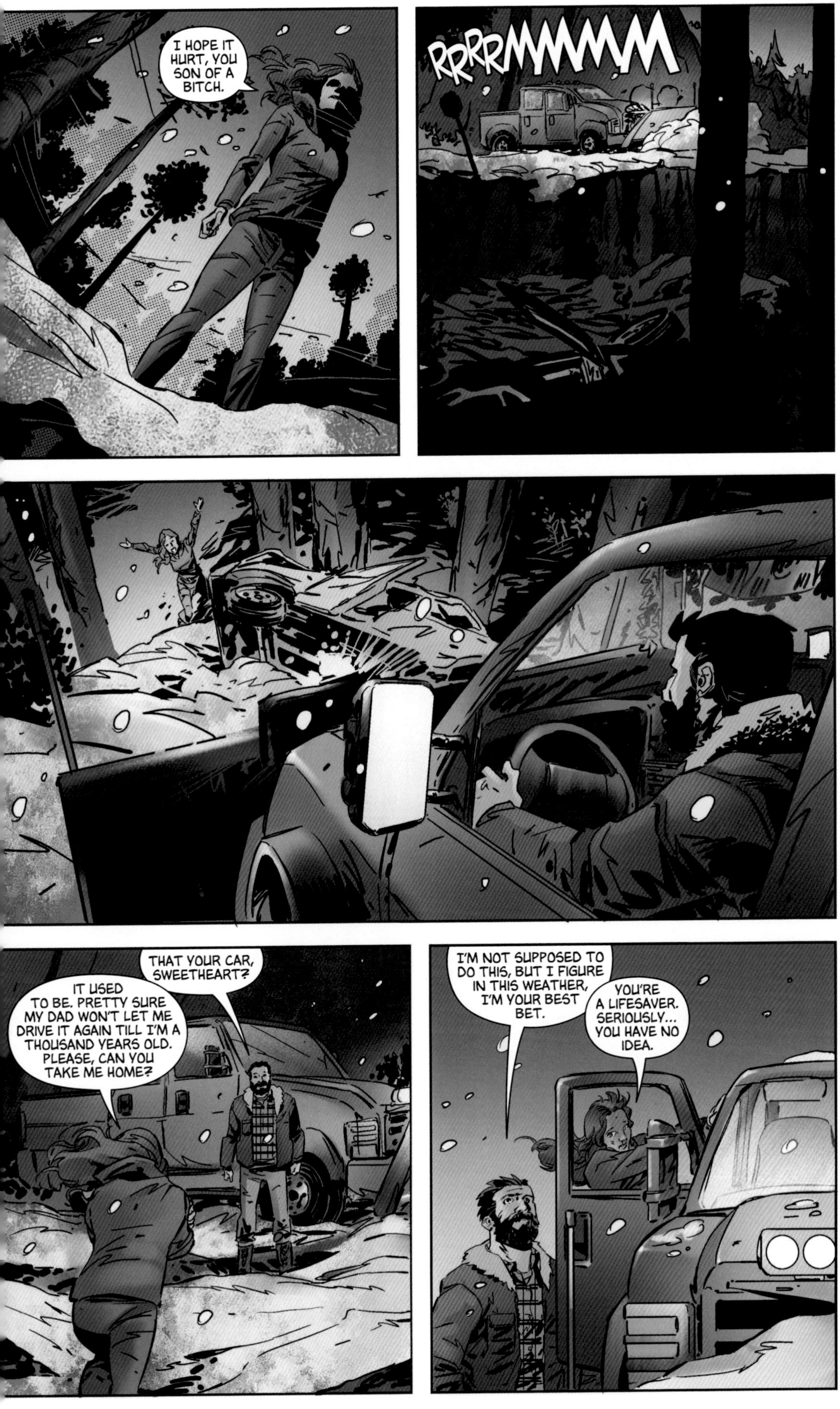
I HOPE IT HURT, YOU SON OF A BITCH.
RRRMMMMMM
THAT YOUR CAR, SWEETHEART?
IT USED TO BE. PRETTY SURE MY DAD WON'T LET ME DRIVE IT AGAIN TILL I'M A THOUSAND YEARS OLD. PLEASE, CAN YOU TAKE ME HOME?
I'M NOT SUPPOSED TO DO THIS, BUT I FIGURE IN THIS WEATHER, I'M YOUR BEST BET.
YOU'RE A LIFESAVER. SERIOUSLY... YOU HAVE NO IDEA.

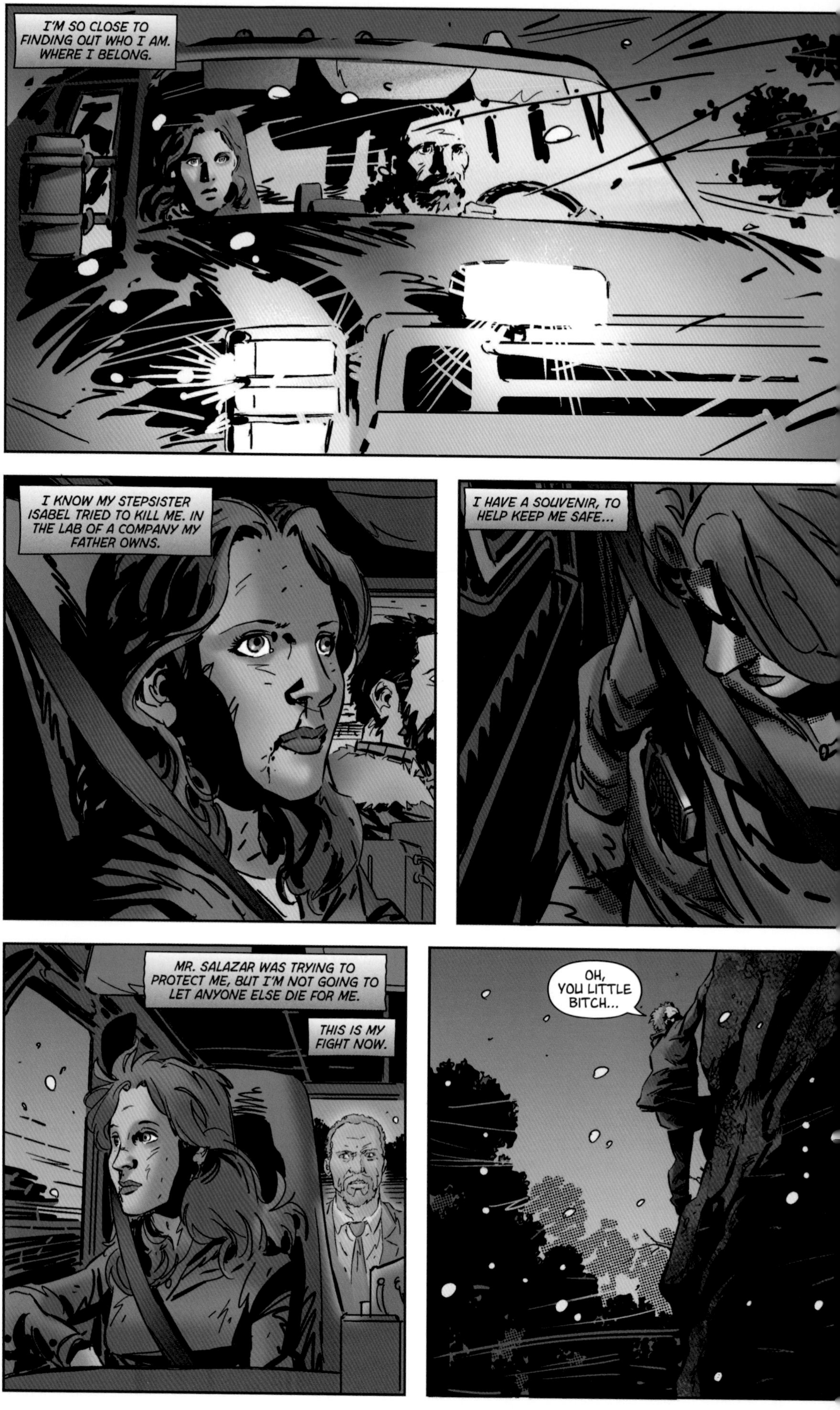
I'M SO CLOSE TO FINDING OUT WHO I AM. WHERE I BELONG.
I KNOW MY STEPSISTER ISABEL TRIED TO KILL ME. IN THE LAB OF A COMPANY MY FATHER OWNS.
I HAVE A SOUVENIR, TO HELP KEEP ME SAFE...
MR. SALAZAR WAS TRYING TO PROTECT ME, BUT I'M NOT GOING TO LET ANYONE ELSE DIE FOR ME.
THIS IS MY FIGHT NOW.
OH, YOU LITTLE BITCH...

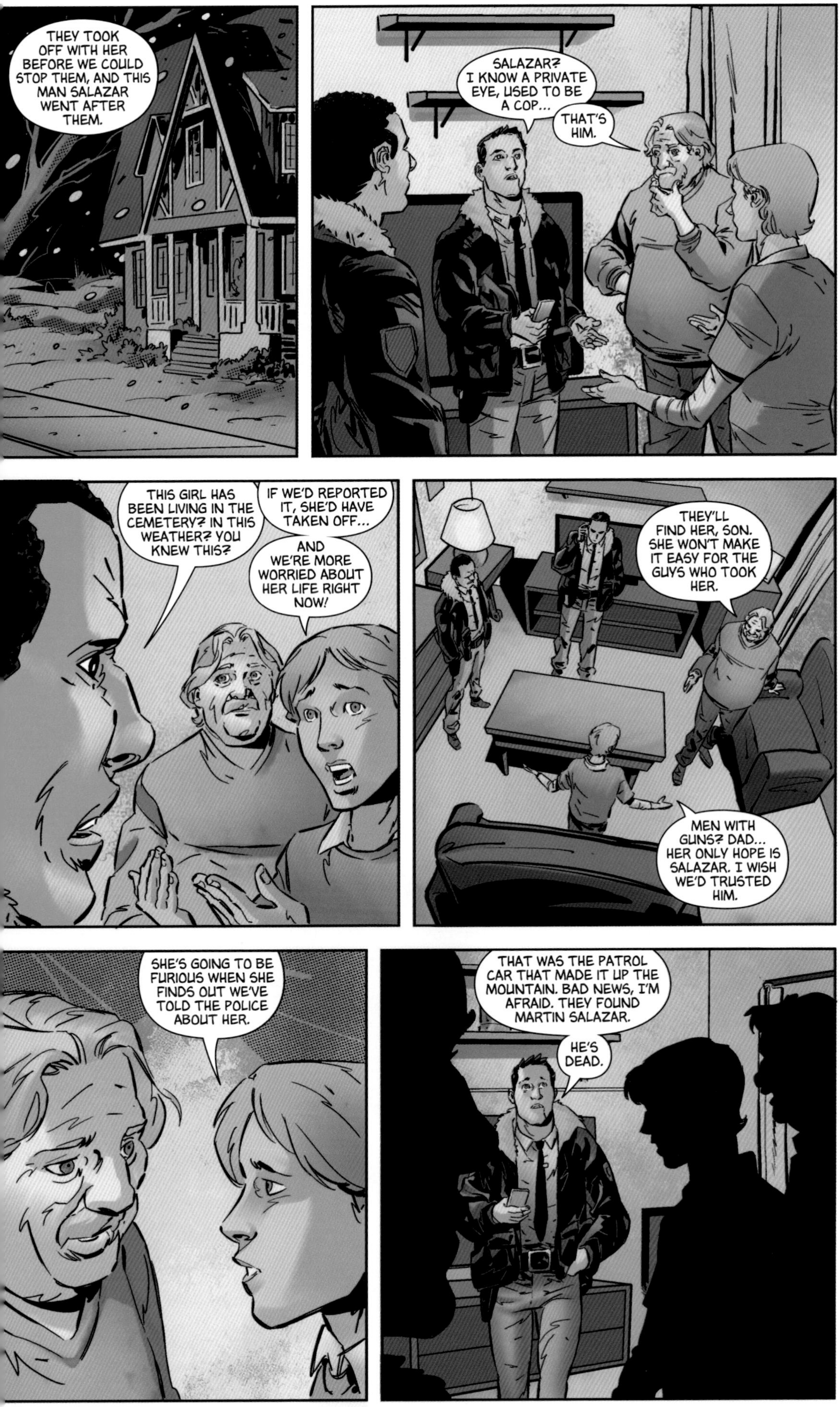
THEY TOOK OFF WITH HER BEFORE WE COULD STOP THEM, AND THIS MAN SALAZAR WENT AFTER THEM.
SALAZAR? I KNOW A PRIVATE EYE, USED TO BE A COP...
THAT'S HIM.
THIS GIRL HAS BEEN LIVING IN THE CEMETERY? IN THIS WEATHER? YOU KNEW THIS?
IF WE'D REPORTED IT, SHE'D HAVE TAKEN OFF...
AND WE'RE MORE WORRIED ABOUT HER LIFE RIGHT NOW!
THEY'LL FIND HER, SON. SHE WON'T MAKE IT EASY FOR THE GUYS WHO TOOK HER.
MEN WITH GUNS? DAD... HER ONLY HOPE IS SALAZAR. I WISH WE'D TRUSTED HIM.
SHE'S GOING TO BE FURIOUS WHEN SHE FINDS OUT WE'VE TOLD THE POLICE ABOUT HER.
THAT WAS THE PATROL CAR THAT MADE IT UP THE MOUNTAIN. BAD NEWS, I'M AFRAID. THEY FOUND MARTIN SALAZAR.
HE'S DEAD.

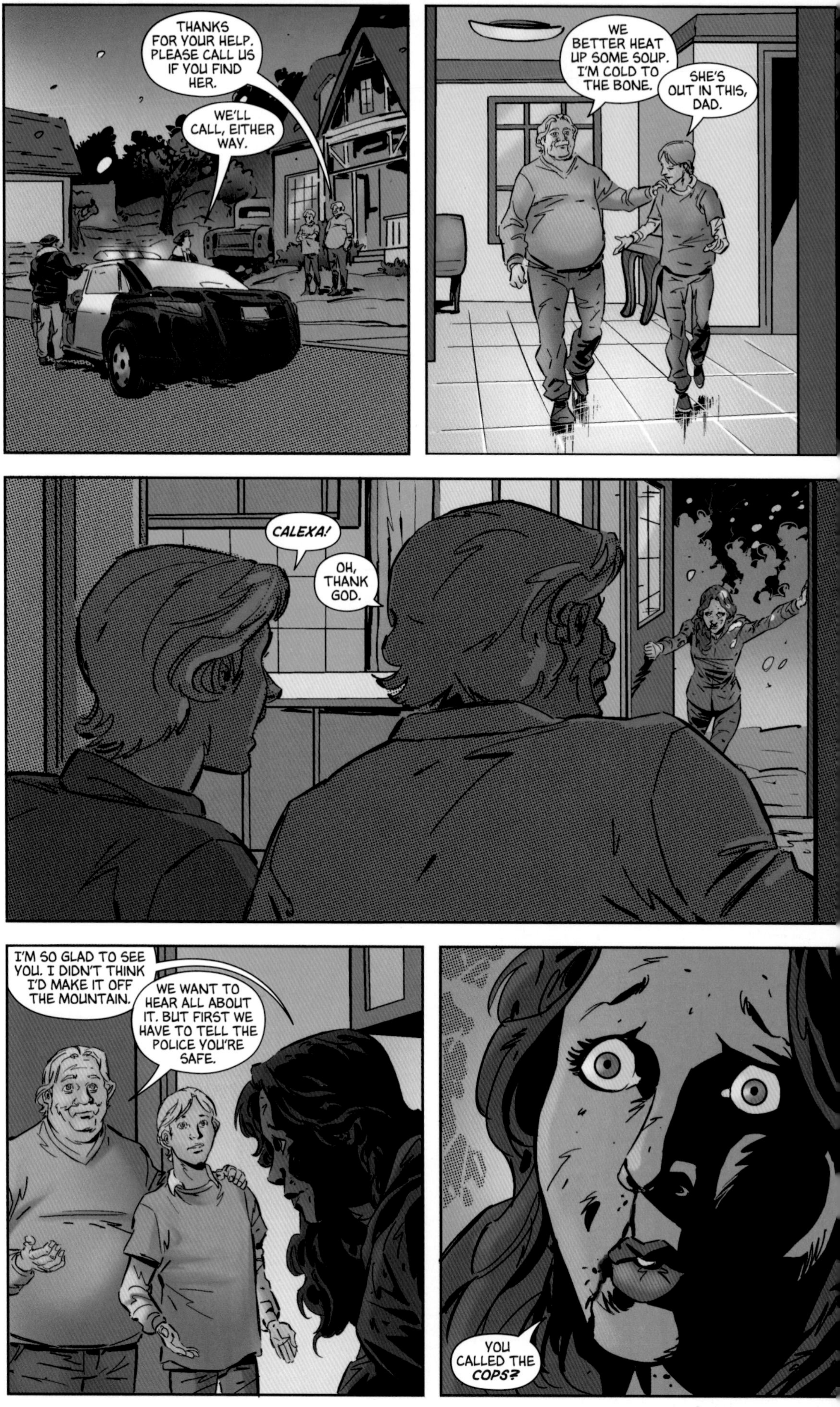
THANKS FOR YOUR HELP. PLEASE CALL US IF YOU FIND HER.
WE'LL CALL, EITHER WAY.
WE BETTER HEAT UP SOME SOUP. I'M COLD TO THE BONE.
SHE'S OUT IN THIS, DAD.
CALEXA!
OH, THANK GOD.
I'M SO GLAD TO SEE YOU. I DIDN'T THINK I'D MAKE IT OFF THE MOUNTAIN.
WE WANT TO HEAR ALL ABOUT IT. BUT FIRST WE HAVE TO TELL THE POLICE YOU'RE SAFE.
YOU CALLED THE COPS?

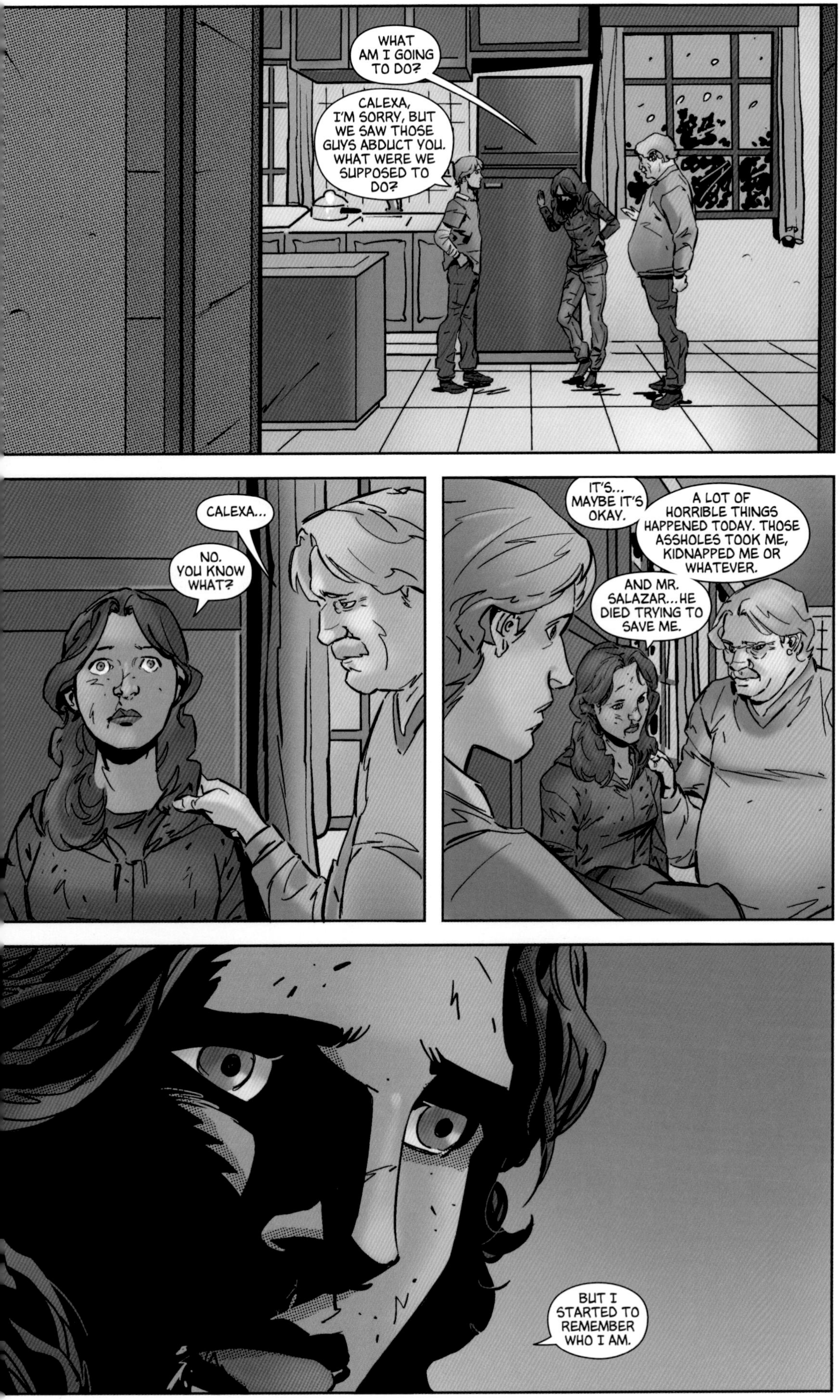

WHAT AM I GOING TO DO?
CALEXA, I'M SORRY, BUT WE SAW THOSE GUYS ABDUCT YOU. WHAT WERE WE SUPPOSED TO DO?
CALEXA...
NO. YOU KNOW WHAT?
IT'S... MAYBE IT'S OKAY.
A LOT OF HORRIBLE THINGS HAPPENED TODAY. THOSE ASSHOLES TOOK ME, KIDNAPPED ME OR WHATEVER.
AND MR. SALAZAR...HE DIED TRYING TO SAVE ME.
BUT I STARTED TO REMEMBER WHO I AM.

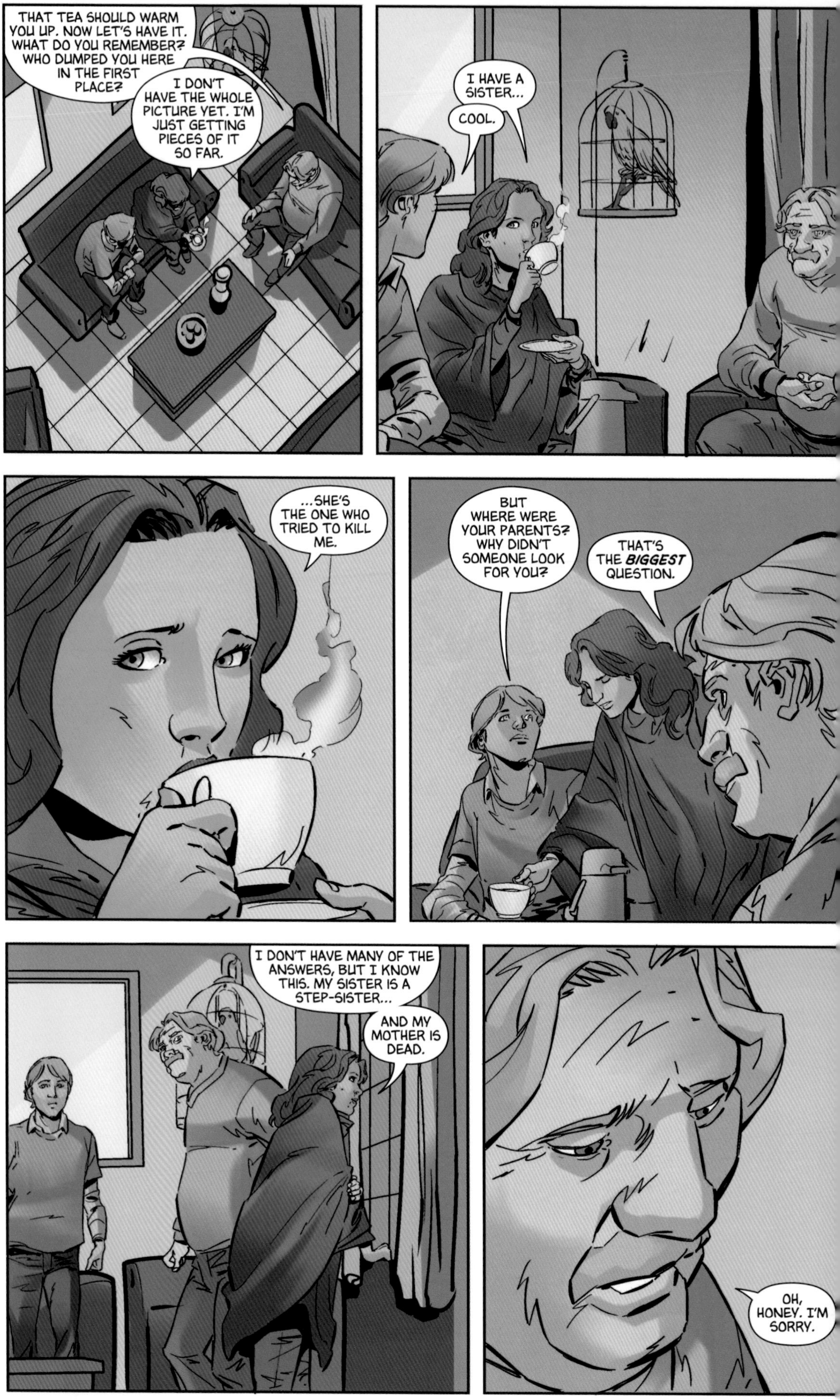

THAT TEA SHOULD WARM YOU UP. NOW LET'S HAVE IT. WHAT DO YOU REMEMBER? WHO DUMPED YOU HERE IN THE FIRST PLACE?
I DON'T HAVE THE WHOLE PICTURE YET. I'M JUST GETTING PIECES OF IT SO FAR.
I HAVE A SISTER...
COOL.
...SHE'S THE ONE WHO TRIED TO KILL ME.
BUT WHERE WERE YOUR PARENTS? WHY DIDN'T SOMEONE LOOK FOR YOU?
THAT'S THE *BIGGEST* QUESTION.
I DON'T HAVE MANY OF THE ANSWERS, BUT I KNOW THIS. MY SISTER IS A STEP-SISTER...
AND MY MOTHER IS DEAD.
OH, HONEY. I'M SORRY.

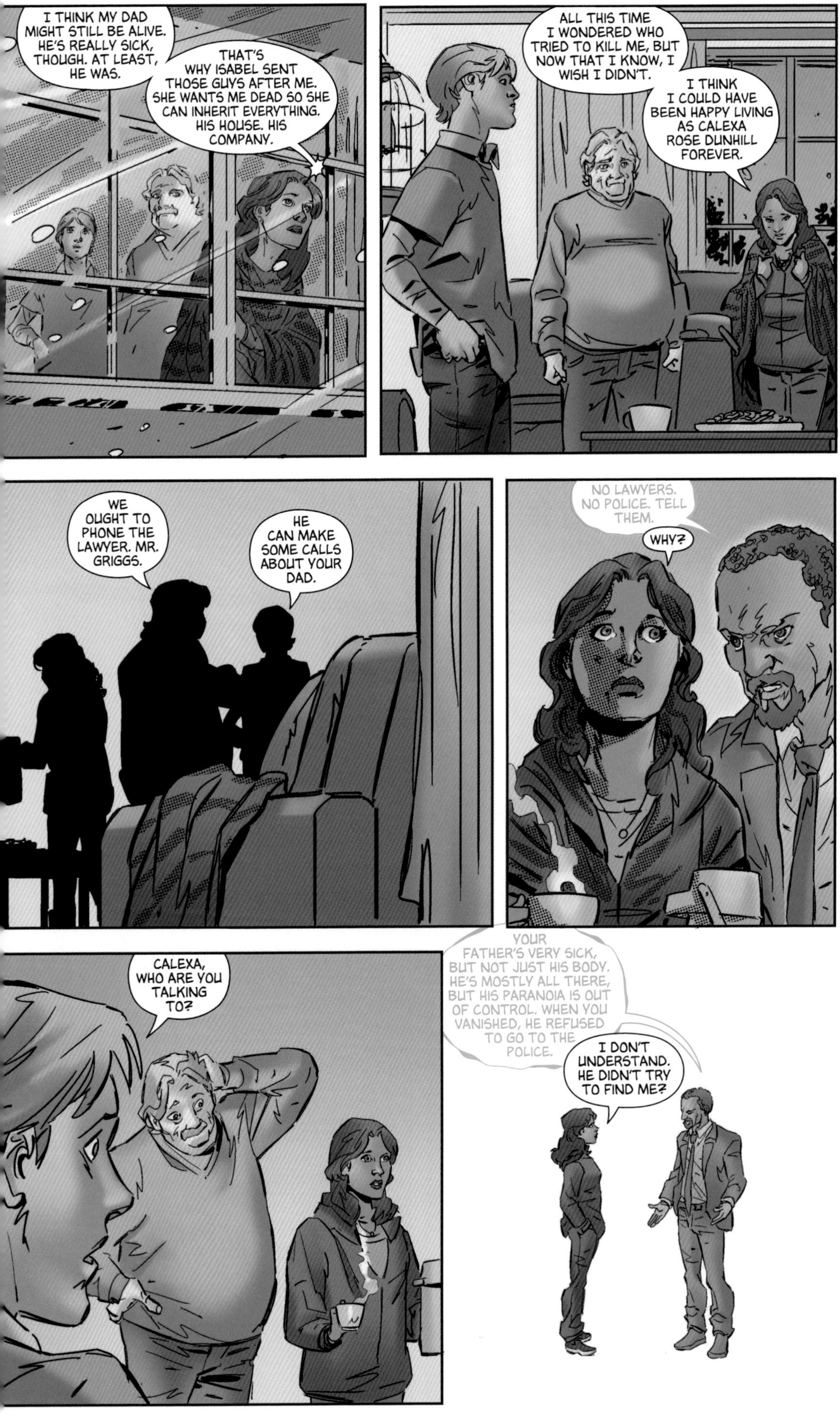
I THINK MY DAD MIGHT STILL BE ALIVE. HE'S REALLY SICK, THOUGH. AT LEAST, HE WAS.
THAT'S WHY ISABEL SENT THOSE GUYS AFTER ME. SHE WANTS ME DEAD SO SHE CAN INHERIT EVERYTHING. HIS HOUSE. HIS COMPANY.
ALL THIS TIME I WONDERED WHO TRIED TO KILL ME, BUT NOW THAT I KNOW, I WISH I DIDN'T.
I THINK I COULD HAVE BEEN HAPPY LIVING AS CALEXA ROSE DUNHILL FOREVER.
WE OUGHT TO PHONE THE LAWYER. MR. GRIGGS.
HE CAN MAKE SOME CALLS ABOUT YOUR DAD.
NO LAWYERS. NO POLICE. TELL THEM.
WHY?
CALEXA, WHO ARE YOU TALKING TO?
YOUR FATHER'S VERY SICK, BUT NOT JUST HIS BODY. HE'S MOSTLY ALL THERE, BUT HIS PARANOIA IS OUT OF CONTROL. WHEN YOU VANISHED, HE REFUSED TO GO TO THE POLICE.
I DON'T UNDERSTAND. HE DIDN'T TRY TO FIND ME?

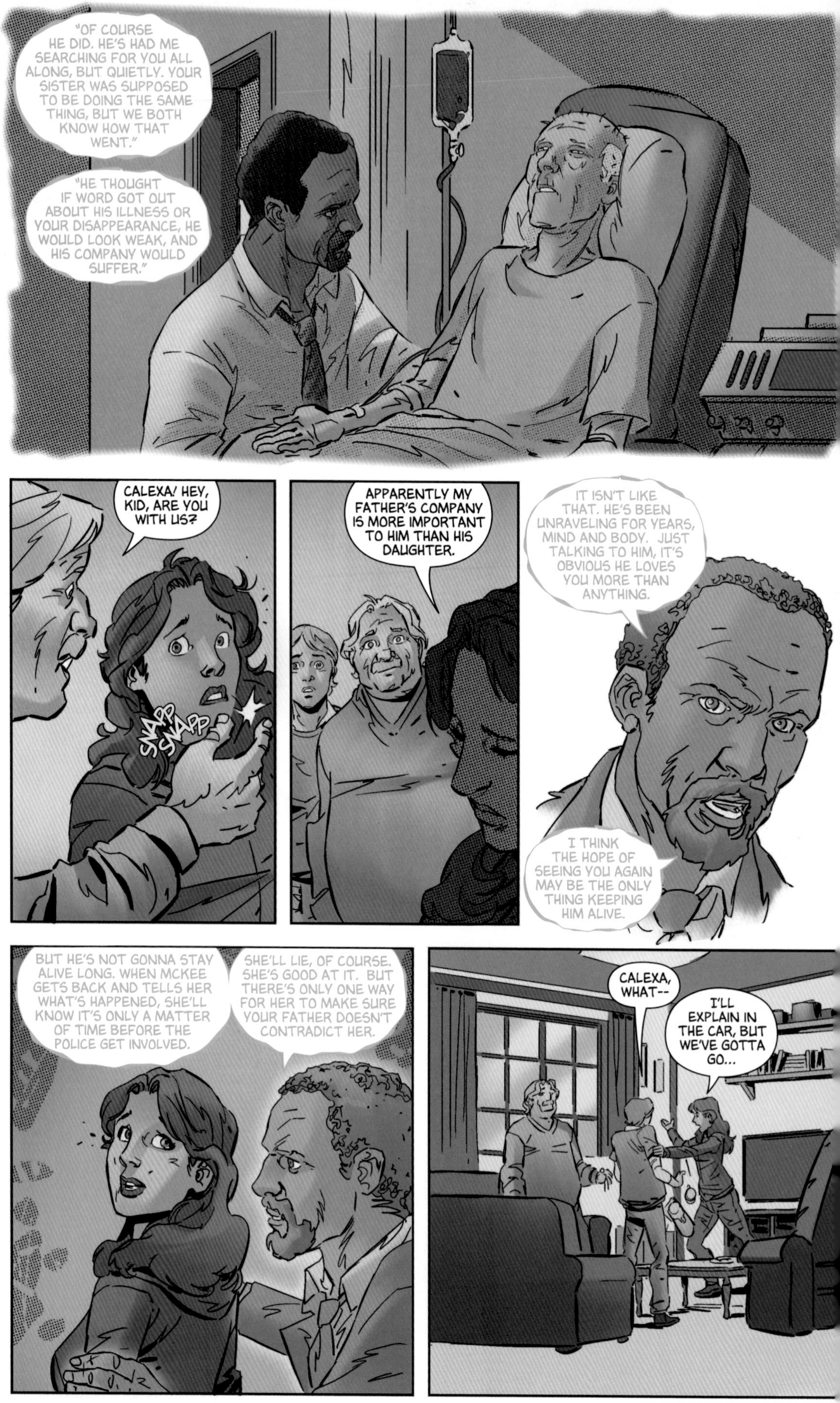
"OF COURSE HE DID. HE'S HAD ME SEARCHING FOR YOU ALL ALONG, BUT QUIETLY. YOUR SISTER WAS SUPPOSED TO BE DOING THE SAME THING, BUT WE BOTH KNOW HOW THAT WENT."
"HE THOUGHT IF WORD GOT OUT ABOUT HIS ILLNESS OR YOUR DISAPPEARANCE, HE WOULD LOOK WEAK, AND HIS COMPANY WOULD SUFFER."
CALEXA! HEY, KID, ARE YOU WITH US?
SNAPP SNAPP
APPARENTLY MY FATHER'S COMPANY IS MORE IMPORTANT TO HIM THAN HIS DAUGHTER.
IT ISN'T LIKE THAT. HE'S BEEN UNRAVELING FOR YEARS, MIND AND BODY. JUST TALKING TO HIM, IT'S OBVIOUS HE LOVES YOU MORE THAN ANYTHING.
I THINK THE HOPE OF SEEING YOU AGAIN MAY BE THE ONLY THING KEEPING HIM ALIVE.
BUT HE'S NOT GONNA STAY ALIVE LONG. WHEN MCKEE GETS BACK AND TELLS HER WHAT'S HAPPENED, SHE'LL KNOW IT'S ONLY A MATTER OF TIME BEFORE THE POLICE GET INVOLVED.
SHE'LL LIE, OF COURSE. SHE'S GOOD AT IT. BUT THERE'S ONLY ONE WAY FOR HER TO MAKE SURE YOUR FATHER DOESN'T CONTRADICT HER.
CALEXA, WHAT--
I'LL EXPLAIN IN THE CAR, BUT WE'VE GOTTA GO...

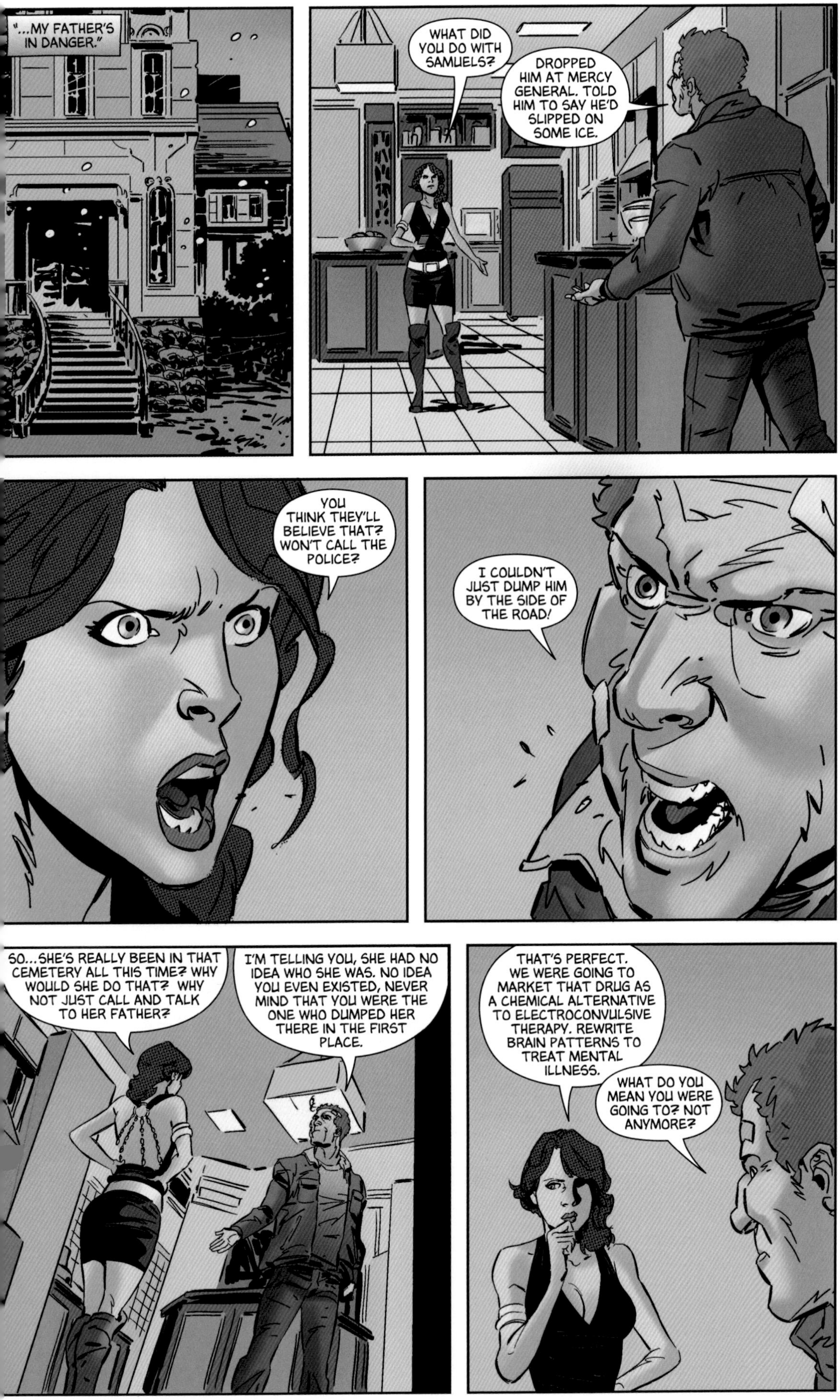
"...MY FATHER'S IN DANGER."
WHAT DID YOU DO WITH SAMUELS?
DROPPED HIM AT MERCY GENERAL. TOLD HIM TO SAY HE'D SLIPPED ON SOME ICE.
YOU THINK THEY'LL BELIEVE THAT? WON'T CALL THE POLICE?
I COULDN'T JUST DUMP HIM BY THE SIDE OF THE ROAD!
SO...SHE'S REALLY BEEN IN THAT CEMETERY ALL THIS TIME? WHY WOULD SHE DO THAT? WHY NOT JUST CALL AND TALK TO HER FATHER?
I'M TELLING YOU, SHE HAD NO IDEA WHO SHE WAS. NO IDEA YOU EVEN EXISTED, NEVER MIND THAT YOU WERE THE ONE WHO DUMPED HER THERE IN THE FIRST PLACE.
THAT'S PERFECT. WE WERE GOING TO MARKET THAT DRUG AS A CHEMICAL ALTERNATIVE TO ELECTROCONVULSIVE THERAPY. REWRITE BRAIN PATTERNS TO TREAT MENTAL ILLNESS.
WHAT DO YOU MEAN YOU WERE GOING TO? NOT ANYMORE?

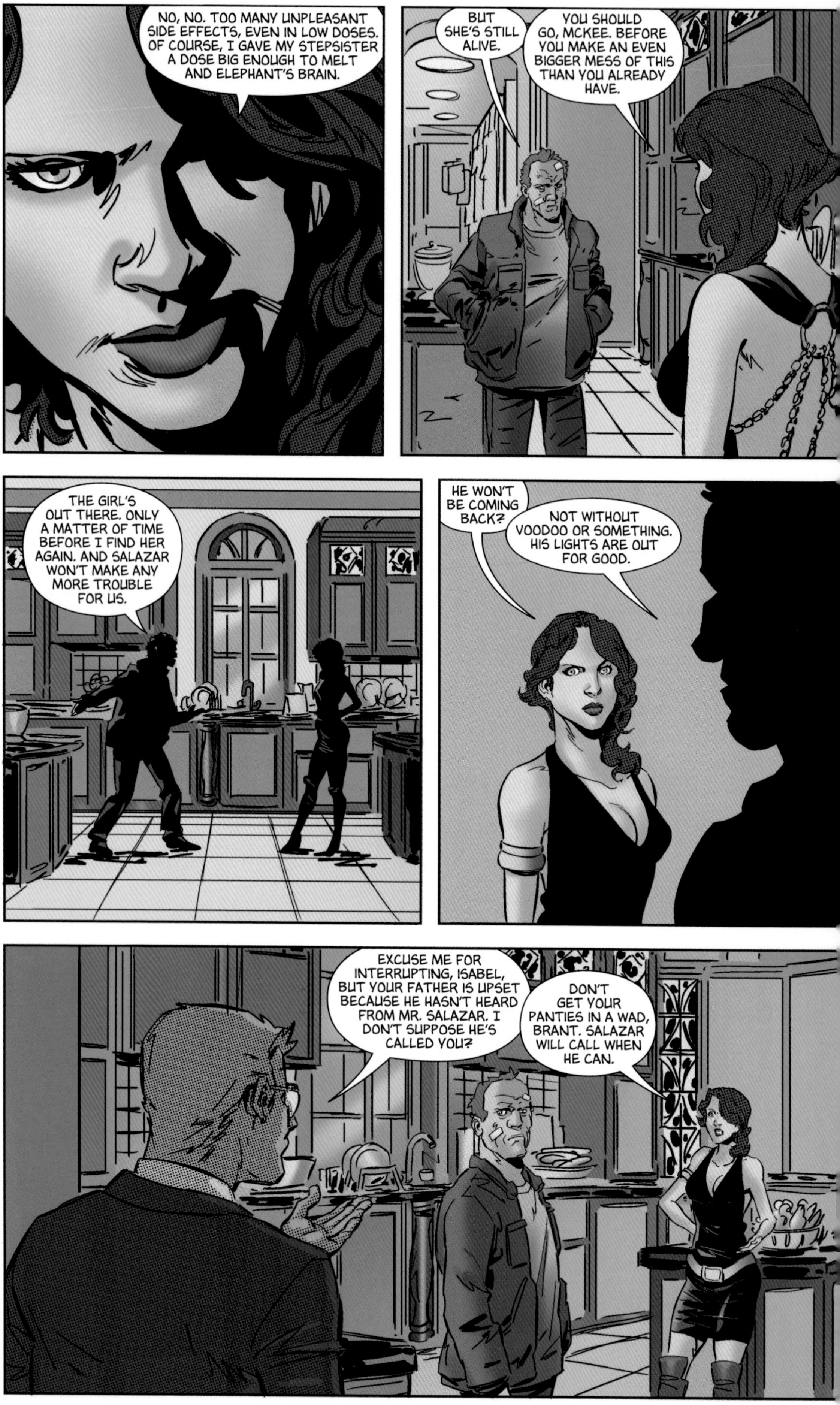
NO, NO. TOO MANY UNPLEASANT SIDE EFFECTS, EVEN IN LOW DOSES. OF COURSE, I GAVE MY STEPSISTER A DOSE BIG ENOUGH TO MELT AND ELEPHANT'S BRAIN.
BUT SHE'S STILL ALIVE.
YOU SHOULD GO, MCKEE. BEFORE YOU MAKE AN EVEN BIGGER MESS OF THIS THAN YOU ALREADY HAVE.
THE GIRL'S OUT THERE. ONLY A MATTER OF TIME BEFORE I FIND HER AGAIN. AND SALAZAR WON'T MAKE ANY MORE TROUBLE FOR US.
HE WON'T BE COMING BACK?
NOT WITHOUT VOODOO OR SOMETHING. HIS LIGHTS ARE OUT FOR GOOD.
EXCUSE ME FOR INTERRUPTING, ISABEL, BUT YOUR FATHER IS UPSET BECAUSE HE HASN'T HEARD FROM MR. SALAZAR. I DON'T SUPPOSE HE'S CALLED YOU?
DON'T GET YOUR PANTIES IN A WAD, BRANT. SALAZAR WILL CALL WHEN HE CAN.

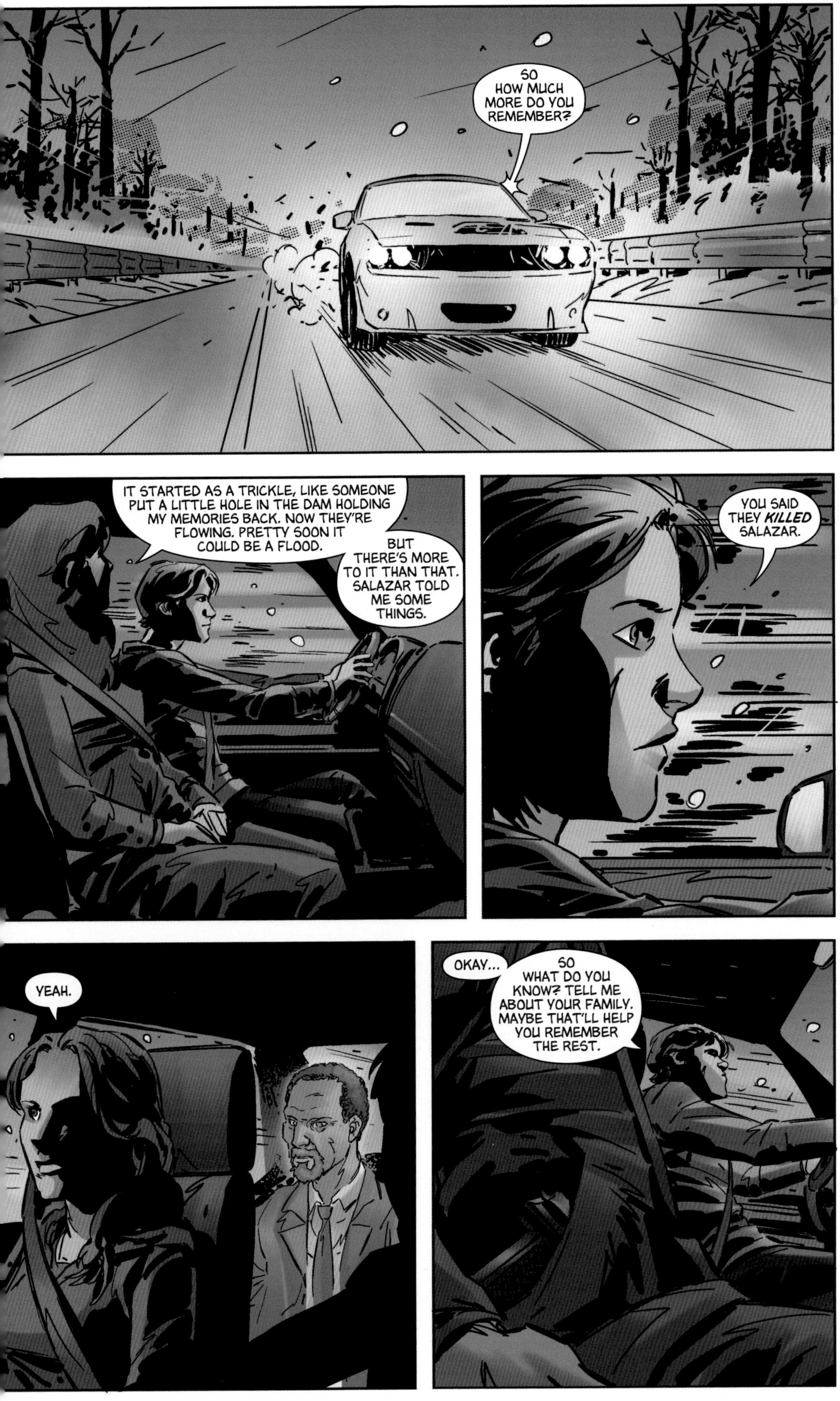
SO HOW MUCH MORE DO YOU REMEMBER?
IT STARTED AS A TRICKLE, LIKE SOMEONE PUT A LITTLE HOLE IN THE DAM HOLDING MY MEMORIES BACK. NOW THEY'RE FLOWING. PRETTY SOON IT COULD BE A FLOOD.
BUT THERE'S MORE TO IT THAN THAT. SALAZAR TOLD ME SOME THINGS.
YOU SAID THEY *KILLED* SALAZAR.
YEAH.
OKAY...
SO WHAT DO YOU KNOW? TELL ME ABOUT YOUR FAMILY. MAYBE THAT'LL HELP YOU REMEMBER THE REST.

MY STEPSISTER ISABEL IS A LAWYER FOR DPC...THE DABNEY PALMETTO CHEMICAL COMPANY.

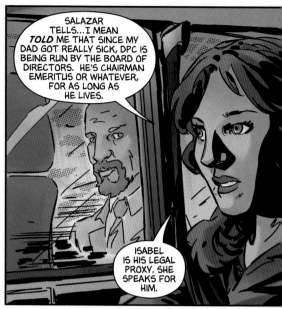

SALAZAR TELLS...I MEAN *TOLD* ME THAT SINCE MY DAD GOT REALLY SICK, DPC IS BEING RUN BY THE BOARD OF DIRECTORS. HE'S CHAIRMAN EMERITUS OR WHATEVER, FOR AS LONG AS HE LIVES.

ISABEL IS HIS LEGAL PROXY. SHE SPEAKS FOR HIM.

BUT SHE'S THE ONE WHO TRIED TO KILL YOU!

MASON, LOOK OUT!

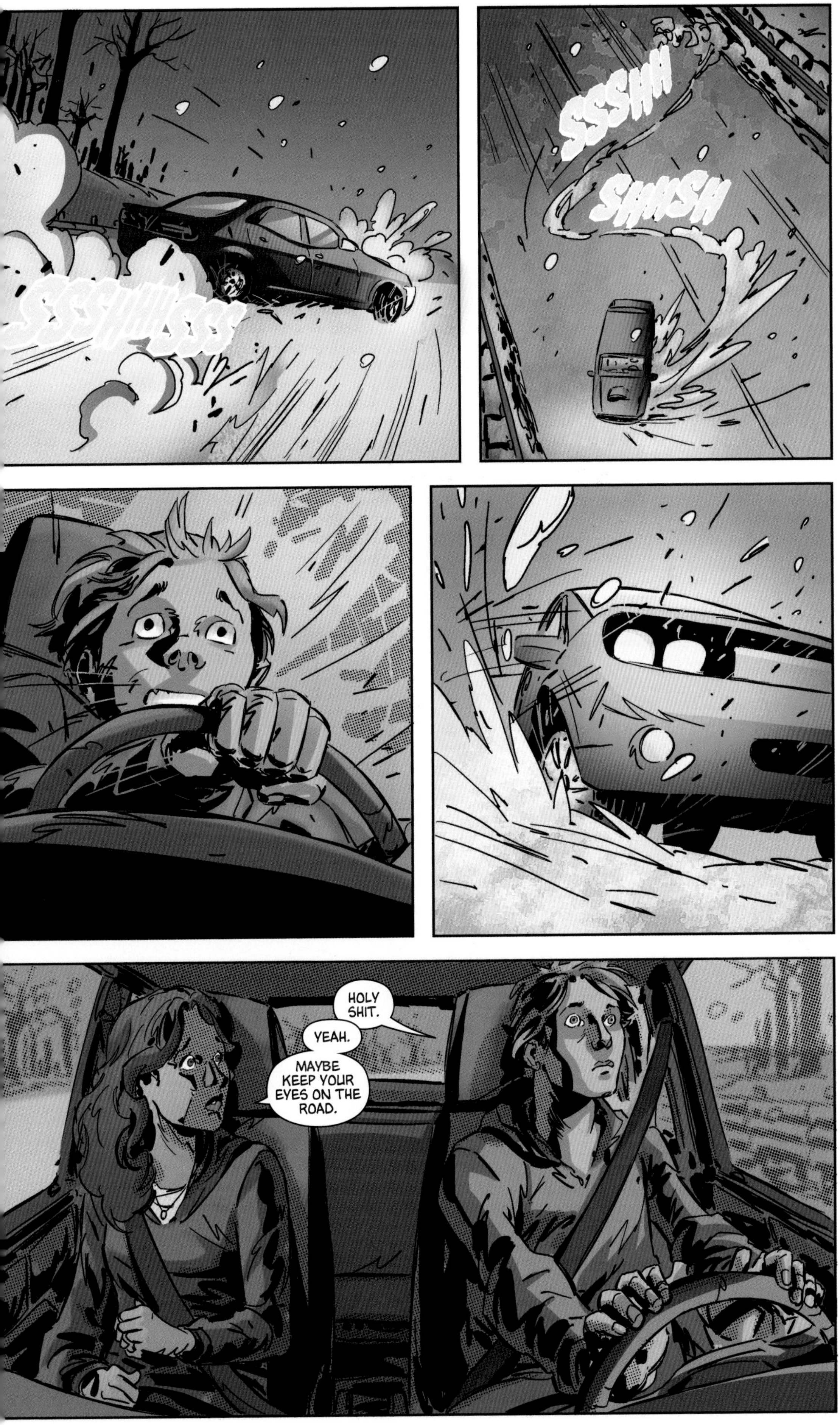
SSSHHSSS
SSSHH
SHHSH
HOLY SHIT.
YEAH.
MAYBE KEEP YOUR EYES ON THE ROAD.

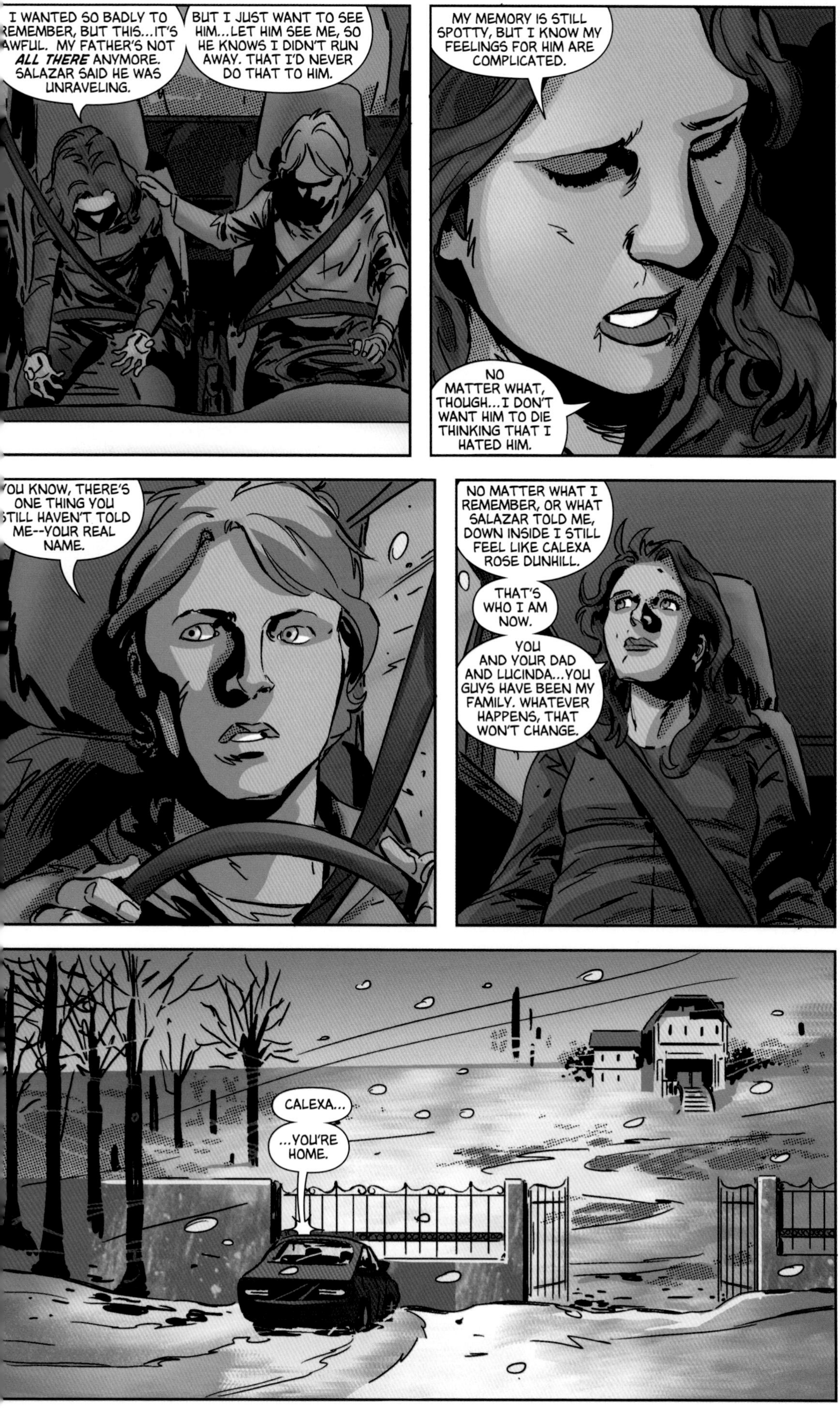
I WANTED SO BADLY TO REMEMBER, BUT THIS...IT'S AWFUL. MY FATHER'S NOT *ALL THERE* ANYMORE. SALAZAR SAID HE WAS UNRAVELING.
BUT I JUST WANT TO SEE HIM...LET HIM SEE ME, SO HE KNOWS I DIDN'T RUN AWAY. THAT I'D NEVER DO THAT TO HIM.
MY MEMORY IS STILL SPOTTY, BUT I KNOW MY FEELINGS FOR HIM ARE COMPLICATED.
NO MATTER WHAT, THOUGH...I DON'T WANT HIM TO DIE THINKING THAT I HATED HIM.
YOU KNOW, THERE'S ONE THING YOU STILL HAVEN'T TOLD ME--YOUR REAL NAME.
NO MATTER WHAT I REMEMBER, OR WHAT SALAZAR TOLD ME, DOWN INSIDE I STILL FEEL LIKE CALEXA ROSE DUNHILL.
THAT'S WHO I AM NOW.
YOU AND YOUR DAD AND LUCINDA...YOU GUYS HAVE BEEN MY FAMILY. WHATEVER HAPPENS, THAT WON'T CHANGE.
CALEXA...
...YOU'RE HOME.

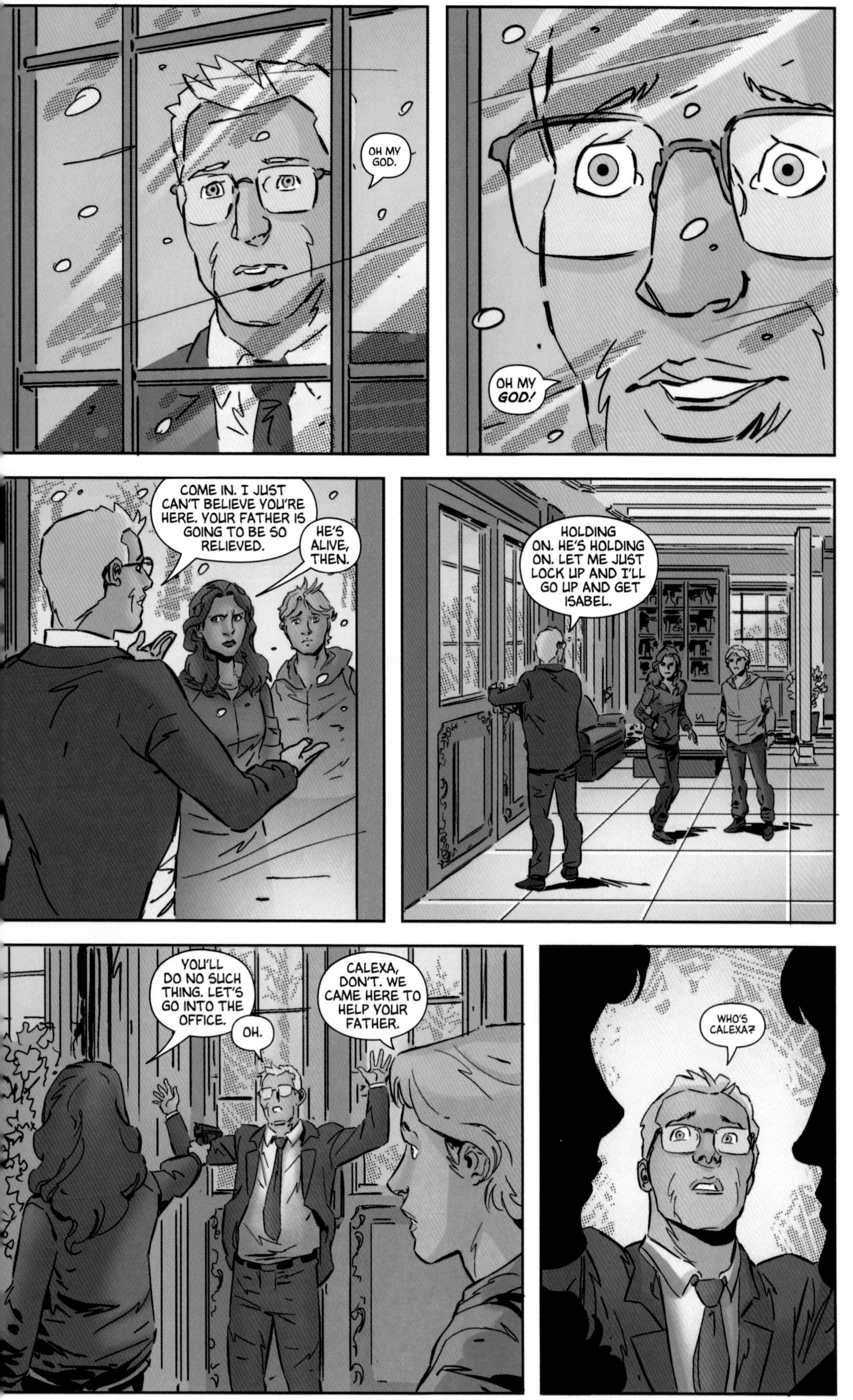
OH MY GOD.
OH MY GOD!
COME IN. I JUST CAN'T BELIEVE YOU'RE HERE. YOUR FATHER IS GOING TO BE SO RELIEVED.
HE'S ALIVE, THEN.
HOLDING ON. HE'S HOLDING ON. LET ME JUST LOCK UP AND I'LL GO UP AND GET ISABEL.
YOU'LL DO NO SUCH THING. LET'S GO INTO THE OFFICE.
OH.
CALEXA, DON'T. WE CAME HERE TO HELP YOUR FATHER.
WHO'S CALEXA?

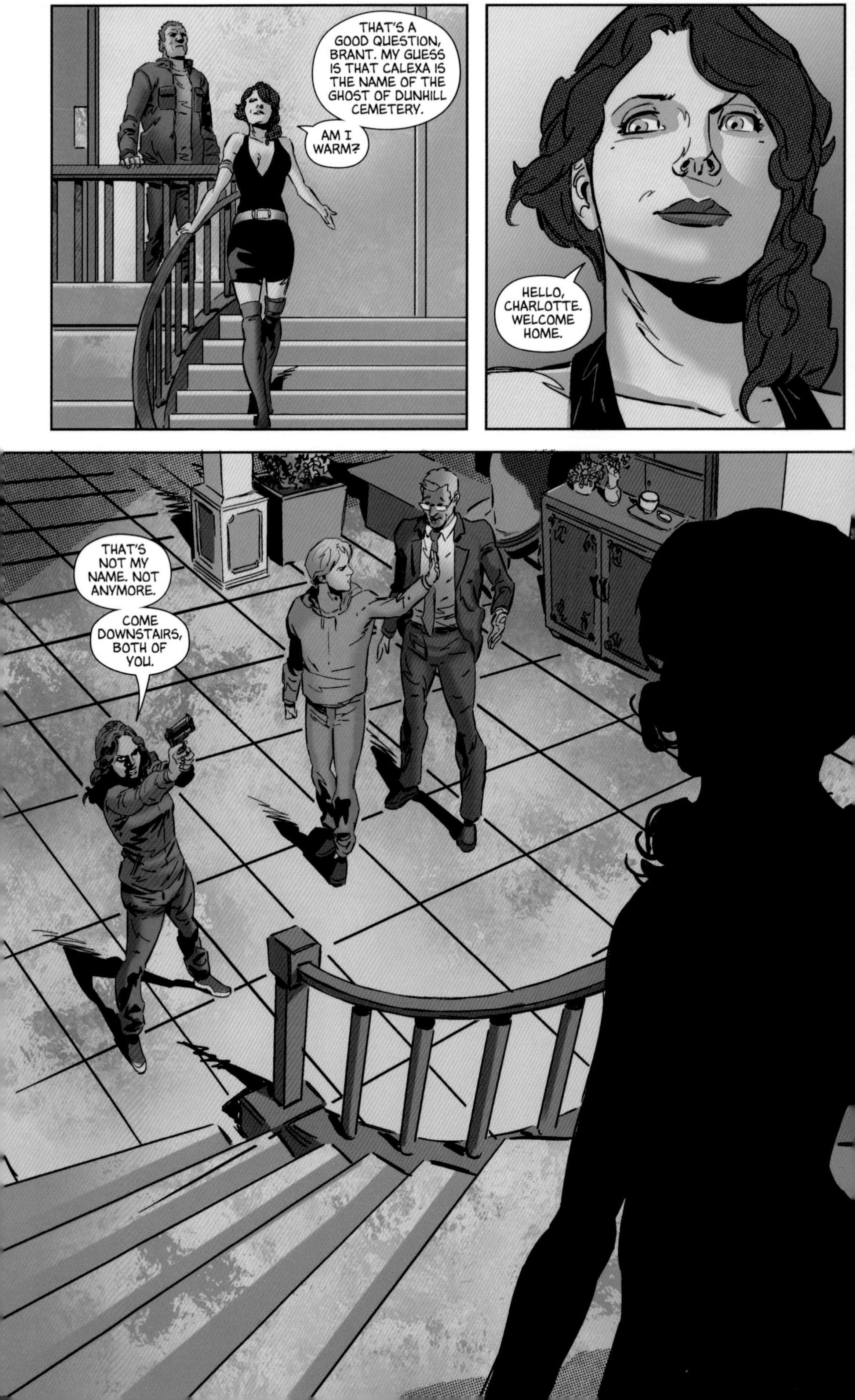
THAT'S A GOOD QUESTION, BRANT. MY GUESS IS THAT CALEXA IS THE NAME OF THE GHOST OF DUNHILL CEMETERY.
AM I WARM?
HELLO, CHARLOTTE. WELCOME HOME.
THAT'S NOT MY NAME. NOT ANYMORE.
COME DOWNSTAIRS, BOTH OF YOU.

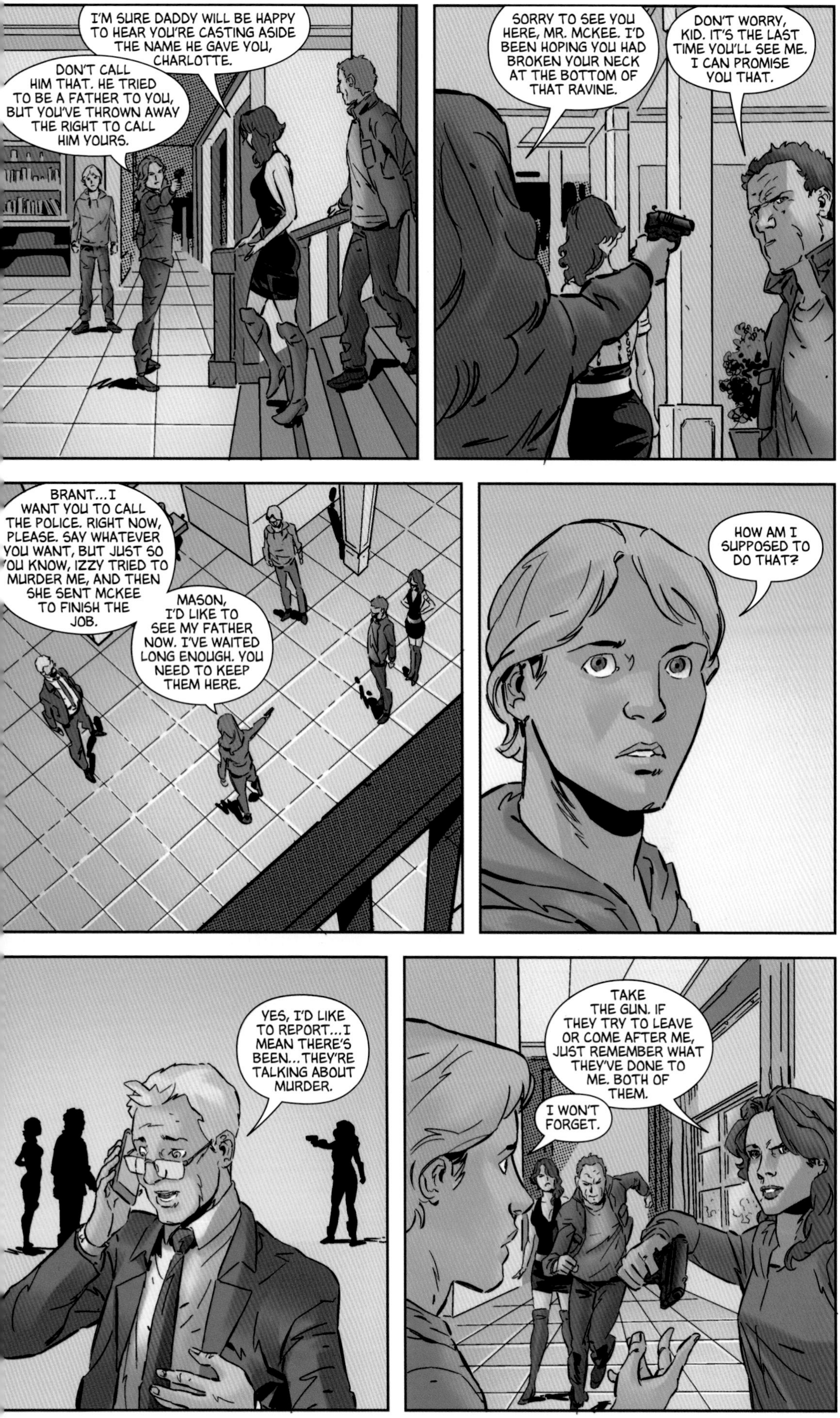
I'M SURE DADDY WILL BE HAPPY TO HEAR YOU'RE CASTING ASIDE THE NAME HE GAVE YOU, CHARLOTTE.
DON'T CALL HIM THAT. HE TRIED TO BE A FATHER TO YOU, BUT YOU'VE THROWN AWAY THE RIGHT TO CALL HIM YOURS.
SORRY TO SEE YOU HERE, MR. MCKEE. I'D BEEN HOPING YOU HAD BROKEN YOUR NECK AT THE BOTTOM OF THAT RAVINE.
DON'T WORRY, KID. IT'S THE LAST TIME YOU'LL SEE ME. I CAN PROMISE YOU THAT.
BRANT...I WANT YOU TO CALL THE POLICE. RIGHT NOW, PLEASE. SAY WHATEVER YOU WANT, BUT JUST SO YOU KNOW, IZZY TRIED TO MURDER ME, AND THEN SHE SENT MCKEE TO FINISH THE JOB.
MASON, I'D LIKE TO SEE MY FATHER NOW. I'VE WAITED LONG ENOUGH. YOU NEED TO KEEP THEM HERE.
HOW AM I SUPPOSED TO DO THAT?
YES, I'D LIKE TO REPORT...I MEAN THERE'S BEEN...THEY'RE TALKING ABOUT MURDER.
TAKE THE GUN. IF THEY TRY TO LEAVE OR COME AFTER ME, JUST REMEMBER WHAT THEY'VE DONE TO ME. BOTH OF THEM.
I WON'T FORGET.

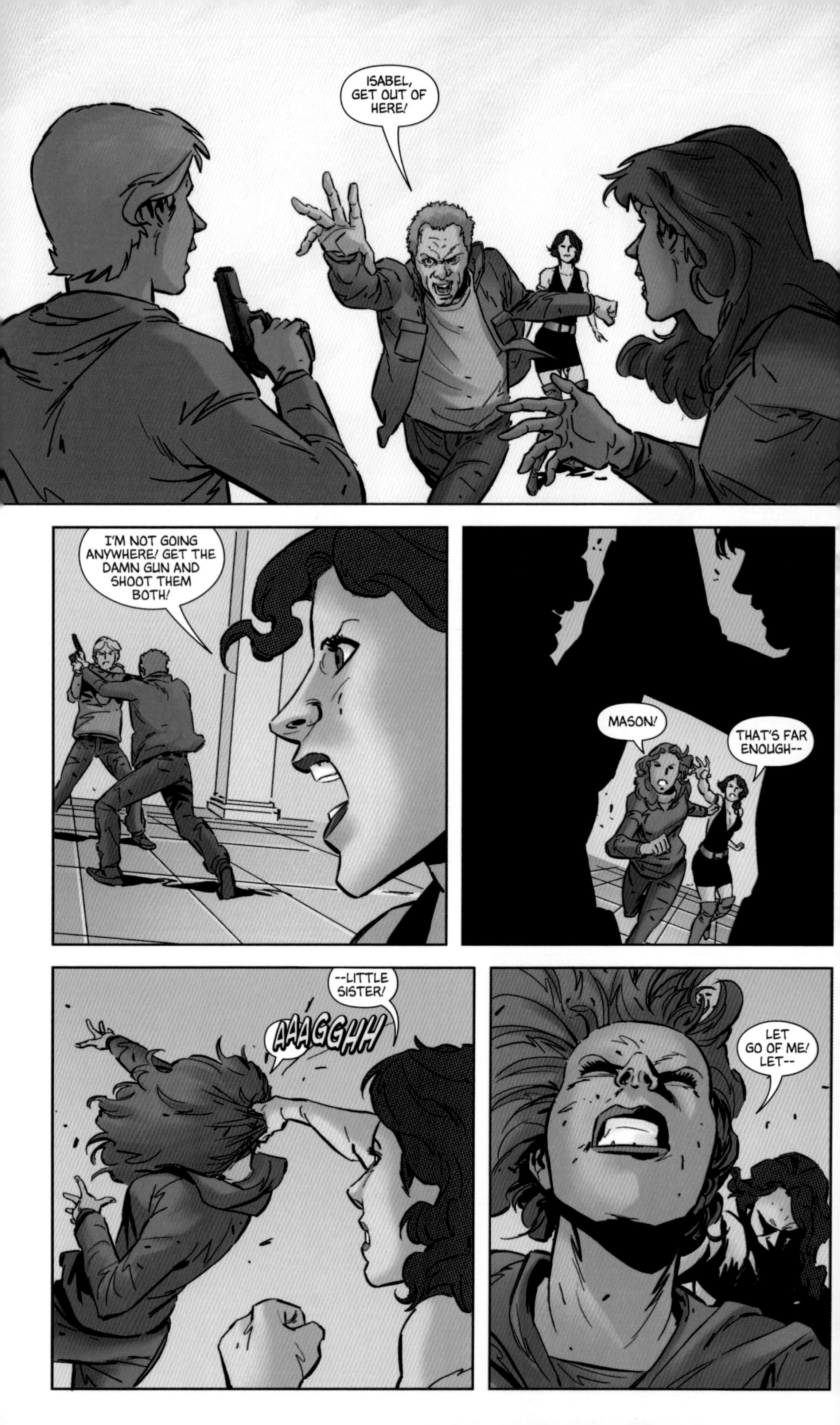
ISABEL, GET OUT OF HERE!
I'M NOT GOING ANYWHERE! GET THE DAMN GUN AND SHOOT THEM BOTH!
MASON!
THAT'S FAR ENOUGH--
--LITTLE SISTER!
AAAGGHH
LET GO OF ME! LET--

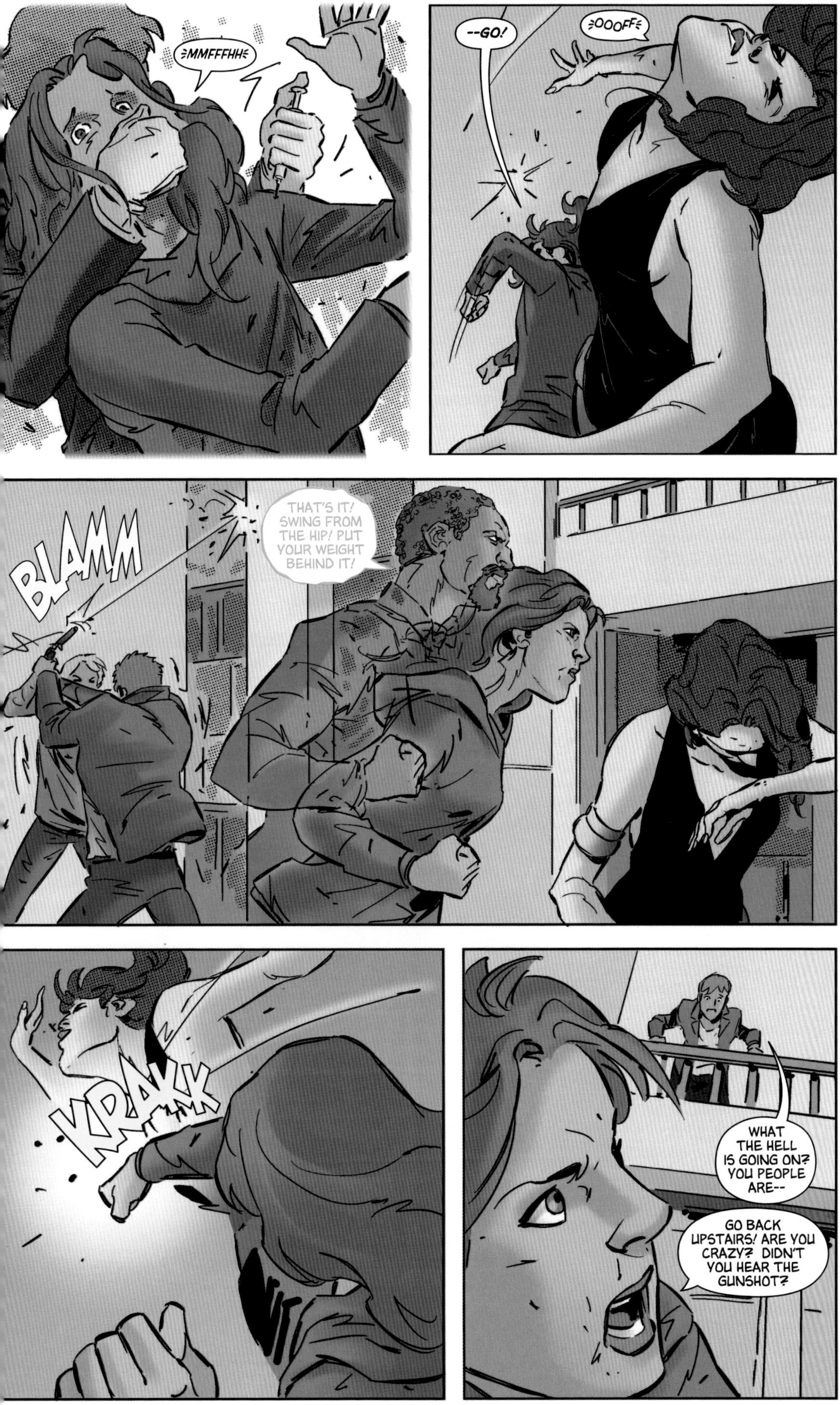
MMFFFHH
--GO!
OOOFF
BLAMM
THAT'S IT! SWING FROM THE HIP! PUT YOUR WEIGHT BEHIND IT!
KRAKK
WHAT THE HELL IS GOING ON? YOU PEOPLE ARE--
GO BACK UPSTAIRS! ARE YOU CRAZY? DIDN'T YOU HEAR THE GUNSHOT?

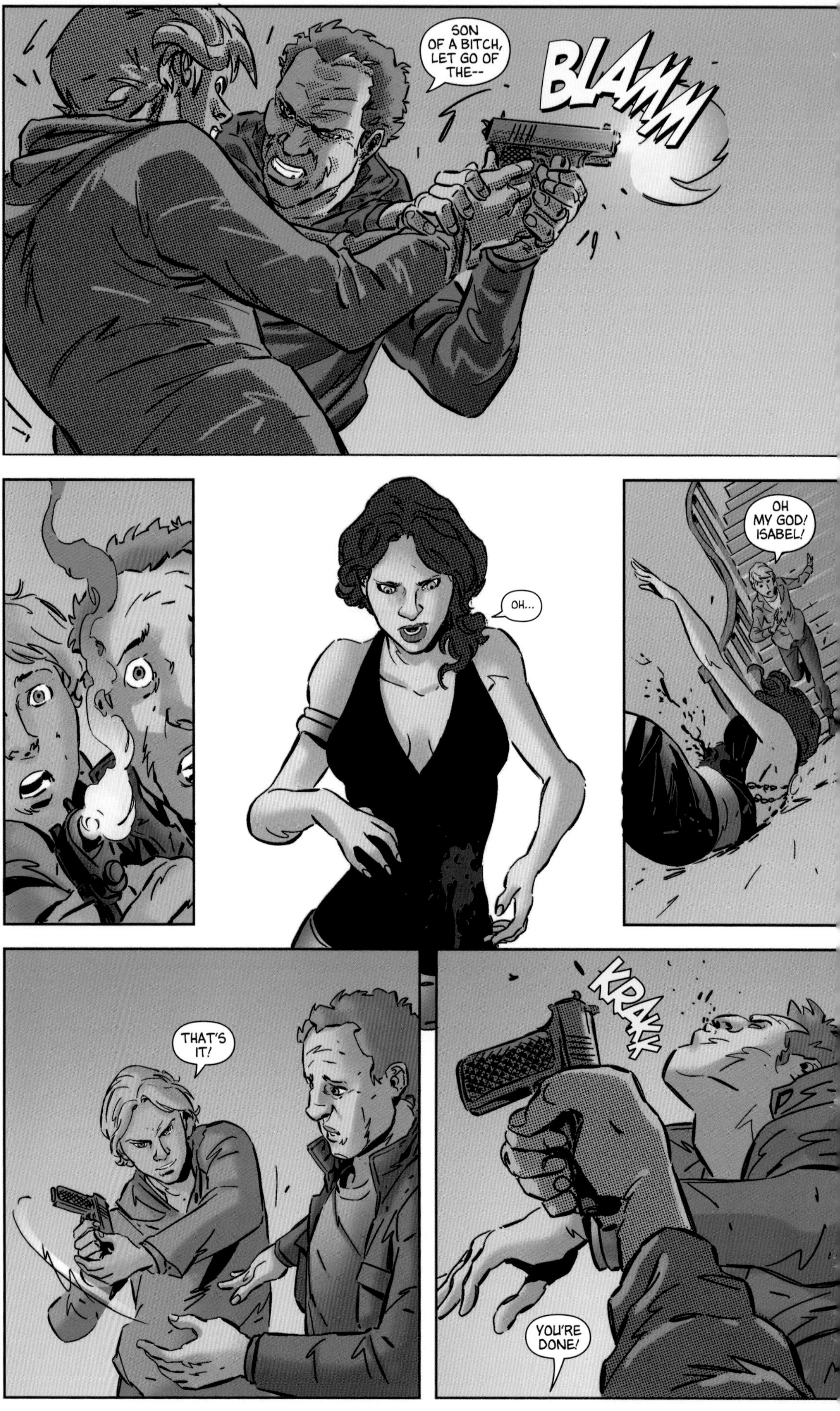
SON OF A BITCH, LET GO OF THE--
BLAMM
OH...
OH MY GOD! ISABEL!
THAT'S IT!
KRAK
YOU'RE DONE!

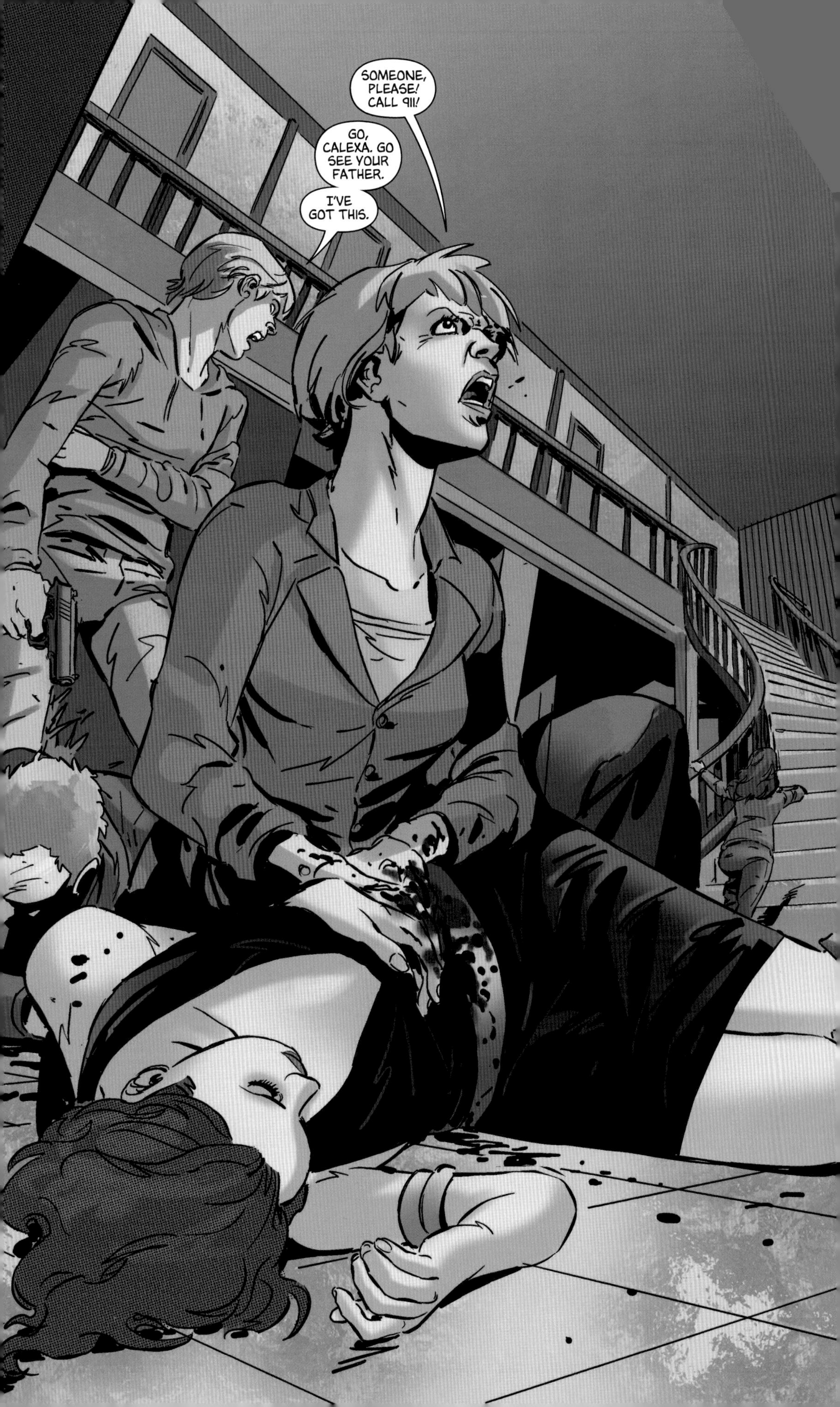
SOMEONE, PLEASE! CALL 911!
GO, CALEXA. GO SEE YOUR FATHER.
I'VE GOT THIS.

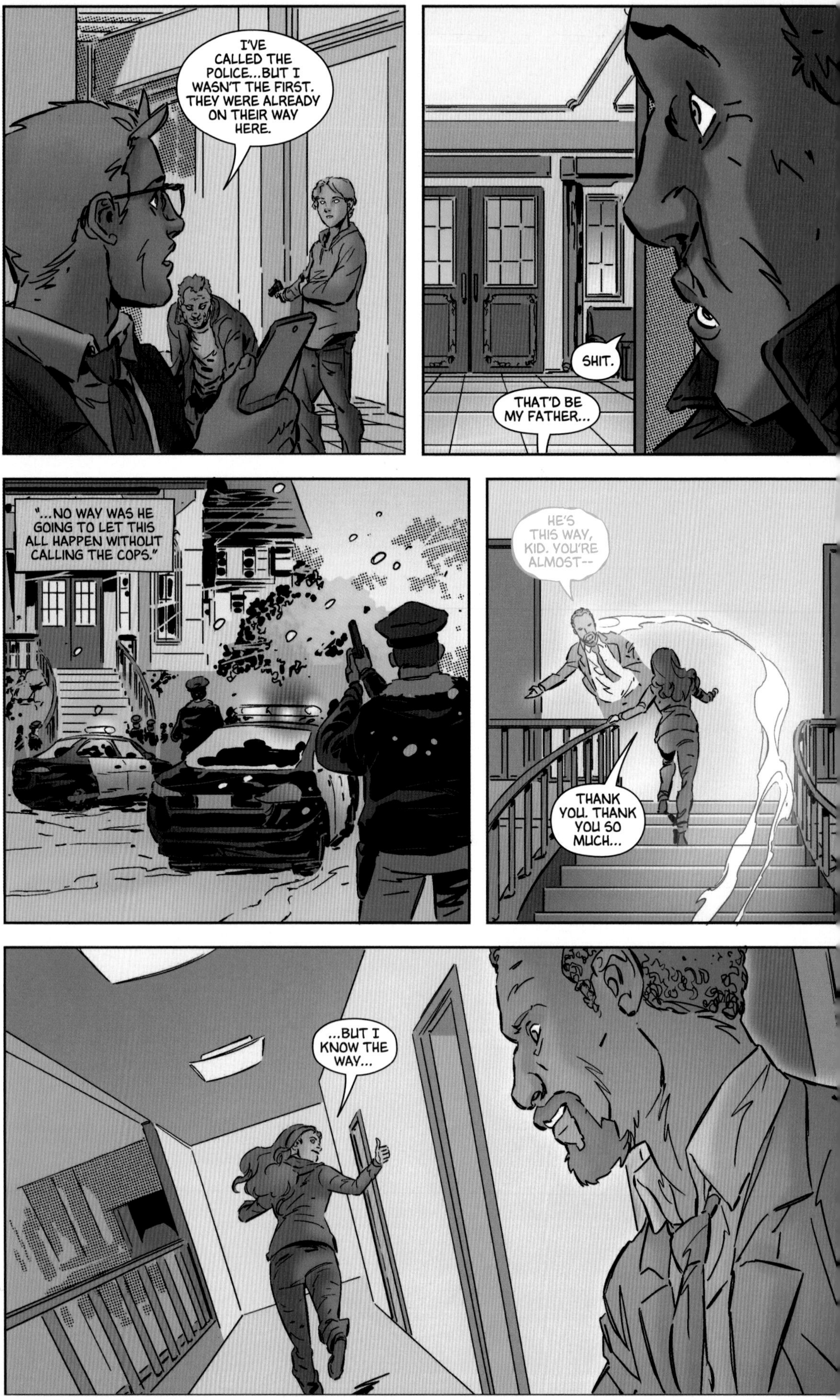
I'VE CALLED THE POLICE...BUT I WASN'T THE FIRST. THEY WERE ALREADY ON THEIR WAY HERE.
SHIT.
THAT'D BE MY FATHER...
"...NO WAY WAS HE GOING TO LET THIS ALL HAPPEN WITHOUT CALLING THE COPS."
HE'S THIS WAY, KID. YOU'RE ALMOST--
THANK YOU. THANK YOU SO MUCH...
...BUT I KNOW THE WAY...

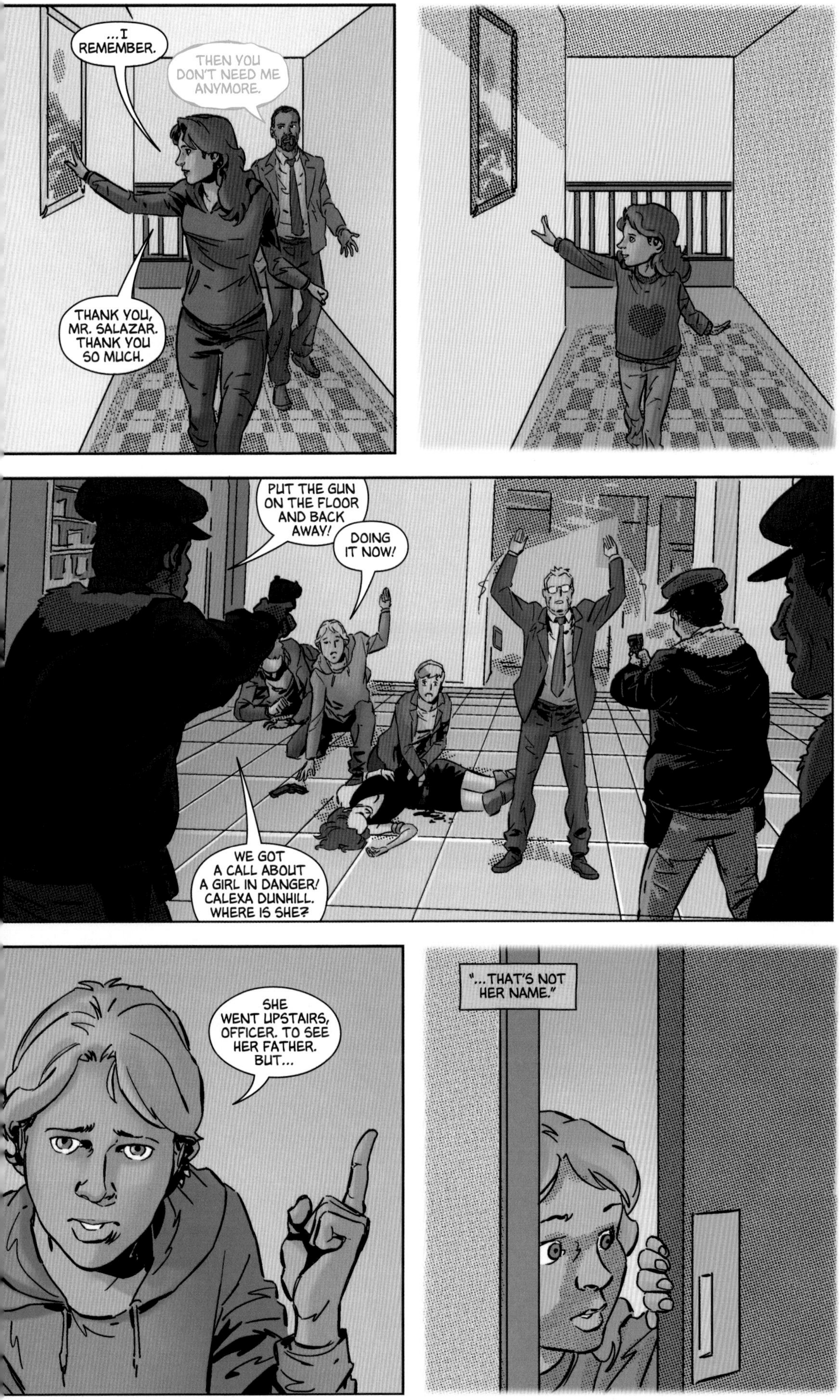

...I REMEMBER.
THEN YOU DON'T NEED ME ANYMORE.
THANK YOU, MR. SALAZAR. THANK YOU SO MUCH.
PUT THE GUN ON THE FLOOR AND BACK AWAY!
DOING IT NOW!
WE GOT A CALL ABOUT A GIRL IN DANGER! CALEXA DUNHILL. WHERE IS SHE?
SHE WENT UPSTAIRS, OFFICER. TO SEE HER FATHER. BUT...
"...THAT'S NOT HER NAME."

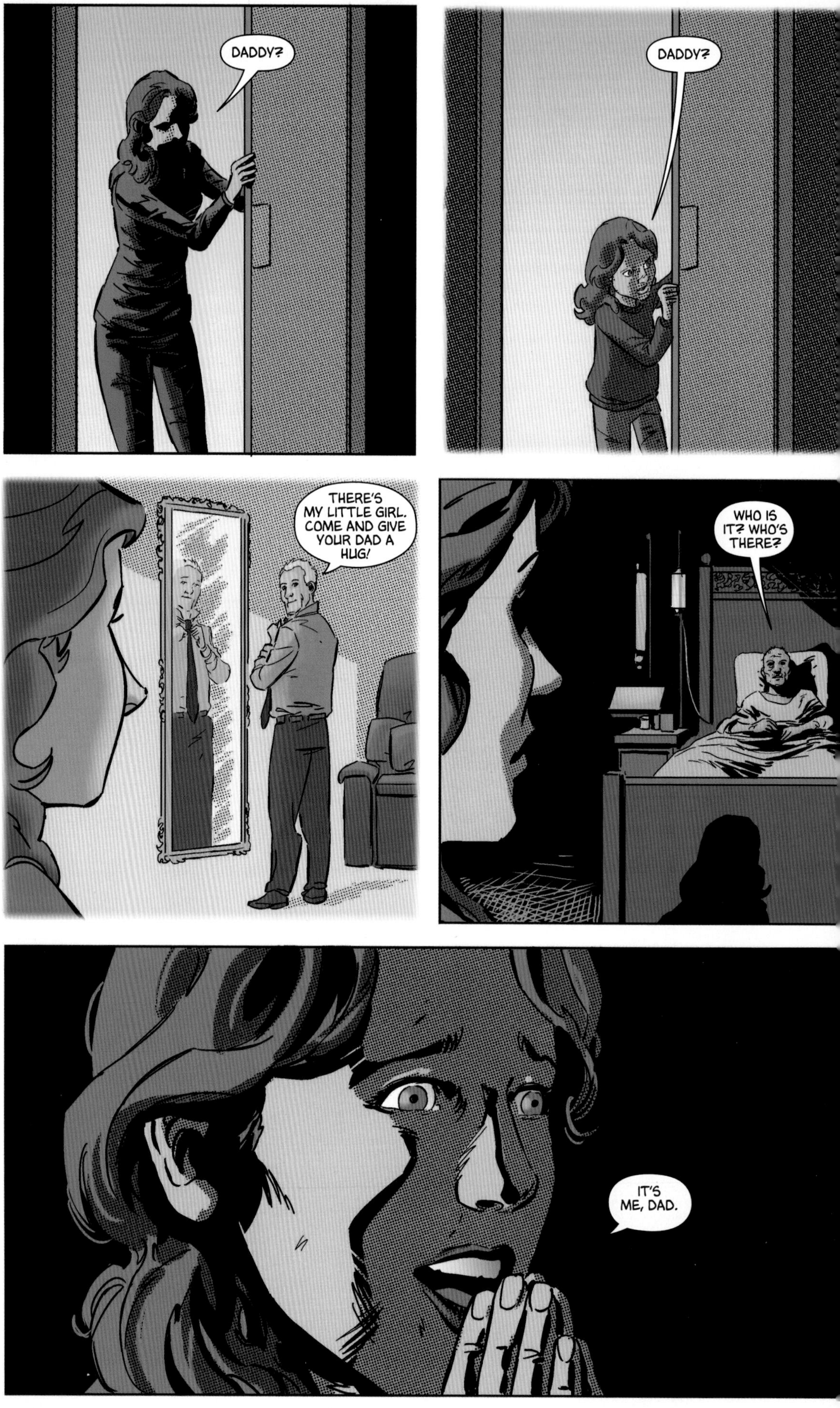
DADDY?
DADDY?
THERE'S MY LITTLE GIRL. COME AND GIVE YOUR DAD A HUG!
WHO IS IT? WHO'S THERE?
IT'S ME, DAD.

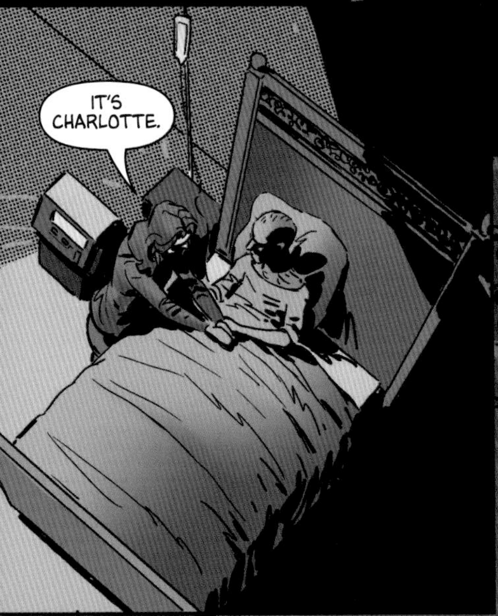
IT'S CHARLOTTE.

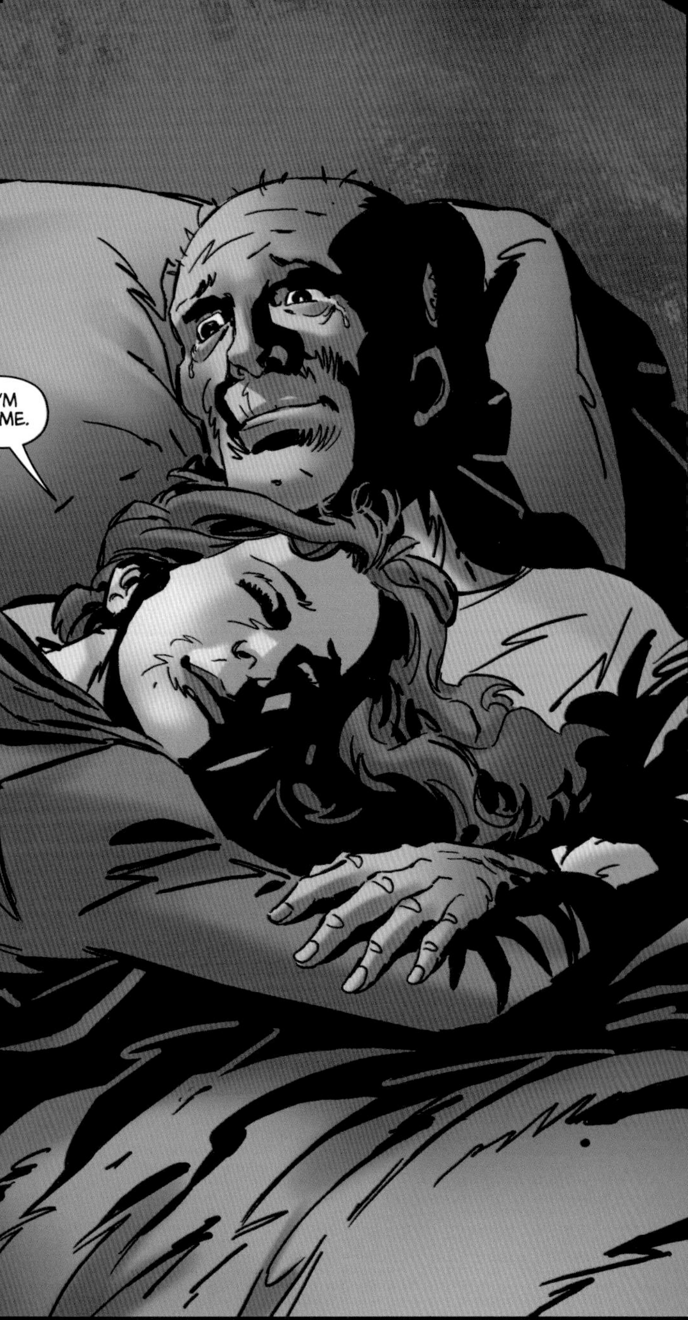
I'M HOME.

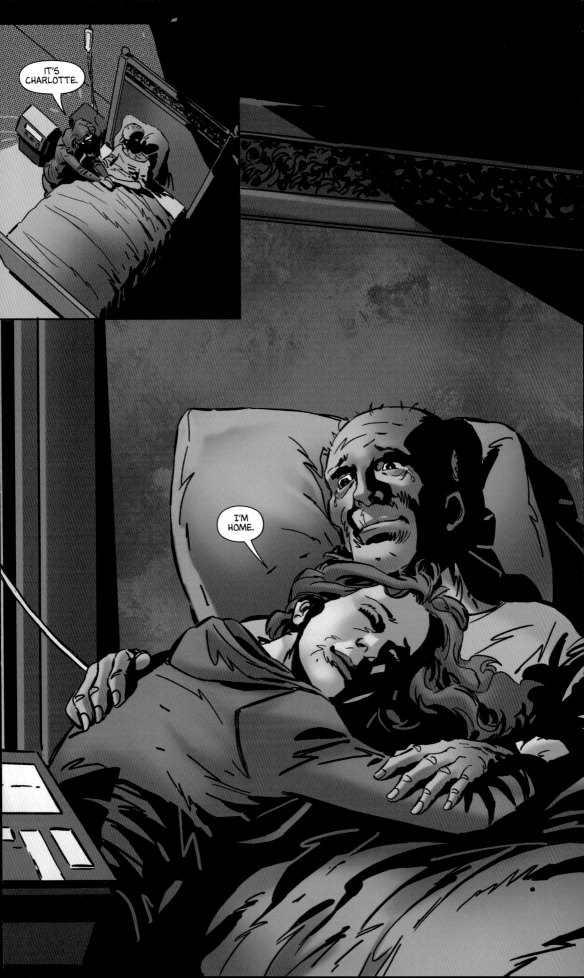

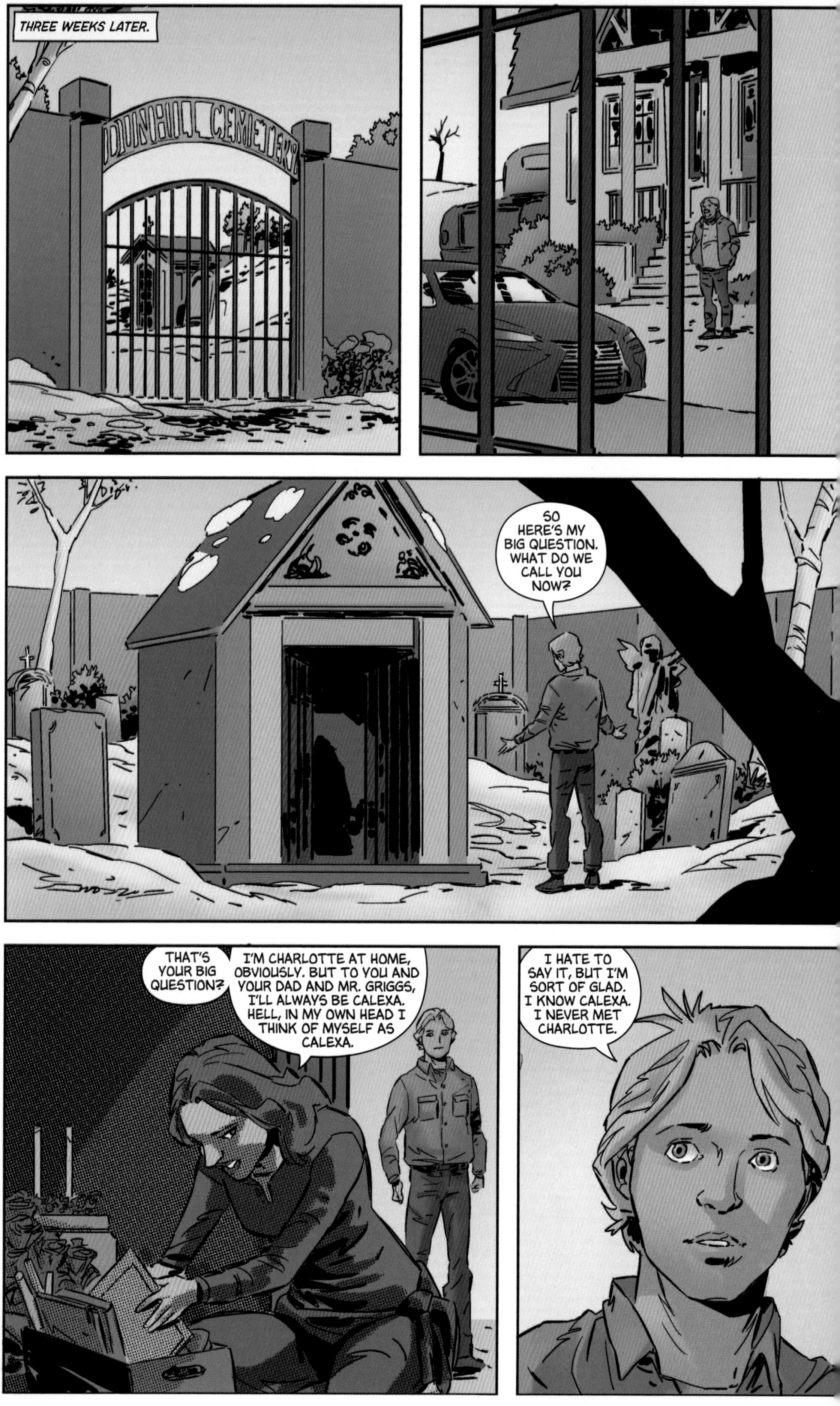
THREE WEEKS LATER.
DUNHILL CEMETERY
SO HERE'S MY BIG QUESTION. WHAT DO WE CALL YOU NOW?
THAT'S YOUR BIG QUESTION?
I'M CHARLOTTE AT HOME, OBVIOUSLY. BUT TO YOU AND YOUR DAD AND MR. GRIGGS, I'LL ALWAYS BE CALEXA. HELL, IN MY OWN HEAD I THINK OF MYSELF AS CALEXA.
I HATE TO SAY IT, BUT I'M SORT OF GLAD. I KNOW CALEXA. I NEVER MET CHARLOTTE.

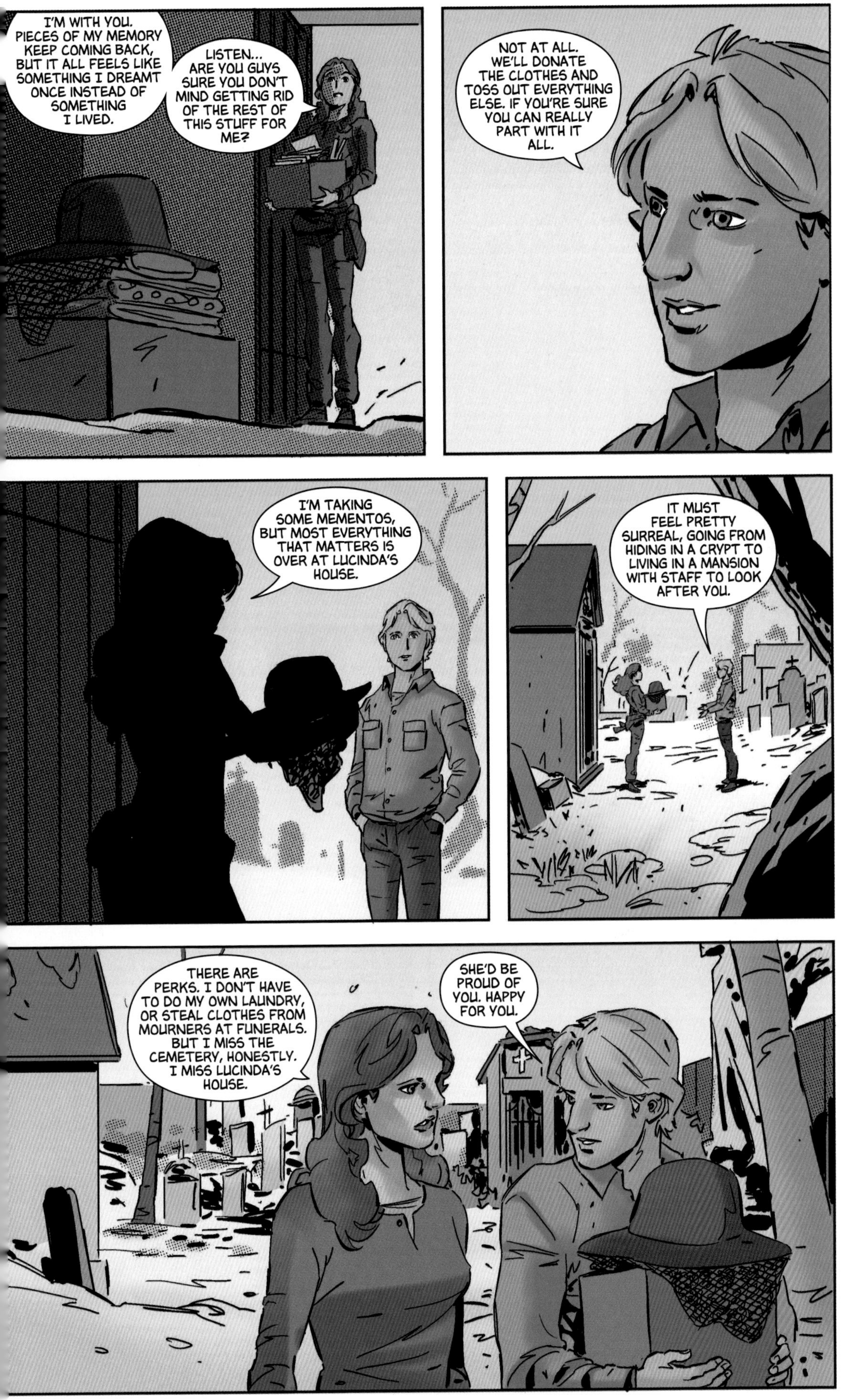

I'M WITH YOU. PIECES OF MY MEMORY KEEP COMING BACK, BUT IT ALL FEELS LIKE SOMETHING I DREAMT ONCE INSTEAD OF SOMETHING I LIVED.
LISTEN... ARE YOU GUYS SURE YOU DON'T MIND GETTING RID OF THE REST OF THIS STUFF FOR ME?
NOT AT ALL. WE'LL DONATE THE CLOTHES AND TOSS OUT EVERYTHING ELSE. IF YOU'RE SURE YOU CAN REALLY PART WITH IT ALL.
I'M TAKING SOME MEMENTOS, BUT MOST EVERYTHING THAT MATTERS IS OVER AT LUCINDA'S HOUSE.
IT MUST FEEL PRETTY SURREAL, GOING FROM HIDING IN A CRYPT TO LIVING IN A MANSION WITH STAFF TO LOOK AFTER YOU.
THERE ARE PERKS. I DON'T HAVE TO DO MY OWN LAUNDRY, OR STEAL CLOTHES FROM MOURNERS AT FUNERALS. BUT I MISS THE CEMETERY, HONESTLY. I MISS LUCINDA'S HOUSE.
SHE'D BE PROUD OF YOU. HAPPY FOR YOU.

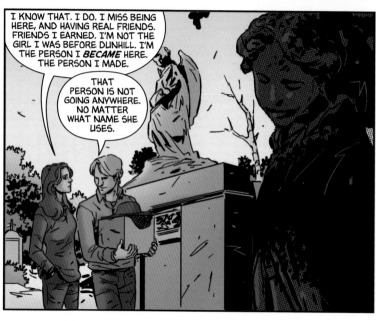

I KNOW THAT. I DO. I MISS BEING HERE, AND HAVING REAL FRIENDS. FRIENDS I EARNED. I'M NOT THE GIRL I WAS BEFORE DUNHILL. I'M THE PERSON I *BECAME* HERE. THE PERSON I MADE.

THAT PERSON IS NOT GOING ANYWHERE. NO MATTER WHAT NAME SHE USES.

CAN WE JUST SIT FOR A MINUTE?

SURE.

OLD FRIENDS... CHARLOTTE'S FRIENDS...HAVE BEEN COMING AROUND.

BUT I FEEL THIS HUGE DISTANCE FROM THEM AND I KNOW THEY FEEL THE SAME. I DON'T KNOW THEM ANYMORE, AND THEY DEFINITELY DON'T *KNOW* ME. I'M STARTING OVER...

THE MOST IMPORTANT THING RIGHT NOW IS THAT I BE THERE TO HELP CARE FOR MY FATHER.

THE DOCTORS GIVE HIM TWO OR THREE MONTHS AND I WANT TO SPEND EVERY ONE OF THOSE DAYS WITH HIM...

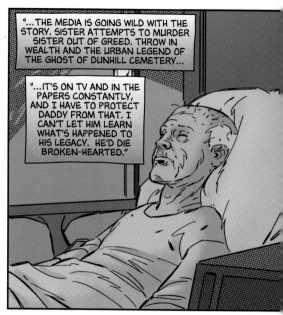

"...THE MEDIA IS GOING WILD WITH THE STORY. SISTER ATTEMPTS TO MURDER SISTER OUT OF GREED. THROW IN WEALTH AND THE URBAN LEGEND OF THE GHOST OF DUNHILL CEMETERY...

"...IT'S ON TV AND IN THE PAPERS CONSTANTLY, AND I HAVE TO PROTECT DADDY FROM THAT. I CAN'T LET HIM LEARN WHAT'S HAPPENED TO HIS LEGACY. HE'D DIE BROKEN-HEARTED."

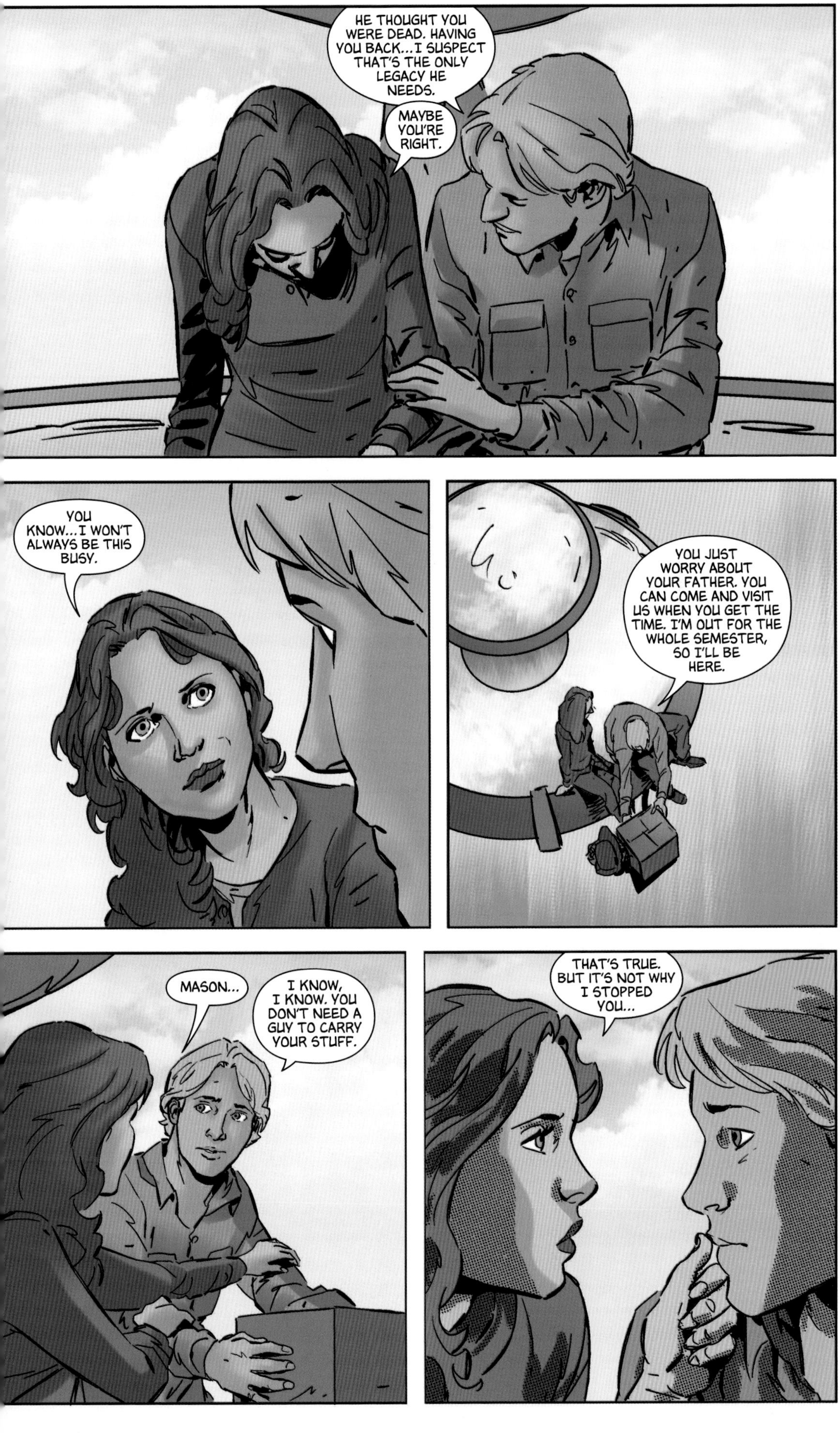
HE THOUGHT YOU WERE DEAD. HAVING YOU BACK...I SUSPECT THAT'S THE ONLY LEGACY HE NEEDS.
MAYBE YOU'RE RIGHT.
YOU KNOW...I WON'T ALWAYS BE THIS BUSY.
YOU JUST WORRY ABOUT YOUR FATHER. YOU CAN COME AND VISIT US WHEN YOU GET THE TIME. I'M OUT FOR THE WHOLE SEMESTER, SO I'LL BE HERE.
MASON...
I KNOW, I KNOW. YOU DON'T NEED A GUY TO CARRY YOUR STUFF.
THAT'S TRUE. BUT IT'S NOT WHY I STOPPED YOU...

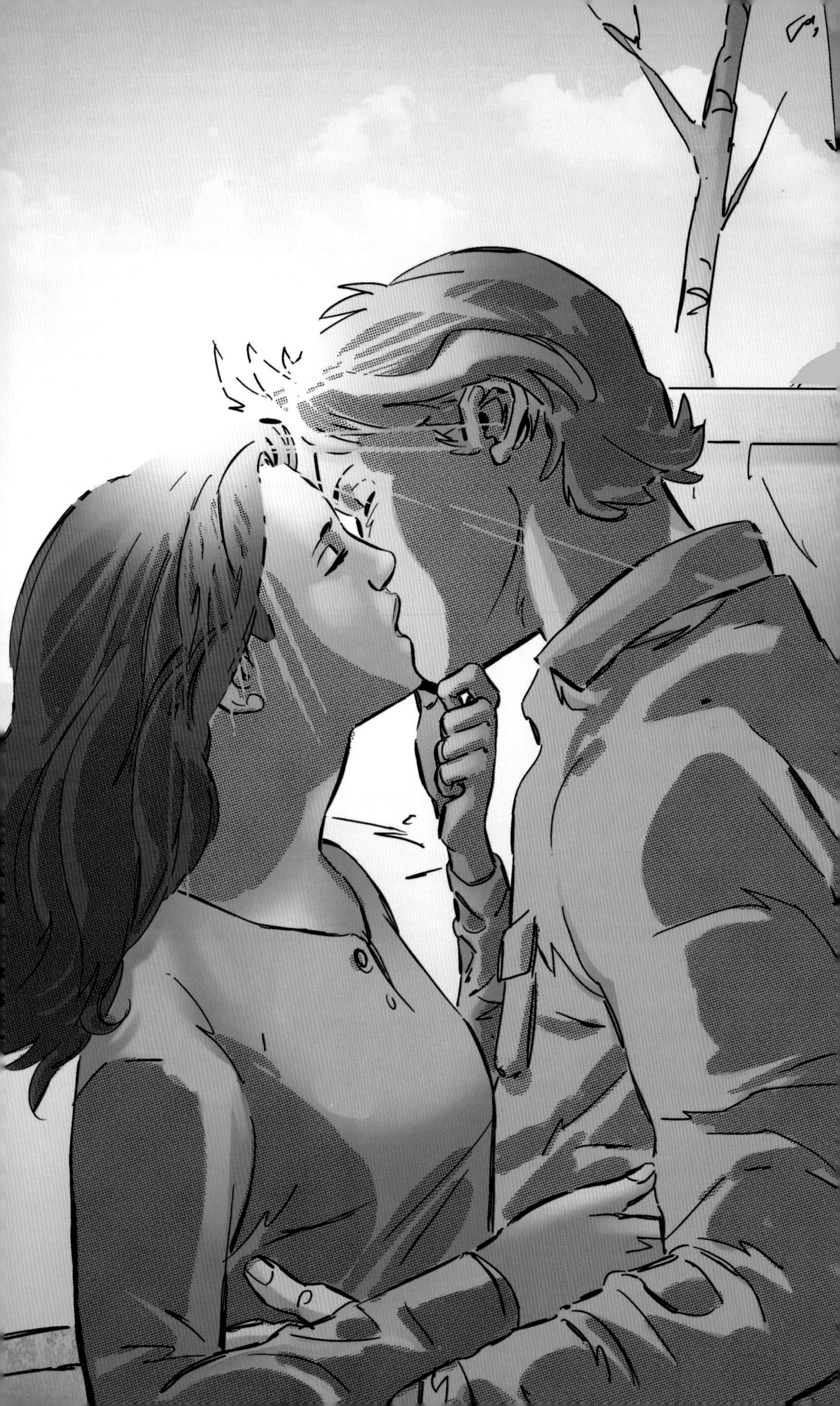

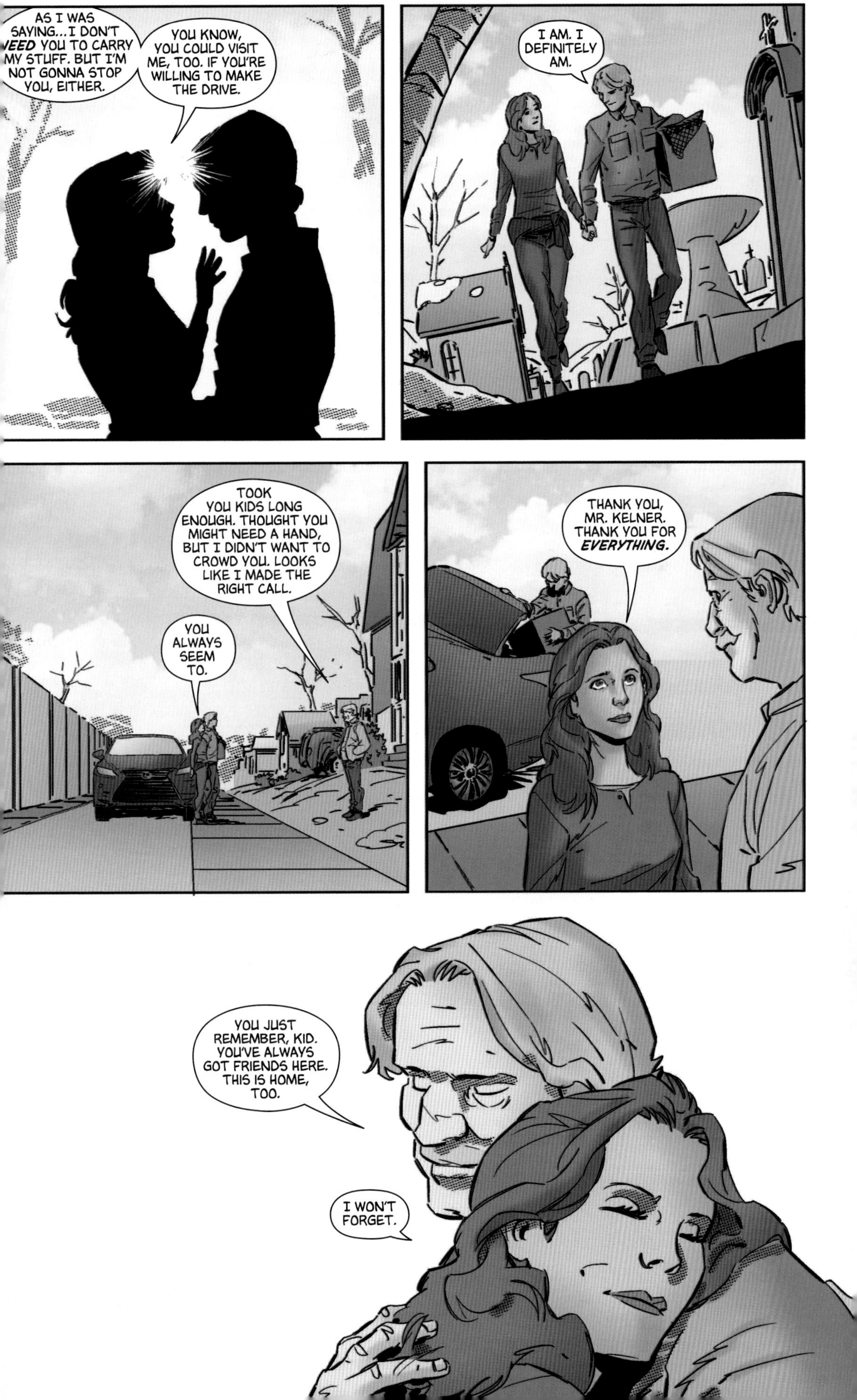
AS I WAS SAYING...I DON'T NEED YOU TO CARRY MY STUFF. BUT I'M NOT GONNA STOP YOU, EITHER.
YOU KNOW, YOU COULD VISIT ME, TOO. IF YOU'RE WILLING TO MAKE THE DRIVE.
I AM. I DEFINITELY AM.
TOOK YOU KIDS LONG ENOUGH. THOUGHT YOU MIGHT NEED A HAND, BUT I DIDN'T WANT TO CROWD YOU. LOOKS LIKE I MADE THE RIGHT CALL.
YOU ALWAYS SEEM TO.
THANK YOU, MR. KELNER. THANK YOU FOR EVERYTHING.
YOU JUST REMEMBER, KID. YOU'VE ALWAYS GOT FRIENDS HERE. THIS IS HOME, TOO.
I WON'T FORGET.

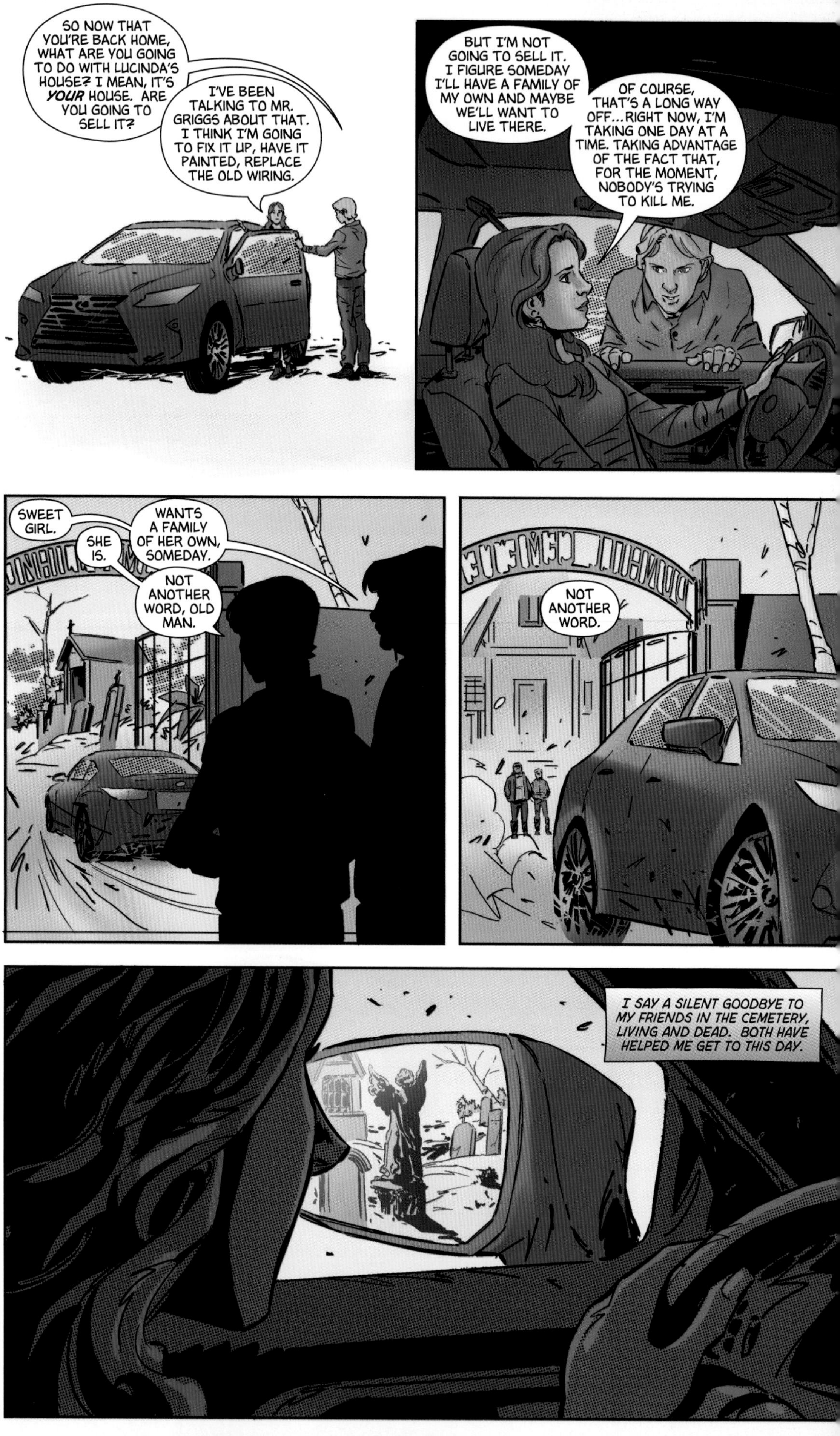
SO NOW THAT YOU'RE BACK HOME, WHAT ARE YOU GOING TO DO WITH LUCINDA'S HOUSE? I MEAN, IT'S YOUR HOUSE. ARE YOU GOING TO SELL IT?
I'VE BEEN TALKING TO MR. GRIGGS ABOUT THAT. I THINK I'M GOING TO FIX IT UP, HAVE IT PAINTED, REPLACE THE OLD WIRING.
BUT I'M NOT GOING TO SELL IT. I FIGURE SOMEDAY I'LL HAVE A FAMILY OF MY OWN AND MAYBE WE'LL WANT TO LIVE THERE.
OF COURSE, THAT'S A LONG WAY OFF...RIGHT NOW, I'M TAKING ONE DAY AT A TIME. TAKING ADVANTAGE OF THE FACT THAT, FOR THE MOMENT, NOBODY'S TRYING TO KILL ME.
SWEET GIRL.
SHE IS.
WANTS A FAMILY OF HER OWN, SOMEDAY.
NOT ANOTHER WORD, OLD MAN.
NOT ANOTHER WORD.
I SAY A SILENT GOODBYE TO MY FRIENDS IN THE CEMETERY, LIVING AND DEAD. BOTH HAVE HELPED ME GET TO THIS DAY.

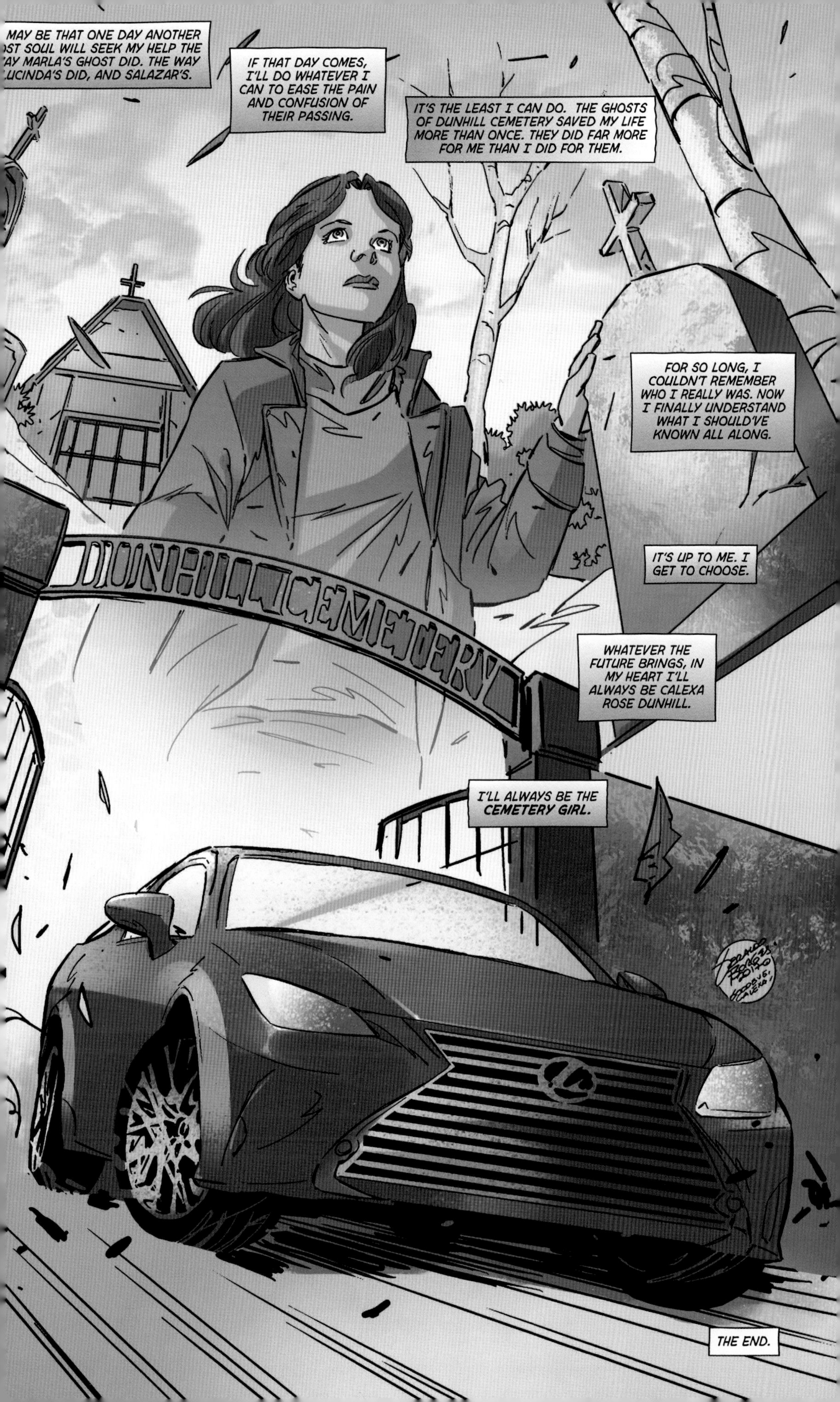
MAY BE THAT ONE DAY ANOTHER
OST SOUL WILL SEEK MY HELP THE
AY MARLA'S GHOST DID. THE WAY
LUCINDA'S DID, AND SALAZAR'S.
IF THAT DAY COMES, I'LL DO WHATEVER I CAN TO EASE THE PAIN AND CONFUSION OF THEIR PASSING.
IT'S THE LEAST I CAN DO. THE GHOSTS OF DUNHILL CEMETERY SAVED MY LIFE MORE THAN ONCE. THEY DID FAR MORE FOR ME THAN I DID FOR THEM.
FOR SO LONG, I COULDN'T REMEMBER WHO I REALLY WAS. NOW I FINALLY UNDERSTAND WHAT I SHOULD'VE KNOWN ALL ALONG.
DUNHILL CEMETERY
IT'S UP TO ME. I GET TO CHOOSE.
WHATEVER THE FUTURE BRINGS, IN MY HEART I'LL ALWAYS BE CALEXA ROSE DUNHILL.
I'LL ALWAYS BE THE CEMETERY GIRL.
THE END.

ENJOY THE FULL SCRIPT TO

Cemetery Girl

BOOK THREE: HAUNTED

BY **CHARLAINE HARRIS** AND **CHRISTOPHER GOLDEN**

CEMETERY GIRL
BOOK THREE: HAUNTED
By Charlaine Harris & Christopher Golden

113 pages

PAGE ONE:

Panel One: Daytime. A cloudy day. Close on Calexa's booted feet as she walks a path in the cemetery. There are some crinkly, old dead leaves on the ground, but a week or more has passed and we're now in mid-December, almost Christmas.

1/CALEXA/CAP: Mid-December, and it's almost cold enough to snow.

Panel Two: Pull back to show her from behind and at a distance, walking past the cemetery's fountain, which is shut down. No water flowing. She has a scarf around her neck and her collar is turned up against the wind, which is blowing her hair. We should get a good sense of the cemetery in this panel, the tombs and graves.

2/CALEXA/CAP: I don't have much of my memory back...just traces. Echoes.

Panel Three: From in front of her now, we see Calexa walking to-ward us. We're looking up at her, so we see her in a kind of iconic image of grim coolness, hair and scarf flowing.

3/CALEXA/CAP: One of those echoes is a general sense of how I feel about Christmas, and about winter.

Panel Four: Glancing around warily, Calexa is using a key to open the side door of Kelner's cottage. His truck is there. The cottage has a fairly pitiful string of Xmas lights up, but they're not plugged in.

4/CALEXA/CAP: There's this crescendo leading up to Christmas, this sense of excitement...which is so strange, because after the holiday, winter truly takes hold...

Panel Five: From outside, we see the cottage door being closed, a few crinkled leaves on the ground.

5/CALEXA/CAP: We're supposed to build up to this...this jubilation...and then the New Year arrives and it's nothing but quiet and rot and depression.

Panel Six: Inside the cottage, she's taken her jacket and scarf off and thrown them on a chair and is sitting in another, kind of hugging herself, staring at nothing, really haunted.

6/CALEXA/CAP: They say Nero fiddled while Rome burned. The holidays are like that. We throw these huge parties and we laugh and we sing...and all the while, we know...

PAGE TWO:

Panel One: Kelner is driving his son Mason's car, looking out through the windshield as he pulls up in front of the hospital where Mason has been treated after the stab wound he sustained in book two.

1/CALEXA/CAP: ...Death is coming.

Panel Two: A more comprehensive establishing shot of the hospital. Winter has arrived in South Carolina. People are wearing jackets, some of them with scarves and gloves.

2/MASON (floating balloon): Y'know, I can actually walk all right.

3/NURSE (floating balloon): You had a knife in your belly, young man, and the docs did a fine job of patching you up...

Panel Three: An attractive, older black nurse is pushing Mason in his wheelchair toward the curb in front of the hospital. Kelner has parked the car at the curb and gotten out and is opening the door. Mason is in sweatpants and a sweatshirt and does not look good.

4/NURSE: You go showing off for the girls and you're liable to tear them sutures open and they'll have to sew you up all over again.

5/MASON: I'm real—

Panel Four: Kelner has gone to take the wheelchair. The nurse has backed again, smiling at Kelner, who has one hand on a wheel-chair handle.

6/KELNER: A fool is what you are, arguing with Nurse Cynthia when she took such good care of you. If you're not in a ton of pain now, it's only 'cause she's got you doped to the gills.

7/NURSE: You listen to your father, Mason. He's a wise man.

Panel Five: Mason, wincing and scowling at the same time.

8/MASON: Don't pay him any mind, Cynthia. He's just flirting with you.

9/MASON: Remember, if I'm a fool, it's only 'cause I had a good teacher.

Panel Six: Kelner is wheeling Mason over so that he's right next to the open car door.

10/KELNER: I thought your car would be easier to climb into, son.

11/MASON: Thanks. Where's—?

12/TONY: She's waiting at the house.

PAGE THREE:

Panel One: All three of them are looking up/around as Martin Salazar (the private detective we saw in the previous book) approaches.

1/SALAZAR: Excuse me, Mister Kelner...

Panel Two: Kelner has moved slightly in front of Mason, protective of his injured son. The nurse is frowning suspiciously at Salazar.

2/KELNER: I told you to stay away.

3/SALAZAR: I'm not here to talk to you, sir. I'd like to speak with the younger Mister Kelner.

Panel Three: Mason has pushed himself slightly forward and up, looking grim and determined, jaw set.

4/MASON: I've already talked to you, Mister Salazar.
Panel Four: A different angle, so we can see all four of them again and read the body language. A standoff.

5/SALAZAR: Just a few more questions.

6/KELNER: We've answered enough of your ridiculous questions about "the ghost of Dunhill Cemetery."

Panel Five: As Kelner is helping Mason into the passenger seat of the car, the nurse glares at Salazar, eyes narrowed.

7/NURSE: Mister Kelner, you want me to call security?

8/KELNER: Don't bother, Cynthia. We're leaving. Thanks for everything.

PAGE FOUR:

Panel One: Salazar has taken a cigarette out of a half crumpled pack he holds in his left hand and is lifting it to his mouth.

1/SALAZAR: Three cops have told me that the kids arrested in the cemetery talked about a girl they chased. The Ghost.

Panel Two: Mason is in the passenger seat now, the empty wheelchair on the curb. The nurse is holding it by its handles. Kelner is about to shut his son's door. Salazar is lighting his cigarette.

2/MASON: Those same kids knifed a girl. You believe scum like them?

Panel Three: Salazar, with lit cigarette in hand. He looks frustrated.

3/SALAZAR: You gentlemen just don't get it. I mean the girl well.

Panel Four: The Kelners are in the car, and Mason is looking out the window, talking to Salazar, who is standing on the curb.

4/MASON: You don't get it, Salazar...

Panel Five: As the nurse wheels the wheelchair back toward the hospital entrance and the Kelners pull away in Mason's car, Salazar takes a drag on his cigarette, watching them go.

5/MASON (floating balloon): ...There's no such thing as ghosts.

PAGE FIVE:

Panel One: The car is in front of Kelner's cottage.
The door of the cottage is open, and Calexa is coming out to greet the two men. The older Kelner is helping Mason from the car. He is obviously hurting, though he's trying to smile.

1/CALEXA: You got released!

2/MASON: Yeah, they kicked me out.

3/KELNER: Let's get you inside...

Panel Two: Calexa, much closer up. She is distressed at the sight of the two men hobbling into the cottage.

4/CALEXA/CAP: I hadn't realized he'd be so weak. And the woman who stabbed him was trying to kill me.

Panel Three: Calexa's face, very close up.

5/CALEXA/CAP: My fault? No. But it sure feels like it.

Panel Four: Inside the cottage, Kelner is helping Mason sit on the couch. Mason is holding his stomach. Through the open door we can see Calexa still outside, her stance depressed.

6/KELNER: Let's hold off telling her about Salazar for now. Girl's got enough on her mind.

7/MASON: Fine by me, but Dad...who could that guy be working for?

Panel Five: The two Kelners are close together, talking intently.

8/KELNER: I don't know. Worries me.

9/MASON: We've got other bad news. Enough for today.

Panel Six: Calexa is coming in the door and the Kelners are a little farther apart.

10/KELNER: It sure upsets me.

11/CALEXA: What upsets you?

PAGE SIX:

Panel One: Kelner is talking to them as he leaves the room. Calexa is squatting in front of Mason.

1/KELNER: I got to open the gates for the Dryden funeral.

2/CALEXA: What's going on, Mason? Is it...are you hurt worse than...

Panel Two: We're intimately close to Mason and Calexa, but with room for the dialogue.

3/MASON: Nothing like that...

4/CALEXA: What, then?

5/MASON: I've got to sit out this semester. Doctor's orders. My dad's not real happy about it.

Panel Three: Pull back, maybe even from above and to one side. Calexa has one hand on her head, maybe with her fingers in her hair, very troubled by this news.

6/CALEXA: But your scholarship!

7/MASON: Coach came to see me. I'd be redshirted this season anyway...

Panel Four: Calexa has stood and turned away, her arms wrapped around herself. She is standing by the parrot's cage.

8/MASON: . . . so a medical leave of absence makes sense.

9/PARROT: AWWWWK!

Panel Five: Calexa's stance has loosened a little, but she's still unhappy.

10/CALEXA: So you'll keep your scholarship?

11/MASON: Yeah. And have until summer to get completely healed.
Panel Six: Calexa is opening the door to leave.
Mason is worried and upset.

12/CALEXA: I have to walk.

13/MASON: Calexa, it's too cold . . .

PAGE SEVEN:

Panel One: Horizontal panel across the top of the page. Calexa is running across the cemetery in that well-established-by-now Calexa way.

1/CALEXA/CAP: I've lived long enough with the dead now that I don't always know what to say to breathing people.

Panel Two: Calexa has stopped running. She's leaning against her crypt.

2/CALEXA/CAP: Ever since I was dumped here in Dunhill Cemetery...

Panel Three: FLASHBACK. The night she was dumped, the killer at the top of the rise, dumping her body down the slope toward the gravestones.

3/CALEXA/CAP: ...and died for a few seconds...

4/CALEXA/CAP: ...I don't know who I am or who wanted me gone for good.

Panel Four: Now she's inside her crypt, and we see her stuff. There are a lot more blankets than before.

5/CALEXA/CAP: I've been mostly living out here since then. My friend Lucinda died and left me her house, but that's...complicated. I can't stay there now.

6/CALEXA/CAP: Soon, it's going to be too cold to sleep out here, but what am I supposed to do?

Panel Five: She's wrapped herself in a blanket, sitting against the wall of the crypt, sad and troubled.

7/CALEXA/CAP: Since they started trying to look out for me, Mason's been stabbed and his father's been questioned by the police. And Lucinda...poor Lucinda.

8/CALEXA/CAP: I'm just bad luck.

PAGE EIGHT:

Panel One: Calexa is reading a book at the open door to the crypt. It's an old paperback, probably left on the front seat of a car during an interment. She's wearing several layers, plus gloves. It's cold.

1/CAP: Two weeks later.

2/CALEXA/CAP: Christmas is days away. I know that should mean something to me. I was hoping it would trigger fresh memories, but...nothing.

Panel Two: Calexa looks up, book forgotten, lost in thought.

3/CALEXA/CAP: All it really means is that it's too freakin' cold to sleep out here anymore.

Panel Three: A close up of her face.

4/CALEXA/CAP: I've tried to limit my stays at Kelner's place. A night, or a meal, every now and then. But now I don't know what to do. I don't want to cause them any more trouble.

Panel Four: Book in hand, Calexa has begun to stand up, facing Mason, who's walking with a cane. He's bundled up, too.

5/CALEXA: Mason! What are you doing out here?

6/MASON: If you won't come to me . . .

Panel Five: She's helping him sit on a raised concrete tomb.

7/MASON: ...then I've got to come to you. We have to talk.

8/CALEXA: I'm listening.

Panel Six: They're turned toward each other, intent. She really cares about him.

9/MASON: Yesterday, we had a visitor at the house. Martin Salazar. Ring a bell?

10/CALEXA: Not even a little one.

PAGE NINE:

Panel One: Mason looks as if he feels a bit guilty. Calexa has her eyes narrowed in confusion.

1/MASON: We've been sort of holding off talking to you about him—my Dad and I. This Salazar guy...he came to see me in the hospital.

2/CALEXA: Why?

Panel Two: She's standing now. Mason is sad to disappoint her.

3/MASON: He's looking for you.

4/CALEXA: What? Why didn't you tell me?

Panel Three: Now she's almost angry; not quite, he's her friend.

5/MASON: Because at first, he was just asking if we'd seen the Ghost of Dunhill Cemetery. We figured he was working for some crazy tabloid or something.

6/CALEXA: Okay. But this time?

7/MASON: This time he showed us a picture . . .

Panel Four: Mason looks worried. Calexa, absolutely on tenterhooks.

8/MASON: . . . a picture of you.

9/CALEXA: Did he tell you my name?

Panel Five: This is an intense conversation and it's obviously taking its toll on them.

10/MASON: What? No!! I would have come to tell you right away.

11/CALEXA: So something spooked you.

Panel Six: Mason is relieved to explain.

12/MASON: Yes. Why doesn't he tell the cops?

13/MASON: And why doesn't he tell us who you are?

14/MASON: Who loses a girl and doesn't report it?

PAGE TEN:

Panel One: They are calmer. They're walking back to Kelner's house through the cemetery. He's taking it slow, using the cane.

1/CALEXA: He's not a reporter? You sure?

2/MASON: No, a P.I. I checked online. He used to be a cop. The question is whether whoever hired Salazar wants to help you...

Panel Two: A different angle...a long shot, giving us bare tree branches and some evergreens amongst the tombstones.

3/CALEXA: ...or hurt me. Just what I was thinking.

4/MASON: Thing is, if he gets suspicious enough, he could just come over the wall some night.

5/CALEXA: Or drive in when there's a funeral.

Panel Three: Mason is getting tired. Calexa is worried, distracted.

6/MASON: Yeah. And it's too cold for you. Out here.

7/CALEXA: But if I stay long-term at your place—

Panel Four: Mason is breathing hard and stops to lean on a cross.

8/MASON: It increases the chances he'll come back while you're there. But our house is better than . . . out here.

9/CALEXA: Come on, just a little way. You need to get inside.

Panel Five: They're in the house now. Mason is in a chair, a hot drink beside him on the table. His feet are propped up.

10/MASON: So much better.

11/MASON: Calexa, you just can't stay out there anymore.

12/CALEXA: Hold on...

Panel Six: Calexa is standing up, troubled, looking down at him.

13/CALEXA: I think I get to decide where I stay.

14/CALEXA: See ya soon, Mason. Keep getting better.

PAGE ELEVEN:

Panel One: She's outside. Cars are coming into the cemetery for a service.

1/CALEXA/CAP: Mason and Kelner are right about one thing.

2/CALEXA/CAP: It's weird this Salazar guy doesn't tell them my name.

Panel Two: Calexa is huddled in her crypt, an old blanket around her. She's got a hat on now, and a scarf and gloves. We can see her breath.

3/CALEXA/CAP: Mason was right about another thing, too. I just didn't want to admit it to him.

4/CALEXA/CAP: It's too damn cold for me to sleep out here.

Panel Three: She's shivering. We're close on her face, and her breath plumes in front of her.

5/CALEXA/CAP: I keep this up, I'll be dead for real.

Panel Four: Calexa's leaving her crypt, blanket draped over the door grate behind her. Around her, we see images of Lucinda, Kelner, and Mason.

6/CALEXA/CAP: I'm nameless . . . but I made myself a name. I don't know my family . . .

7/CALEXA/CAP: But I've created one.

Panel Five: Calexa is at a pay phone, putting coins in the slot. It's the one she used in the previous book.

8/CALEXA/CAP: And I'm homeless . . . but I have a house. If I can figure out a way to use it.

Panel Six: The phone is ringing in Grigg's office. His secretary (we've seen her before) is answering.

9/SECRETARY: Law office of Harold Griggs, Martha Reynolds speaking.

10/CALEXA (electric balloon coming from the phone): This is Calexa Rose Dunhill . . . I was a friend of Lucinda Cameron's.

PAGE TWELVE:

Panel One: The secretary is standing in the doorway of Griggs' office. He is sitting behind a cluttered desk, looking up as she gestures at him, pointing to the phone on his desk.

1/MARTHA: It's her! On the phone...right now!

Panel Two: Griggs is gleeful. He's picked up his phone.

2/GRIGGS: Ms. Dunhill? I'm glad you've called back. We were worried about you.

3/CALEXA (electronic balloon, voice coming over the phone): That's kind of nice to hear.

Panel Three: We're back with Calexa now, at the pay phone.

4/GRIGGS (electronic balloon coming over the phone): Can we set a time for you to come in to talk to me?

5/CALEXA: Yes. I'm ready to do that.

Panel Four: Griggs has just hung up. He's talking to Martha, still in the doorway.

6/GRIGGS: The mystery girl is coming in tomorrow morning at eight-thirty.

7/MARTHA: You haven't gotten here that early in ten years.
Panel Five: Griggs has gone from elated to serious. He is the main character in this panel, though we may see a bit of Martha.

8/GRIGGS: It's the only time I had free. And she sounds like she's in trouble.

PAGE THIRTEEN:

Panel One: That night, the cemetery is quiet. This shot shows the silent beauty of the place.

Panel Two: Inside Kelner's cottage, Mason and his father watch It's a Wonderful Life on TV.

1/MASON: We can't just leave her out there.

2/KELNER: We can't force her, either.

Panel Three: Mason is at the window, staring out at the night, one hand over the place where he was stabbed. He's in some pain still. Kelner is looking at him, frowning.

3/MASON: Temperature's going to drop tomorrow night. Word is we could have a hell of a snowstorm. I'm not going to sit in here, safe and warm, with her out there.

4/KELNER: No...I guess I'm not either.

Panel Four: Close on Kelner, deeply troubled.

5/KELNER: If she doesn't come to her senses tonight, we'll go and talk to her in the morning.

Panel Five: Inside her crypt, Calexa huddles beneath a ton of blankets, wearing her hat and gloves and scarf.

6/CALEXA/CAP: That private detective...Someone paid him to find me, just like I always hoped...and now I'm afraid to know who hired him.

7/CALEXA/CAP: Someone who loves me...or the person who tried to kill me?

Panel Six: Closer shot on her face (but with room for the text), and we see tears on her cheeks.

8/CALEXA/CAP: Going to see Mr. Griggs seems like the only choice, but I'm so scared.

9/CALEXA/CAP: So scared...and so, so cold.

PAGE FOURTEEN:

Panel One: The next morning, an exterior shot of Griggs' office building and the street outside. No sign of Calexa.

Panel Two: A shot of a clock on the wall of Griggs' office. It's 8:35.

Panel Three: Martha sets a Starbucks cup down on Griggs' desk with her left hand. She has her own coffee in her right.

Panel Four: Martha is sipping her coffee as Griggs picks up his own.

1/GRIGGS: She'll be here.

Panel Five: At the cemetery, Kelner comes out of Calexa's crypt, a troubled look on his face. Mason is waiting outside.

2/KELNER: She's not here.

3/MASON: Where could she have gone? Do you think she slept at Lucinda's?

Panel Six: The two men looking at each other, very worried.

4/MASON: Wait...you don't think Salazar caught up to her.

5/KELNER: I don't know, son. I just don't know.

PAGE FIFTEEN:

Panel One: Calexa comes into the main door of Griggs' office, into the reception area. She looks "bag lady," or as much as a young and attractive girl can. Not dirty, but disheveled. She is wearing a hoodie, important later. Martha looks up as Calexa enters, a little surprised. Calexa is hesitant and scared.

1/MARTHA: Good morning! Are you Calexa Dunhill?

2/CALEXA: Yes ma'am.

3/MARTHA: Come in, honey. I wasn't sure you were going to make it in.

Panel Two: Close on Calexa, so nervous.

4/CALEXA: Neither was I.

Panel Three: Martha is opening the inner door, and we see a slice of Griggs's office.

5/MARTHA: Cold this morning isn't it?

6/CALEXA: It's been cold all night.

7/MARTHA: Then let me get you a cup of coffee or tea.

Panel Four: This is a double panel. We see a plate of doughnuts on Griggs's desk. There is a steaming mug in front of Calexa, and a little plate, strewn with crumbs or bits of sugar, indicating she has had more than one doughnut. Griggs is eyeing her, smiling slightly, as she clutches the mug. Calexa is warm and comfortable and fed now, and she's relaxing.

8/GRIGGS: I can send Martha for some more chocolate filled, if you'd like.

9/CALEXA: I couldn't eat another bite. Thanks.

Panel Five: They're both leaning back now, eyeing each other.

10/GRIGGS: Please tell me your story, Ms. Dunhill. How did you get to know Lucinda?

11/CALEXA: If you're ready to hear something . . . crazy.

Panel Six: Griggs has seen it all. His eyebrows are raised, and he looks fine with hearing a crazy story.

12/GRIGGS: Lucinda was a good judge of character. I'm all ears.

13/CALEXA: You may change your mind about that, Mister Griggs. Because I met Lucinda when I was stealing food from her kitchen...

PAGE SIXTEEN:

Panel One: Calexa is finishing her recitation. Griggs looks very thoughtful.

1/CALEXA: ...So that's my history...at least all of it that I remember.

Panel Two: Griggs is standing, looking thoughtfully out the window. Calexa is sitting in her chair in a way only the young can do; maybe she has her legs tucked up under her.

2/GRIGGS: Fascinating. So what do we know about you?

3/CALEXA: Not much.

Panel Three: Griggs has swung around to face her, and he's counting off on his fingers.

4/GRIGGS: Au contraire. You're well-educated. You're athletic. You've had good dental and medical care, apparently.

5/CALEXA: Oh. Well . . . true.

Panel Four: Griggs is looking troubled.

6/GRIGGS: That makes it all the more puzzling that you haven't been reported missing.

7/CALEXA: Maybe I'm from far away?

Panel Five: This is a three-quarters panel Griggs sits again, regarding her seriously.

8/GRIGGS: But you were dumped in Dunhill. By car.

9/CALEXA: So that means I can't have come from far away?

10/GRIGGS: That's a reasonable assumption. Not very far, in any case.

Panel Six: Griggs sits on the end of his desk, looking down at Calexa with fatherly concern.

11/GRIGGS: I understand your fears, Calexa, and I promise I'll do everything I can to keep you safe while we start unraveling the mystery of you.

12/GRIGGS: If you're to inherit Lucinda's home and estate, we've got to figure out who you really are. But there are some things we can do right away to help you.

PAGE SEVENTEEN:

Panel One: Closeup on Griggs. He's using an intercom to call his secretary in.

1/GRIGGS: Martha?

Panel Two: Martha is in the doorway, Calexa has turned to look at her, and Griggs is making notes on a piece of paper.

2/GRIGGS: I'm the executor of Lucinda's estate, and she gave me instructions. I'm giving you the keys to the house.

3/CALEXA: We can...you can just do that, before you know who I am?

Panel Three: Griggs has come around to hand Martha the piece of paper, and both of them are looking at Calexa kindly.

4/GRIGGS: I'll also establish an account for groceries and incidentals. The bills will come here.

5/MARTHA: I'm on it.

Panel Four: Calexa, warming up to this now. She's unsure, but hopeful. Griggs smiles.

6/CALEXA: Can . . . can I have enough money for a phone?

7/GRIGGS: That's a very good idea. Martha will take care of it.

Panel Five: They're all in transition. Calexa is up and moving toward the doorway into the outer office. Griggs is out from behind the desk and following her. Martha is in the lead, halfway through the door.

8/CALEXA/CAP: A telephone!

9/GRIGGS: The most important task is determining your age. Your identity may take a little time, but if we could figure out how old you are...

10/MARTHA: Couldn't a dentist confirm her age by examining her teeth?

PAGE EIGHTEEN:

Panel One: They've emerged into the outer office. Griggs looks thoughtful. Martha is going to her desk.

1/GRIGGS: That's an idea, Martha. I'm honestly not sure it works outside of TV cop shows, but it's worth looking into.

Panel Two: Martha has pulled a small metal cash box from a drawer in her desk.

2/MARTHA: Calexa, I'm going to give you a hundred and twenty dollars out of petty cash. That's enough for one of those no-contract phones, plus some prepaid minutes...

Panel Three: Calexa is taking the cash from Martha with a happy, dazed look on her face. Griggs watches happily.

3/MARTHA: ...and you should have enough left over for a bite of lunch.

4/CALEXA: I don't know how to thank you both.

Panel Four: Griggs is shaking hands with Calexa, with Martha in the background. Calexa looks relaxed in a way we've rarely seen her, smiling, a bit dazed.

5/GRIGGS: You can thank us by keeping in touch. Lucinda wanted me to look out for you the same way I would for her, and I intend to do just that.

6/GRIGGS: When you get your phone, please call Martha and give her your number.

7/CALEXA: Of course. Thank you so much!

Panel Five: Calexa is walking down the street, keys clutched in her hand.

8/CALEXA/CAP: I'll be sleeping in a warm bed tonight. And I don't have to worry about where my food is coming from!

9/CALEXA/CAP: It's nice to have Kelner and Mason worrying about me, but even better not to have to make them worry anymore.

PAGE NINETEEN:

Panel One: We see Calexa in a convenience store buying a phone. It's Christmas to her.

1/CALEXA/CAP: I feel like a real person! And I know where I'm going next.

Panel Two: Calexa is pushing open the door to Big Al's, the restaurant she went to in previous books.

2/CALEXA/CAP: I ate doughnuts at Griggs's office, but what I'm really craving for lunch . . .

Panel Three: Calexa is in line. In front of her is a mom with a toddler, and in front of the mom is SALAZAR. He's talking to Big Al himself, a beefy guy wearing an apron over his orange shirt and khakis. Salazar is showing Big Al a photograph.

3/CALEXA/CAP: ...is a Big Al Burger!

4/SALAZAR: --looking for a missing girl. She's in her teens. Hard to tell by the photo, but her hair's sort of red-ish.

Panel Four: Calexa is leaning out from behind the mom to get a good look at the detective. Big Al sees her.

5/CALEXA/CAP: Oh, you have got to be freakin' kidding me. Is this the guy looking for me?

6/BIG AL: Sorry, mister. Haven't seen her.

7/SALAZAR: Strange.

Panel Five: Calexa hurries over to a booth.

8/SALAZAR: Every teenager in the area comes into this place. I've been watching.

9/BIG AL: Don't mean I look at 'em.

Panel Six: We see Calexa's wide eyes as she's sitting in a booth with her back to the entrance, her hood pulled up around her face to conceal her hair.

10/SALAZAR: I'm leaving you my card. Call me if you see her.

11/BIG AL: Righhht.

PAGE TWENTY:

Panel One: Wide horizontal panel. Salazar is leaving. Behind him we see Big Al loading a tray with food and a drink. A teenage worker has stepped up to take the mom's order. Calexa is still hunched in her booth.

1/CALEXA/CAP: If this guy is the one the Kelners mentioned—Salazar—he's definitely getting more determined. I just wish I knew who he was working for.

Panel Two: We're right by Calexa's booth. Big Al is placing a tray in front of her. It's the order he was loading up in the previous panel. She is so grateful.

2/BIG AL: Hey, girlie, he's gone. It's a double cheese with pickles and onions, right?

3/CALEXA: You don't remember my face, but you know what I usually order?

Panel Three: Big Al sits opposite her, but in such a way as to make it clear he is only perching there for a second. She's unwrapping her hamburger.

4/BIG AL: He seems like an all right guy, this private detective.

5/CALEXA: I just...I don't know what he wants from me, and I'm afraid...

Panel Four: We're closer to them.

6/BIG AL: You don't have to explain, darlin'. You seem like a good kid and I'm not going to make any trouble for you. But I always thought you looked like you could use a friend.

Panel Five: Big Al has gotten up to go back to work. He looks concerned.

7/BIG AL: You want, you can meet the guy here, find out what he wants. I'll watch out for you.

8/CALEXA: Let me think on it, okay? But maybe.

9/CALEXA: And hey...I never paid you.

Panel Six: Big Al is smiling in close up.

10/BIG AL: You can pay when you're done. Take all the time you need.

PAGE TWENTY-ONE:

Panel One: Establishing shot of Lucinda's house. One car parked on the street (nothing suspicious about it—just to give some texture). Maybe a man walking a big dog, a plastic clean-up-after-your-mutt bag in his hand.

1/CALEXA/CAP: When I woke up in the cemetery without any memory, Lucinda Cameron was the first person to offer me kindness. Her friendship helped me start forging a new life.

2/CALEXA/CAP: Then she was killed by a greedy neighbor over a property dispute.

Panel Two: Calexa stands in front of Lucinda's house, on the lawn, just a few steps from the front stairs, with the keys in her hand.

3/CALEXA/CAP: The first time we ever met, I was stealing from her...and now she's left her house to me. I'm inheriting her estate.

Panel Three: Calexa has the key in the lock and the door swung partway inward, but she's paused in a moment of emotion, of grief and relief.

4/CALEXA/CAP: I miss you so much, Lucinda. But this is an amazing feeling.

5/CALEXA: I owe you everything.
Panel Four: Calexa is doing the necessary things. Here, she's cleaning out the refrigerator.

6/CALEXA/CAP: Garbage pickup is tomorrow, I think . . .

Panel Five: Calexa is changing the sheets on Lucinda's bed.

Panel Six: Calexa sweeping the kitchen.

PAGE TWENTY-TWO:

Panel One: Calexa shaking off a throw rug on the front steps, a broad smile on her face.

Panel Two: Calexa vacuuming the stairs, whistling to herself.

1/CALEXA: (musical notes to indicate whistling)

Panel Three: Calexa adjusting the position of an old Queen Anne chair (fabric, comfy, but old-fashioned).

2/CALEXA: Perfect.

Panel Four: She's making her first phone call. We can't see Mason, so his response is unintelligible.

3/CALEXA: It's me! I have a telephone!

4/MASON: (jumble of sounds)

5/CALEXA: Can you and your dad come over and see?

Panel Five: Calexa's standing in the doorway, and Kelner is walking with Mason up to the front steps. Mason is walking with a cane, but doing significantly better today. Mason's car is parked at the curb.

6/CALEXA: Welcome to my house!

7/KELNER: Never thought I'd hear that.

Panel Six: They are sitting in the living room. Of course, it's dated. And there are little reminders of Lucinda everywhere: a pair of reading glasses, a copy of AARP or Good Housekeeping, things like that. On the coffee table are several mugs they've used, maybe even a little tea service.

8/CALEXA: . . . so that's everything Mr. Griggs said.

9/MASON: So I guess we won't be seeing you anymore?

PAGE TWENTY-THREE:

Panel One: Calexa is picking up coffee cups. She is the hostess.

1/CALEXA: Are you kidding? Who's gonna help me fix the leaky faucet upstairs? Who's gonna recommend a good home inspector?

2/KELNER: Interesting you should think of a house inspection. Good idea.

Panel Two: Calexa is leading the way up the stairs. She looks back anxiously at Mason, who is managing, though grimacing a bit uncomfortably.

3/CALEXA: Can you handle these stairs?

4/MASON: Sure. Gotta see the house!

Panel Three: Kelner and Calexa are jammed into the bathroom. He's got the cabinet open under the sink and is reaching into it, on his knees. Calexa is smiling so happily. Mason leans against the door jamb, watching. A little bit in love.

5/KELNER: Should be easy enough to fix. I can get my tools, but—

6/CALEXA: Let's check the garage. I'm sure Lucinda...I mean, I'm sure I've got whatever you'll need. Oh my God that's so weird to say.

Panel Four: Close on Mason, still with that wow-this-girl-is-something look on his face.

7/MASON: I've gotta tell you, Calexa...you've got a killer smile.

8/MASON: It's great to see you happy.

Panel Five: As Kelner glances up, noting the tone of the exchange with a raised eyebrow, Mason and Calexa share a sweet look together.

9/CALEXA: And it's great to see you motoring under your own steam, more or less.

10/CALEXA: If you can manage a trip to the market, I thought I'd make you two some dinner tonight. How does chicken marsala sound?

Panel Six: Kelner is standing, wiping his hands on a rag. He's half-smiling, not sure he approves of this growing attraction.

11/KELNER: I'd say that sounds just about perfect. Mason can drive down to the store while I'm fixing this sink...

PAGE TWENTY-FOUR:

Panel One: Salazar has parked his car in front of a building that says COUNTY MORGUE on a sign out front. He's getting out, glancing up at the building.

Panel Two: A car draws up a little ways behind Salazar's as Salazar walks toward the morgue's steps or front door.

Panel Three: Inside the car, we see a pair of grim thugs, McKee and Samuels. Samuels is a thirtyish black guy with carefully sculpted beard stubble. McKee is a former soldier whose nose has been broken more than once. Irish bar brawler. They are watching Salazar.

1/SAMUELS: You think this means the girl is dead?

2/MCKEE: I damn well hope not. We'd lose our payday.

Panel Four: We see Salazar in the morgue. An attendant has pulled open a body bag. Salazar's looking down at a dead girl. She's a teenager, and she's obviously suffered a beating.

3/SALAZAR: It's not her.

4/MORGUE ATTENDANT: Damn it. I was sure this time. I'm gon-na collect that money eventually.

Panel Five: Salazar glances at the morgue attendant in revulsion.

5/SALAZAR: What, you're hoping for more dead girls?

6/MORGUE ATTENDANT: Aw, you know that ain't what I meant.

PAGE TWENTY-FIVE:

Panel One: Salazar walking down a tiled corridor away from an open door where the attendant stands half in the hall, door propped open, looking annoyed.

1/SALAZAR: Just remember, Harry. Keep this to yourself or you don't get a dime, even if you do find the girl.

2/MORGUE ATTENDANT: Yeah, yeah. I got it.

Panel Two: Salazar walking out the door of the morgue building. The daylight is fading.

3/SALAZAR: This just isn't working.

Panel Three: McKee and Samuels, in their car, watching Salazar get into his car.

Panel Four: Salazar is looking at a laptop while he's in his car.

4/SALAZAR: All these dead girls. No names. Murdered, over-dosed, abandoned. But none of them is her.

5/SALAZAR: I should be saying "thank God" for that, I guess, but I can't decide what would be worse—finding her dead or never finding her at all.

Panel Five: We're in McKee and Samuels' car, watching with them as Salazar's car pulls away. McKee is firing up the engine.

6/SFX: VVRRMMMM

7/MCKEE: I'm gonna hang back some. We know where he's going and we can't risk him spotting us. The man's good at his job.

PAGE TWENTY SIX:

Panel One: At the cemetery, as the sun goes down, Calexa is coming out of her crypt with an armload of clothes and books from inside. Kelner has some as well, waiting for her outside the crypt. Calexa looks troubled, but Kelner is smiling.

1/CALEXA: I hated to leave Mason at the house.

2/KELNER: He's not much for hobbling around right now, but he'll do a fine job cutting up mushrooms for your marsala. Try not to miss him too much.

U: Close on Calexa, looking caught.

3/CALEXA: What's that mean?

Panel Three: Kelner, smiling as they both start walking back through the cemetery. Calexa looks irritated.

4/KELNER: Don't worry, sweetheart. He's been watching you the very same way you've been watching him.

5/CALEXA: I haven't been "watching" him.

Panel Four: They're carrying her things over a small rise, below which we can see Kelner's car parked on one of the narrow roads that go through the cemetery. Calexa's blushing fiercely now. (Coloring note.)

6/KELNER: Nothing wrong with it, Calexa. Kind of sweet, if you ask me.

Panel Five: Calexa and Kelner getting out of Kelner's car with the stuff. They're parked in Lucinda's driveway.

7/CALEXA: You're not going to say anything, are you?

8/KELNER: Not a word. There's no telling what the future holds, but us older folks have to keep out of the way and let you young people figure it out for yourselves.

PAGE TWENTY-SEVEN:

Panel One: Calexa and Kelner come into the kitchen and we can see that Mason has put his cane aside (it's leaning against the counter) and is cutting up a bunch of peppers and is making a salad.

1/CALEXA: Well, you kept yourself busy.

Panel Two: Mason has turned to smile sweetly at her.

2/MASON: I did.

3/MASON: Welcome home.

Panel Three: Calexa is smiling, a bit shyly.

4/CALEXA: Thanks.

Panel Four: She is carrying her armload of stuff out of the kitchen, turning toward Kelner as she goes. She looks flustered.

5/CALEXA: I'm just...uhm...I'll dump this stuff upstairs. You can just put that bunch anywhere and I'll get it later.

6/KELNER: All right.

Panel Five: As Kelner sets his armload of stuff on a kitchen chair, Mason watches him, frowning.

7/MASON: What's got her all flustered?

8/KELNER: I haven't a clue, son. Not a one.

PAGE TWENTY-EIGHT:

Panel One: The next day, the sun barely peering through some clouds. Salazar has parked in front of a beautiful mansion and is walking toward the front door, where a maid stands in the open doorway awaiting him.

1/CAP: The next day.

2/MAID: It looks like rain. I wish it'd snow.

3/SALAZAR: Weatherman says you're gonna get your wish. We don't get a lot of major snowstorms around here, especially this early in winter, but it looks like a big one.

Panel Two: Inside the mansion Salazar is going up stairs, lavish and wide, and he passes a uniformed nurse (modern scrub-type uniform) along the way.

4/SALAZAR: How's he doing?

5/NURSE: Lucid.

Panel Three: Salazar is walking down a hall; there are bedroom doors on one side, and the other side is open save for a railing. One of the bedroom doors is open and a woman is coming out. She is in her late twenties, pretty, and smiling like she's glad to see Salazar. She is ISABEL. He is more guarded.

6/ISABEL: Martin, hi! Is Dad keeping you busy?

7/SALAZAR: Always something to do.

Panel Four: She's put her hand on his shoulder, stopping him. She's definitely flirting, and he's attracted, all right, but bound to secrecy.

8/ISABEL: I don't think he needs to be worried right now.

9/SALAZAR: He's my boss, Isabel. He calls, I report.

Panel Five: She's looking at him, trying to appeal to him, and he's feeling cornered.

10/ISABEL: He won't be for much longer.

11/SALAZAR: Then I'll be working for someone else.

PAGE TWENTY-NINE:

Panel One: A wide horizontal panel. We see further along the hall, a door is open and a young man in a suit is standing there, waiting impatiently. This is the assistant, BRANT MEDFORD. Salazar steps past Isabel, who stares at his back, her expression not nearly so pleasant.

1/ISABEL: (very quietly) That someone's gonna be me.

2/BRANT: He's waiting, Mr. Salazar.

Panel Two: Another large horizontal panel. Inside the bedroom of Tucker Dabney. He is only in his late fifties, but he has cancer and he is in the process of dying. The very large bedroom is decorated tastefully, and it is the one he shared with his deceased wife, so it is not overbearingly masculine. It is also full of medical equipment.

3/SALAZAR: Mr. Dabney? How are you doing?

4/DABNEY: Dying, as you can see. What news?

Panel Three: A closer shot of the two men as Salazar approaches the bed. There is a picture of Tucker and his first wife on view; Tucker, though now hairless, had red hair when he was well. They are much younger. There is also a picture of Tucker and second wife, also deceased. She is blonde, like Isabel.

5/SALAZAR: No one matching her description is in any morgue or hospital in this state. I'm asking questions about any story I hear, no matter how weird.

6/DABNEY: Keep looking.

7/SALAZAR: It would help if I could explain to people why I'm looking.

Panel Four: Salazar is closer to Dabney, and their conversation is intense. Dabney is imperious, the way many wealthy men are.

7/DABNEY: No! You know this, Martin! No one can know she's missing. I won't have this in the press, where the world can see what's become of me!

8/SALAZAR: Mr. Dabney . . . why not involve the police? So many more eyes looking! They could work it quietly—

Panel Five: Salazar is trying to make his point, but Dabney, in pain, is having none of it. His eyes are wide, one corner of his mouth lifted. He looks a little crazy, and he is, after cancer and chemotherapy have taken a toll on his mind.

9/DABNEY: I don't trust anyone not on my payroll.

10/SALAZAR/CAP: So your pride is more important than your daughter?

PAGE THIRTY:

Panel One: Salazar makes an appeal. Dabney is firm, and maybe a little crazy.

1/SALAZAR: What if I bribed a cop to look into it, paid him to share information only with us?

2/DABNEY: No one more crooked than a cop on the take. No.

Panel Two: The argument continues. The nurse has come back in, and she is taking Dabney's pulse.

3/SALAZAR: This damned ghost story at Dunhill Cemetery is the last lead to follow. If that's nothing, I'm at a dead end.

4/DABNEY: Go after it, Martin. Hurry. It won't be long before I'm the ghost.

Panel Three: Outside the room. Isabel has her ear glued to the door.

Panel Four: The secretary has approached the door, startling Isabel.

5/BRANT: Was he calling for me?

6/ISABEL: I thought I heard him, but I guess not. He's just losing patience with Salazar.

Panel Five: She's walking away, and Brant is looking after her, troubled.

Panel Six: Isabel is in her room, right down the hall. She is on her cell phone.

7/ISABEL: Salazar's going to be leaving in a minute. Follow him.

8/VOICE: (jumble of noise, unintelligible to us)

9/ISABEL: Grab her if you see her! Don't screw this up, McKee.

PAGE THIRTY-ONE:

Panel One: We're back at Dunhill Cemetery. It's in the afternoon, the late afternoon. The wind is howling, and it's obvious there's going to be a storm. Light rain has begun to fall. Through the window, we see Salazar is in the cottage, talking to Kelner and Mason.

1/SALAZAR: I have to talk to this girl. You must see that!

Panel Two: Now we're in the room with Salazar, Kelner, and Mason. We see that the kitchen door is almost pulled shut, and maybe we can see what Salazar cannot. There's someone standing there, eavesdropping. In the living room, the men are all sitting down. Salazar is leaning forward, looking tense. Kelner and Mason are making an effort to look relaxed. Mason looks better than he did the last time we saw him. In the corner, the parrot is in his cage.

2/MASON: Who do you work for?

3/SALAZAR: I can't tell you.

4/KELNER: Why are you trying to find her?

5/SALAZAR: I can't tell you that, either.

Panel Three: Now we're in the kitchen with Calexa, who's wearing a coat. She's obviously come in the back way and paused at seeing they have a guest. She's got her eye fixed to the little gap in the door.

6/MASON'S VOICE: What can you tell us, then?

7/SALAZAR: All I can say is that I'm on her side. I've been looking for months.

Panel Four: Back in the living room.

8/KELNER: But why aren't there flyers out?

9/MASON: Why no stories in the media?
Panel Five: Calexa, in the kitchen, leaning against the wall, listening.

10/CALEXA/CAP: Yes, detective. Why?

11/SALAZAR (floating balloon): Mr. Kelner, just answer one question for me.

12/KELNER: Let's hear it.

Panel Six: Back in the living room.

13/SALAZAR: Have you ever seen the girl in the picture I showed you?

14/MASON: And if we have?

15/SALAZAR: Then I can help her.

PAGE THIRTY-TWO:

Panel One: Close up on the PARROT, in his cage.

1/PARROT: Calexa! Calexa!

Panel Two: In the kitchen, Calexa is startled and bumps against something: a cookie jar, the breakfast table, a chair. Whatever's reasonable given the views of the kitchen we've had before.

2/SFX: BUMMP!

3/CALEXA (small letters): Damn it!

Panel Three: All the men in the living room jump up and turn to the kitchen. Mason is looking worriedly at his father.

4/SALAZAR: Who's there?

Panel Four: Calexa throws open the back door, rushing out as she looks over her shoulder at the door to the living room. It's dusk.

Panel Five: Salazar has started to move toward the Kitchen but Kelner is blocking his way, one hand out, lying to him.

5/KELNER: Relax, Mr. Salazar. It's just Rick, the groundskeeper. He knows where I keep my Hydrox cookies.

Panel Six: Close on Salazar, head cocked, frustrated.

6/SALAZAR: You expect me to believe that?

PAGE THIRTY-THREE:

Panel One: Kelner, despite his age, looks fairly intimidating as he squares up to Salazar. Mason is looking on worriedly, reaching for his father's arm.

1/KELNER: Unless you want to call me a liar, but I wouldn't recommend it.

2/MASON: Dad...

Panel Two: Calexa has come out that kitchen door and is looking back toward is as she walks out toward the cemetery, prepared to flee. But McKee and Samuels are there in the cemetery, parked on the road (inside the cemetery) that passes by Kelner's cottage.

3/SAMUELS: Son of a bitch, it's really you!

4/CALEXA: Shit!

Panel Three: Calexa starts running, with McKee and Samuels giving chase. McKee is already nearly on her in this panel.

5/MCKEE: Finally!

6/CALEXA: Leave me alone!

Panel Four: McKee catches Calexa by the hair. She's yelling in pain as he snags her and her head is yanked back.

7/CALEXA: AAAIIGGGHH

8/MCKEE: Sorry, honey...we been hunting you too long.

Panel Five: Inside the living room, Mason has looked around, frowning, as Kelner and Salazar are still facing off. Salazar is being super sarcastic.

9/MASON: Did you guys hear that? Sounded like a scream.

10/SALAZAR: Maybe it's "Rick, the groundskeeper."

PAGE THIRTY-FOUR:

Panel One: Calexa elbowing McKee in the face as Samuels rushes to grab her.

1/SFX: KRAKK!

2/CALEXA: Mason! Kelner! I need you!

3/MCKEE: Ungghhh!

Panel Two: Samuels has an arm around her the throat from behind, wrestling her backward toward the car. Calexa is struggling. McKee is hurrying after them.

4/SAMUELS: Hey, hey....It doesn't have to be like this.

5/CALEXA (small letters): ...let me...just let me breathe...

Panel Three: Now Samuels is on one side of her and McKee on the other. Samuels has a fistful of her hair and McKee is opening the car door. She's struggling still, fighting hard.

7/CALEXA: NOOOOOO!!

Panel Four: Calexa has one foot on the car and one on the door, preventing them from putting her in. The guys are having a much harder time with her than they'd imagined.

8/MCKEE: Get her in the car! She's just a damn girl!

9/CALEXA: Kelner! I need—

Panel Five: Samuels punches her in the kidneys, HARD.

10/CALEXA: unnhffhh

PAGE THIRTY-FIVE:

Panel One: Kelner, Salazar, and Mason (in that order) come bursting out of the cottage as Calexa is being manhandled into the car at last.

1/MASON: Stop! Let her go!

2/KELNER: Leave the girl alone you bastards!

Panel Two: Samuels jumps behind the wheel as McKee closes the back door. He has climbed back there with Calexa. We catch a glimpse of her face—in serious pain—as the door is closing.

3/MCKEE: Go, go, go!

Panel Three: Salazar, Mason, and Kelner as the car tears away from them, toward the open cemetery gates.

4/SALAZAR: Son of a bitch. It's really her.

5/KELNER: How did this happen?

Panel Four: As the car tears out through the gates, Mason shoves Salazar back a bit. Kelner is looking on, bereft.

6/MASON: This is you! You must have led them here!

7/SALAZAR: Are you...If you'd just been honest with me...

Panel Five: Close on Salazar, looking determined.

8/SALAZAR: I can't do this now. I've got to go after her.

PAGE THIRTY-SIX:

Panel One: As Mason stares at Salazar, the detective is racing toward his own car in the driveway. Kelner is headed back for the door to his cottage.

1/KELNER: Do what you want...I'm calling the police!

2/SALAZAR: No! You want her back in one piece?
Panel Two: Salazar stands next to the open driver's door of his car, looking over the top of the vehicle at them.

3/SALAZAR: Give me two hours to get this sorted out...to get her back. You don't hear back from me by then, call in every cop in the state.

Panel Three: Salazar is tearing out of the cemetery in his car. Behind him, in the little driveway of the cottage, the Kelner men can only watch.

Panel Four: Close on Mason and Kelner.

4/MASON: What the hell do we do?

5/KELNER: Depends if we believe him.

6/MASON: Crazy thing is, I think I do.
Panel Five: Calexa's in the back seat. McKee has a gun on her now. Samuels is driving. Her face is crinkled in pain.

7/CALEXA: ungghh

8/MCKEE: Sorry about that, honey, but you had to do it the hard way.

Panel Six: Still in pain, Calexa sits up slightly, moving away from him on the seat.

9/CALEXA: You've got to let me out.

10/McKEE: You're a smart girl. You've gotta know I can't do that.

PAGE THIRTY-SEVEN:

Panel One: McKee's car driving past a restaurant and a gas station, as if on the outskirts of the town, with mountains in the distance and the forested foothills very close. The dusk is fading to night time.

1/CALEXA/CAP: Night comes on quickly, as if to help hide these men and what they've done.

Panel Two: The car driving up a steep hill through a thickly wooded area, heading up into the mountains.

2/CALEXA/CAP: I'm more worried about what they intend to do next...

Panel Three: In the back seat, Calexa sits sullenly, staring sidelong at McKee, trying to figure out what the hell is going on. McKee has the gun on his lap, almost relaxed about it. Samuels is driving.

Panel Four: Close on Calexa, looking pissed and determined.

3/CALEXA: So are you gonna tell me who you are or what you want with me?

Panel Five: In the front seat, Samuels frowns and glances in the rearview mirror.

Panel Six: In the back seat, McKee has turned toward Calexa, sort of scowling.

4/MCKEE: Don't pull that shit. You know me.

PAGE THIRTY-EIGHT:

Panel One: Calexa is biting her lower lip, fighting the urge to cry... fighting and failing, as her eyes begin to well with tears.

Panel Two: She has turned toward McKee, angry and afraid.

1/CALEXA: I don't have the first clue who you are. I don't remember you.

Panel Three: From through the side windows, we can see Samuels glancing back at them incredulously. McKee is staring at Calexa, too.

2/CALEXA: I don't even remember myself, so I sure as hell don't remember why you tried to kill me in the first place, or dumped me back in that cemetery.

Panel Four: Close on McKee.

3/McKEE: You're not kidding, are you?

Panel Five: Calexa, wincing as she reaches around to touch her bruised kidneys, is staring at the gun in his hand.

4/CALEXA: You've got a gun in your hand. Does this seem like a time when I would be kidding about pretty much anything?

Panel Six: Close on Samuels at the wheel.

5/SAMUELS: It doesn't matter, man. The job's the job.

PAGE THIRTY-NINE:

Panel One: McKee has lifted his gun and is pointing it at Calexa, frowning.

1/MCKEE: I know that. Don't you think I know that?

2/MCKEE: For the record, though, honey...

Panel Two: Close on McKee.

3/MCKEE: Whatever happened to you before, it wasn't us who done it.

Panel Three: Through Calexa's window, we can see her, very confused. She's wiping at her tears.

4/CALEXA: I don't understand. You weren't the ones who gave me the drugs...who put me in the trunk...
Panel Four: McKee looks disgusted, almost insulted.

5/McKEE: Naw, I don't mess with drugs.

Panel Five: Calexa is facing her situation more calmly, with some dignity. She's facing him, and in this panel we can see all three of them.

6/CALEXA: So, what are you going to do with me now?

7/McKEE: What we've been paid to do.

8/CALEXA: You're going to kill me, aren't you?

PAGE FORTY:

Panel One: Salazar in his car. You can tell he's in the mountains, too. He's got a headset on, and he's talking on the telephone. It's full night.

1/CAP: "Not if you don't piss us off. You're worth plenty alive."
2/SALAZAR: Yes, I saw her! But one of the guys who hauled her away—

Panel Two: Salazar, up close, grim.

3/SALAZAR: He looked an awful lot like Ross McKee. Your 'friend' from Security.

Panel Three: Isabel, in her bedroom in the mansion. She is lying.

4/ISABEL: I don't remember any McKee.

Panel Four: Salazar, looking very skeptical.

5/SALAZAR: That so? I heard you two were involved. That you spent weekends in the mountains together.

Panel Five: Isabel, angry. Sitting on her bed, looking petulant.

6/ISABEL: Like I care what my dad's personal thug thinks.
Panel Six: From outside the car, we see a grimly determined Salazar. We're slightly in front of the car and we can see that he's driving with the headlights OFF. Snow has begun to fall very lightly.

7/SALAZAR: This thug thinks the guy you 'don't remember' is taking her to your cabin.

PAGE FORTY-ONE:

Panel One: Isabel has gotten up and is looking out the window as night arrives fully. She knows this information, but she's pretending she doesn't.

1/ISABEL: To our family cabin on Mt. Eben?

2/SALAZAR (electronic bubble from the phone): Exactly. I'm dropping back now because I don't want them to spot me, but given the route that's got to be where they're headed.

Panel Two: An aerial shot of the road winding through the trees up the mountain, with Salazar's car and then, WAY ahead, headlights on, McKee's car. The snow is beginning to fall harder.

3/ SALAZAR (balloon from Salazar's car): I don't know how they found her. McKee's company security, but he doesn't seem smart enough to hack my files.

4/SALAZAR (balloon from Salazar's car): Has the old man gotten a ransom call?

Panel Three: Close on Salazar.

5/SALAZAR: You still there?

6/ISABEL: Sure. And no...not that I know of.

Panel Four: Isabel pretends to be upset. Since the focus is on her, the response from Salazar is unintelligible.

7/ISABEL: Martin, bring her back to me!

8/SALAZAR (electronic balloon): That's the plan.

Panel Five: Isabel with her back to her bedroom door, still on the phone.

9/ISABEL: If I get a ransom demand, I'll call right away.

Panel Six: Isabel has the phone in both hands like it's something precious. She's smiling thinly, head down, as if her plan is all coming together perfectly.

PAGE FORTY-TWO:

Panel One: Isabel is frowning, slightly turned toward the door as she hears a knock.

1/SFX: KNOCK KNOCK!

2/ISABEL: Come in.

Panel Two: Brant Medford has come in the room behind Isabel, looking troubled. He keeps one hand on the door knob.
3/BRANT: He's asking for you.

Panel Three: Isabel still has her back to him, not even giving him the courtesy of facing him.

4/ISABEL: Tell him I'm coming. I've got to make a call.

5/BRANT: All right.

Panel Four: Brant lingers in the door. Isabel has turned to glare at him.

6/ISABEL: Is there something else?

Panel Five: Brant looks hopeful.

7/BRANT: Do you think she's still alive?

Panel Six: Close on Isabel, who is glaring at him.

8/ISABEL: No. I really don't...

PAGE FORTY-THREE:

Panel One: Brant moving down the corridor, looking chastened.

1/CAP/ISABEL: "...and you shouldn't be getting his hopes up."

Panel Two: We're back with Samuels and McKee and Calexa. It's getting gloomier, and the snow is swirling over the road.

2/CALEXA: Why didn't anyone look for me?

Panel Three: Calexa in the back seat, looking worriedly out the window.

3/CALEXA: Until recently, I mean. Till this guy Salazar started poking around, I didn't think anyone was trying to find me. And when he showed up, it spooked me.

4/CALEXA: Guess I should've talked to him, huh?

Panel Four: Samuels, behind the wheel. From this angle we can see McKee in the back seat. They are both silent.

Panel Five: McKee, in the back seat, reacting as his cell phone begins to ring. He's reaching into his coat to get it, keeping the gun pointed at Calexa.

5/McKEE'S TELEPHONE: (music) "Party like a rock star . . . party like . . ."

Panel Six: Close on McKee.

6/McKEE: Yeah?

PAGE FORTY-FOUR:

Panel One: Isabel is at her bedroom door, looking out to make sure the corridor is clear and no one is eavesdropping.

1/ISABEL (small letters): Salazar called me. He's on your trail.

2/McKEE (electronic balloon/small letters): He knows where the cabin is?

Panel Two: Isabel has closed her door and is leaning against the wall.

3/ISABEL: My father had Salazar bring him up there after the last round of chemo—part of his "farewell tour," I guess.

Panel Three: McKee's car winding its way up through a narrower mountain road, trees overhanging on both sides.

4/McKEE (balloon from the car): You're breaking up, Isabel. But don't worry, we'll take care of Salazar.

5/MCKEE (balloon from the car): Listen, which batch of the stuff did you give her?

Panel Four: Isabel frowning, still on the phone.

6/ISABEL: The fourth trial. Why?

Panel Five: McKee and Calexa in the back seat. He's on the phone, gun aimed at her, and he's smiling. She has her arms crossed and is staring out the window as if he's not even there.

7/MCKEE: She's actually lost her memory. Seriously. That shit worked better than the lab ever imagined.

Panel Six: Isabel is leaving her room, walking into the hallway.

8/ISABEL: None of that matters now.

9/ISABEL: Just call me when it's done.

PAGE FORTY-FIVE:

Panel One: Calexa is looking at McKee:

1/CALEXA: Who's Isabel?

2/McKEE: You don't need to know.

Panel Two: Isabel, smiling in a very unpleasant way, is looking down at Tucker, the old man in the bed. His eyes are closed, and he is either deep asleep or unconscious. BRANT is in the background, and he looks troubled.

3/BRANT: I don't know how much longer he's got.

Panel Three: Calexa is shouting at them.

4/CALEXA: WHO AM I?

Panel Four: We're looking into the car from the side now. We can see the snow coming down, and we can see Samuels, the driver.

5/SAMUELS: You really don't remember?

6/McKEE: You've gone this long without knowing . . .

Panel Five: Close up on McKee. Cold-hearted bastard.

7/McKEE: You can go forever.

Panel Six: Calexa thinking, trying to sort it all out.

8/CALEXA: You said you kidnapped me for ransom. So tell me this much...who'd pay?

PAGE FORTY-SIX:

Panel One: McKee is smiling, almost laughing, kind of amazed at his own answer.

1/MCKEE: Weirdly, lots of people.

Panel Two: Samuels at the wheel.

2/SAMUELS: Some to have you back alive...some to have you dead.

Panel Three: Calexa is looking over the seat at the reflected eyes of Samuels in the rearview mirror.

3/CALEXA: Like . . . Isabel?

Panel Four: McKee and Samuels both laugh. Calexa stares at them, full of hate. McKee still has his gun.

4/MCKEE: HA HA HA!

5/SAMUELS: HEH HEHEHH!

Panel Five: McKee has leaned toward her, gun aimed at her face, very sinister and imposing now.

6/MCKEE: Isabel wouldn't pay a dime for you. Not alive, anyway.

PAGE FORTY-SEVEN:

Panel One: Small panel in the center...the only square panel on the page and the only one colored normally—Calexa, shock in her eyes as some memories come rushing back to her.

1/CALEXA (small letters): Isabel...

Panel Two: The rest of the page. You could do the broken mirror effect that Don did in the previous volumes. Calexa has MEMORIES. She sees a woman, partially in the darkness, screaming at her. She sees a tremendous physical fight, during which she's struggling for her life. She sees someone holding her down, kneeling on her, while injecting her with a drug. [There is a shot in BOOK TWO in which Isabel (though we couldn't see who it was then and we can now) has a gloved hand over Calexa's mouth and is injecting her in the neck.] She sees herself being shoved into a car trunk and looking up at a face. And that face is ISABEL'S.

PAGE FORTY-EIGHT:

Panel One: Calexa is still in the car. She's leaning over, swamped by this wave of memory. This panel is just her.

1/CALEXA/CAP: Why did she do this to me? Who is she to me?
Panel Two: She's asking McKee because there's no one else to ask, turning toward him, totally bereft.

2/CALEXA: Who is Isabel to me? You know! Please, just tell me that much!

Panel Three: From outside, seeing the car pass by. Calexa is pleading now.

3/CALEXA: At least tell me what my real name is.

4/SAMUELS: Poor baby, doesn't have a name!

Panel Four: We're looking at Calexa and McKee as if from the front seat. Calexa tries again. McKee remains cold.

5/CALEXA: Why won't you tell me?

6/McKEE: It'd be a waste of our breath.

Panel Five: Samuels is leaning forward, looking through the windshield at a looming shape ahead in the snow. The headlights make it clear that it is snowing pretty damn hard now.

7/SAMUELS: We're here.

PAGE FORTY-NINE:

Panel One: A nice big panel establishing the cabin. The car has pulled up in front of it. It's pretty rustic in appearance, but it's actually a very nice place . . . the mountain cabin of a rich family. McKee is getting Calexa out of the back seat. **Throughout this whole scene, the snow continues to fall**

1/CALEXA/CAP: Not that I believed them in the first place—not really—but it's pretty obvious now...

2/MCKEE: Come on, girl.

Panel Two: Calexa trying to pull away from McKee...looking frightened and sad.

3/CALEXA/CAP: There's no ransom plan.

4/CALEXA: You don't have to do this!

Panel Three: Samuels is getting a shovel from the trunk.

5/SAMUELS: We do if we want to get paid.

Panel Four: Calexa is tugging away from McKee, making it hard for him to pull her along toward the woods. They're still by the car.

6/CALEXA/CAP: They're going to kill me here.

7/CALEXA: NO!

Panel Five: McKee shoves her to the snow. Samuels is walking over, the shovel over his shoulder casually.

8/MCKEE: Don't get me any trouble, bitch.

9/CALEXA: Why are you doing this?

Panel Six: The two men are looking down at Calexa. There is no pity in them. Calexa has gotten up on one knee (she's about to lunge, but they don't know that).

10/McKEE: You outta the way, Isabel's got a clear path. She'll own everything free and clear.

11/CALEXA: Own what? I don't even know what you're talking about!

12/McKEE: I actually think I believe you, kid. Shame of it is, we gotta kill you anyway.

PAGE FIFTY:

Panel One: Calexa lunges at Samuels, putting her shoulder into his gut like a football player and slamming him against the car.

1/SAMUELS: unnfff

Panel Two: Small panel of her hands snatching the shovel from his hands.

Panel Three: She smashes the handle (holding it like a fighting staff) into his mouth, his head rocked back by the blow.
2/SFX: krakk

Panel Four: McKee is pulling out his gun, furious that she would dare.

3/MCKEE: You stupid—

Panel Five: Calexa smashes him across the head with the flat of the shovel blade, swinging it like a baseball bat. He is dropping his gun.

4/SFX: KRUNNKK

5/MCKEE: ungghh

PAGE FIFTY-ONE:

Panel One: Calexa drops the shovel, backing away from them, wide eyed.

Panel Two: Calexa has turned and started to bolt for the woods. Samuels—bleeding from his mouth—is reaching for McKee, who is on his knees in the snow, one hand clapped to his head and obviously in a lot of pain.

1/SAMUELS: unnghh...shit, man, are you o—

2/MCKEE: Go after her, you idiot...

Panel Three: McKee is scrambling in the snow for his gun as Samuels turns to give chase. There is no sign of Calexa.

3/MCKEE: GO AFTER HER!

Panel Four: Calexa is running through the snowy woods, glancing over her shoulder in terror.

Panel Five: Samuels draws his gun as he follows her footsteps into the woods.

4/SAMUELS: Come on, kid. You know how this is gonna end.

PAGE FIFTY-TWO:

Panel One: McKee, now with his gun, is heading into the woods behind Samuels. He's bleeding from his forehead/temple where the shovel connected and it's already swelling.

1/MCKEE: You got lucky, little girl! But rich-girl self defense classes are only gonna get you so far!

Panel Two: Calexa, moving with difficulty through the trees and the snow. She's frowning.

2/CALEXA/CAP: Rich girl?

Panel Three: Salazar pulls his car up behind McKee's at the cabin. He's looking through the windshield and sees the other car with its trunk open.

3/SALAZAR: Oh, shit...

Panel Four: Salazar is climbing quickly from his vehicle. We can still see the thugs' car, with its trunk open.

4/SALAZAR: Pray God I'm not too late.

Panel Five: Salazar hears shouts in the woods.
He's drawn his gun as he turns toward the noise.

5/McKEE (small letters): Shoot her, damn it!

6/SALAZAR: She's still alive.

PAGE FIFTY-THREE:

Panel One: We see Calexa hiding behind a tree, frightened, as Samuels and McKee move through the woods in the falling snow.

1/MCKEE: Can you still see her tracks?

2/SAMUELS: In the dark, in the woods, in this storm? What am I, the last friggin' Mohican?

Panel Two: Samuels has paused and is looking at some disturbed snow.

3/SAMUELS: Wait a second...

Panel Three: They're turning toward Calexa, who has her head out from behind the tree, eyes wide with the realization that they've spotted her.

4/CALEXA/CAP: No.

5/MCKEE: Come on, girl. You got nowhere to run.

Panel Four: Calexa bolts from behind the tree, crashing through some small branches, arms in front of her for protection as she barrels through the woods.

4/SFX: kkrasshh

Panel Five: McKee and Samuels give chase, racing past the tree where she was hiding.

5/MCKEE: Damn it, girl! The more you make us run, the more I'm gonna have to hurt you!

PAGE FIFTY-FOUR:

Panel One: McKee tackles Calexa in the snow as they burst from the trees into a small clearing.

1/CALEXA: Unngghhh!

Panel Two: McKee is on top of Calexa and punches her in the face.

2/MCKEE: Told you not to run!

3/SFX: smakk

Panel Three: At the edge of the clearing, off to one side (not coming from the way they'd come) Salazar has appeared, gun pointed at McKee. The snow is falling.

4/CALEXA: Please, no! Get off—

5/SALAZAR: Ross, let her go!

Panel Four: McKee stands up, but keeps a boot on Calexa's arm. He's got his hands up. Salazar has moved closer.

6/McKEE: Martin, you need to mind your own business. Isabel ain't gonna like you interfering.

7/SALAZAR: I work for the old man, not Isabel.

Panel Five: There's a shadowy form coming up behind Salazar. It's Samuels, but Salazar does not know he's there. McKee is standing with a foot still on Calexa's arm and now his gun is pointed at her. We're seeing this over McKee's shoulder, so we have a view of Salazar and of Samuels coming up behind him.

8/McKEE: I'm warning you one last time.

PAGE FIFTY-FIVE:

Panel One: Samuels has emerged completely and is right behind Salazar. McKee has bent to pull Calexa up, and incidentally, to get out of the line of fire. He still has his gun on her so she doesn't do anything.

1/SALAZAR: I'm taking her back with me.

2/McKEE: Don't try any of your Special Forces shit, Martin.

Panel Two: They are in the same positions, except Calexa has turned her head to see Salazar better . . . and Samuels is ready to fire.

3/CALEXA: Behind you!

Panel Three: Salazar turns—he's good at this—and snaps a kick at Samuels' gun hand that knocks it back (Samuels doesn't drop the gun) and the gunshot goes wide.

4/SALAZAR: Son of a—

5/SFX: BLAMM!

Panel Four: McKee has Calexa from behind, his arm around her throat, and he fires several times at Salazar. One bullet is hitting Salazar in the side (he's turned sideways, having just kicked Samuels).

7/CALEXA: NO!

8/SFX: BLAMM BLAMM BLAMM!
Panel Five: A bullet smashes into Salazar's head, snapping his head to the side, blood and bone spraying out the other side.

9/SFX: BLAMM!

10/SALAZAR: hnnh

PAGE FIFTY-SIX:

Panel One: Salazar is falling to ground, dead on his feet, and his spirit is rising from his body in a way we've seen before.

1/SALAZAR GHOST: uunnhhhoooooooo

Panel Two: Samuels is standing nearby, gun dangling in his hand.
2/SAMUELS: Got the son of a bitch! Nice shot!

Panel Three: Calexa is still being held by McKee in the same way as the previous page. She's crying as she watches Salazar's ghost come speeding toward her.

3/CALEXA: No, no. Please don't!

4/MCKEE: It's already done.

Panel Four: The spirit essentially crashes into Calexa, diving into her chest, and it's with enough force that it is knocking both her and McKee backward, toppling them.

5/CALEXA: Nooo—

6/MCKEE: What the—

Panel Five: Samuels running across the snowy clearing toward McKee and Calexa, both of whom are still on the ground.

PAGE FIFTY-SEVEN:

Panel One: Calexa lying on the snow, SURROUNDED by the fragmented glass shard images of Salazar's life...including picking oranges at the age of twelve, playing football in high school, in uniform at army basic training, in uniform as part of the Special Forces in a bombed out building in Iraq during the middle of a firefight, and standing by the beside of the old man (Tucker, Calexa's father).

1/CALEXA/CAP: Oh, no...not again...I don't want this...

Panel Two: McKee, dragging Calexa up by a fistful of her hair. She's struggling to stand.

2/MCKEE: What was that? What just happened?

Panel Three: Calexa, held up by her hair, is being forced to face McKee. Samuels has come up beside McKee.

3/CALEXA: You...killed him...

4/SAMUELS: No shit.

PAGE FIFTY-EIGHT:

Panel One: McKee lets go of her hair, kind of shoving her head so she staggers back a step, and has his gun on her. Salazar's ghost has started to detached from her slightly, so we see him kind of branching off from her, looking sad and worried.

1/MCKEE: Whatever. Go on, girl. This is as good a place as any.

2/SALAZAR: What...what is this?

Panel Two: Close on Calexa, though we can see Samuels and McKee behind her. Salazar's ghost is half-looking at Calexa, trying to fig-ure out what's happened.

3/MCKEE: We were gonna make you dig your own grave, but—

4/CALEXA: You're dead.

Panel Three: Just Calexa and Salazar's ghost, staring at each other.

5/CALEXA: But I need your help. I need your skill. Show me what to do.

6/SALAZAR: I think I understand.

Panel Four: McKee coming toward her with his gun out. Samuels hangs back a little, gun at his side.

6/MCKEE: You tell me I'm a dead man and then you want my help? You're more screwed up than I—

Panel Five: Calexa does the same spin kick that Salazar did on Samuels, knocking the gun from his hand. She is silhouetted by the ghost of Salazar.

PAGE FIFTY-NINE:

Panel One: Still silhouetted, Calexa steps in with a precision move, using the base of her palm to smash McKee's nose (slightly from one side), breaking it. Samuels is looking on in shock, starting to raise his gun.

1/SFX: kkrnnchh

2/MCKEE: Unnffffhh
Panel Two: Still silhouetted, Calexa spins and smashes an elbow into Samuels' throat.

3/SFX: hhhurrrkkk

Panel Three: As the two men are recovering from this swift attack, Calexa is running back into the woods, no longer silhouetted by the ghost.

4/CALEXA: Ohmigod, thank you. Thank you!

Panel Four: Close on Calexa, running and crying, with Salazar's ghost again somewhat detached from her, upper ghostly body looming beside her.

5/SALAZAR: This wasn't supposed to happen. None of this.

Panel Five: Calexa bursts from the woods near the cabin, the two cars still there, some snow having accumulated on them now.

6/CALEXA: There! The other car...is that yours?

7/FLOATING BALLOON (ghostly blue lettering): The front right wheel well...there's a spare key in a magnetic container...get it!

PAGE SIXTY:

Panel One: Calexa is snatching the little plastic container magnetically attached to the wheel well of the front driver's side wheel of Salazar's car.

1/CALEXA: I can't remember if I know how to drive!
Panel Two: Calexa is behind the wheel, starting the car. The door is still hanging open.

2/SFX: VVRRMMMM

3/CALEXA: I guess I remember that much at least!

Panel Three: Samuels and McKee storm out of the woods, guns in hand. McKee's nose is bleeding. Samuels has dried blood on his chin.

4/SAMUEL (rough, small letters): I'm gonna kill the little bitch.

5/MCKEE: Don't talk, just drive!
Panel Four: They're in the car, Samuels behind the wheel, tearing after her down the snowy road.

6/MCKEE: Faster!

Panel Five: Calexa behind the wheel, eyes wide, hands white-knuckled on the wheel. The windshield wipers are going. The snow is practically a whiteout.

7/CALEXA: Oh God, oh God!

8/FLOATING BALLOON (ghostly blue letters): You've got to slow down.

PAGE SIXTY-ONE:

Panel One: Calexa glancing in the rearview mirror. The headlights of the following car are there.

1/CALEXA: I can't!

Panel Two: A shot of the beautiful, deadly scene...the two cars in the chase down the mountain road, trees on either side, too much snow.
No plow has been by here.

Panel Three: Calexa's car is going around a corner, the rear tires slewing, kicking up snow.

2/SFX: SSSSHHHHH

Panel Four: McKee's car fishtailing into a spin.

3/SFX: VVVMMMMMM

Panel Five: Small panel, inside the car, as McKee and Samuels hold on.

4/MCKEE: OOHHH SHIIIIIIIIIIT....

PAGE SIXTY-TWO:

Panel One: Calexa glancing in the rearview mirror again, seeing the thugs' car spin out in the snow and slide off the road.

1/CALEXA: YES!

Panel Two: Calexa looks up and sees a stop sign ahead—she's still on a mountain road, but there's another road that crosses it before it continues down on the other side.

2/CALEXA: Crap!

3/FLOATING GHOSTLY BALLOON: No, don't—

Panel Three: Calexa's foot jammed on the brake.

4/FLOATING GHOSTLY BALLOON: --Brake!

Panel Four: Calexa's car sliding diagonally through the intersection.

5/SFX: SSSHHHHHHHH

PAGE SIXTY-THREE:

Panel One: Her car slides off the road into some small trees and between two big ones.

1/SFX: KRRNNCHHH
Panel Two: McKee and Samuels come slipping and sliding on foot down the hill toward the stop sign.

2/MCKEE: Enough of this. I'm cold and bleeding and pissed off. Kill this bitch.

3/SAMUELS: Right there with you.

Panel Three: Calexa climbs out of Salazar's useless car, glancing over at the men coming across the intersection.

4/CALEXA/CAP: Can't stop moving.

Panel Four: Calexa running into the woods with the two men racing toward the wrecked car behind her. They're not going to be far behind once they reach the woods.

5/MCKEE: Give up, bitch! Lie down and die!

Panel Five: Close on Calexa. Salazar's ghostly face floats just above her—this time, in her mind, talking to her.

6/CALEXA (small letters): Why? If you're there, tell me that much! Why do they want me dead? Who the hell are these guys?

7/SALAZAR: The guy shouting is named Ross McKee...and he works for your sister...

PAGE SIXTY-FOUR:

(This page and the next one should be designed the way Don designed many of the memory pages—in the center of each page will be the panels taking place in the present, with Calexa sneaking through the snowy woods, trying to elude her pursuers, while the panels above and below will be the memory panels.)

Panel one: FLASHBACK—These three panels are across the top of the page. In Salazar's memory, he's talking to Isabel in a sitting room in her father's mansion.

1/ISABEL: I'm sorry to keep you waiting, Mr. Salazar. My father didn't tell me he'd asked you to pay him a visit.

2/SALAZAR: He called this morning, but didn't say a word about why he wanted to see me. Can you shed any light on it for me?

Panel two: FLASHBACK—In Salazar's memory, he's following Isabel up the stairs in the mansion.

3/ISABEL: I'm sure he'd rather have that conversation with you himself.

Panel three: FLASHBACK—In Salazar's memory, at the top of the stairs, we see McKee waiting outside Tucker Dabney's room as Isabel and Salazar top the steps. He's glaring at Salazar with obvious dislike and suspicion but not making any move to stop him.

4/ISABEL: He's the one who invited you, after all.

Panel four: At the center of the page, this horizontal panel shows Calexa running in a crouch from one tree to another.

Panel five: FLASHBACK—This and the next panel are the bottom of the page. In Salazar's memory he has stepped into Tucker Dabney's room and is closing the door behind him. Outside in the corridor he can see Isabel and McKee talking conspiratorially.

Panel six: FLASHBACK—In Salazar's memory, he's approaching Tucker's bed, the ailing man slightly propped up (the bed is one of those whose upper half can be raised and lowered). Tucker's not as sick looking as we saw him earlier because this memory predates those scenes.

5/SALAZAR: Mr. Dabney?

6/TUCKER: Come in, Martin. I need to speak with you...

PAGE SIXTY-FIVE:

Panel one: In Calexa's memory—the panels for which should have more fractured looking outlines—we see five year old Calexa on a swingset, the silhouette of a man with his back to us watching her swing. (This is her father, younger and obviously not yet suffering from cancer.)

1/DABNEY/CAP: "...about my daughter."

2/YOUNG CALEXA: Higher, Daddy! Higher!

Panel two: In Calexa's memory, she's ten years old and riding a horse, dressed in the formal attire that goes along with equestrian riding.

Panel three: In Calexa's memory, she's thirteen and pushing

through the door to her father's study/office at home (though we don't see him in this panel). She's smiling and has a cupcake with a lit birthday candle in it.

3/CALEXA AT 13: ...Happy birthday, dear Dad...Happy birthday to you!

Panel four: Horizontal panel across the middle...in the present, Calexa has stopped behind a tree, her back against it, eyes wide with shock. In the background, far away but moving toward us, McKee and Samuels are searching the snowy woods with their guns drawn, ready to kill her.

4/CALEXA (small letters, whispering): Dad?

Panel five: In Calexa's memory, she stands in her father's study, presenting him the cupcake. He's smiling at her, beaming with love and pride, and we see that Tucker Dabney loved his daughter. (Remember, this is about five years before the present.)

5/TUCKER: You spoil me.

Panel six: In Calexa's memory, continuing on from the previous panel, she and her father are both turning toward Isabel (five years younger than in the present), who is leaning against the door frame, smiling at them. She's probably 21 or 22 here, if I recall correctly, but looks stylish and professional.

6/ISABEL: She's just returning the favor.

7/ISABEL: Happy birthday, Dad.

PAGE SIXTY-SIX:

Panel one: In the present, Calexa is stumbling between a pair of trees, overcome with her memories. She's snapping off a couple of small branches.

1/SFX: KRAKK SNAPP KRAKK

Panel two: McKee and Samuels reacting to the sound. McKee is pointing off to the right.

2/SAMUELS: You hear that?

3/MCKEE: Damn right. You head that way. I'll go around the other. Try to get on either side of her.

Panel three: Calexa is staggering blindly as memories crash into her mind.

Panel four: FLASHBACK—Calexa walking up to her father's house in the dark, the same age she was when she was dumped in the cemetery. There's a silver Lexus in the driveway.
Panel five: In the present, Calexa in close-up, snapping her head up as Salazar's voice rings out inside her head.

4/SALAZAR (floating balloon): CALEXA!

Panel six: We see that she has nearly walked right into a ravine, maybe seven feet across and twenty feet deep, with tree roots and rocks and such sticking out, and snow at the bottom, of course.

5/CALEXA (small letters, whispering): oh…

PAGE SIXTY-SEVEN:

Panel one: Samuels moving swiftly and professionally through the trees, gun at the ready, glancing around for her.

Panel two: Calexa has found the head of the ravine and is moving around it so she can continue deeper into the woods.

Panel three: FLASHBACK—Calexa has paused behind a tree or at the edge of her father's house, because Isabel has gotten out of the passenger side of the silver Lexus while a man perhaps thirty-five and very wealthy looking is getting out the driver's side. Calexa is curious…watching.

1/ISABEL: Thank you, Bryan. It was a lovely night.

2/BRYAN: The pleasure is always mine.

Panel four: FLASHBACK—Isabel and the driver and in an embrace, kissing.

Panel five: FLASHBACK—Calexa is pressed up against the tree or house or whatever, cringing at how awkward this moment is.

3/CALEXA (small letters, whispering): Awkward.

PAGE SIXTY-EIGHT:

Panel one: FLASHBACK—Isabel and Bryan are still embracing, but they've pulled back from each other a bit and he's looking at her with a smug smile.

1/ISABEL: So you know what you need to do, right? I won't have to refresh your memory?

2/BRYAN: I'm not a fool, Isabel. Once I've done the dirty work, your father will have to resign as chairman. You just make sure you've got the votes amongst the board to take his place.

Panel two: FLASHBACK—Calexa in her hiding spot, gasping in shock at what she's just heard.

3/CALEXA (small letters): Oh my God!
Panel three: FLASHBACK—Isabel glances over...she heard...and catches sight a bit of Calexa's hair around the side of the tree or house.

4/BRYAN: What is it?

5/ISABEL: Nothing. You do your part, that's all. I'll take care of the rest.

Panel four: FLASHBACK: Calexa running around the back of the house.

Panel five: FLASHBACK—Calexa at the back door, using a key to let herself in.

Panel six: FLASHBACK—Calexa rushing into the kitchen.

PAGE SIXTY-NINE

Panel one: FLASHBACK—Isabel striding down the corridor toward the back of the house, inside, looking grim.

Panel two: FLASHBACK—Isabel pokes her head into the kitchen, where Calexa is standing by the counter, pouring herself a glass of milk, an open package of OREOs beside the glass.

1/ISABEL: There you are. Did you have fun at Jessica's?

2/CALEXA: Yeah, of course. How, um...how was your date?
Panel three: FLASHBACK—Mid-shot of a suspicious Isabel.

3/ISABEL: Nothing special. And now it turns out I have to run back to the lab for something. Dad's not back until tomorrow, so why don't you come for the ride?

Panel four: FLASHBACK—Calexa making a face as Isabel gazes at her expectantly.

4/CALEXA: I'm not eight years old. I don't need a babysitter.

5/ISABEL: No argument from me. But I could use the company.

Panel five: FLASHBACK—Calexa walking after her out of the kitchen and into the corridor. We can see the front door way ahead, at the end of the hall.

6/CALEXA: Okay, I guess.

Panel six: FLASHBACK—They're going out the front door into the dark. Calexa goes down the steps as Isabel uses her keys to lock the door.

7/ISABEL: Come on, am I really that bad?

PAGE SEVENTY:

Panel one: Back in the present, Calexa has ducked down behind a huge fallen tree, peering over the top in search of McKee and Samuels. Salazar's ghost stands beside her, transparent and obviously unafraid of anyone seeing him.

1/CALEXA (small letters, whispering): These guys...they work for this Isabel? My...my sister?

2/SALAZAR: Step-sister, actually.

Panel two: McKee moving through the trees and falling snow.

We're looking at him through the trees, as if we're in Calexa's POV, so he's a distance away, off to the right.

Panel three: Close on Calexa.

3/CALEXA (small letters, whispering): She sent them to kill me. To finish the job.

Panel four: Salazar's ghost, frowning. Calexa has sat down behind the fallen tree, her pursuers forgotten, just in shock.

4/SALAZAR: Isabel tried to kill you before? That's why you ran away?
5/CALEXA (small letters, whispering): I didn't run away. I died...

Panel five: FLASHBACK—Calexa and Isabel getting out of Isabel's car in the otherwise empty parking lot of DABNEY CHEMICAL, a five-story office building/pharmaceutical company in an office park type environment. Note that Isabel is wearing the same gloves that we've seen on her attacker in flashbacks such as the one on page 5 of book two.

PAGE SEVENTY-ONE:

Panel one: FLASHBACK—The sisters walk into a room that's part laboratory. There were glimpses of this in books one and two, so let's make sure the shelves/cabinets shown there are in here, as well as a desk/computer setup. One wall is a freezer full of test tubes and such. Isabel looks intent as she strides across the room toward the freezer, dropping her keys on a table or desk. Calexa is troubled, hanging back a little, obviously dubious.

1/CALEXA: I thought we were going to your office. What'd you forget down here?

Panel two: FLASHBACK—Isabel has the freezer open and is taking a test tube out with her left hand. Calexa is behind her, looking on with reluctant curiosity.

2/ISABEL: This is amazing stuff. Still in the testing phase. It's going to make the company billions...

3/CALEXA: What does it do?

Panel three: FLASHBACK—With the test tube in her left hand, Isabel elbows Calexa hard in the gut. Calexa is doubling over in pain, all the air going out of her.

4/ISABEL: You want to know?

5/CALEXA: unnnhfffff

Panel four: FLASHBACK—A bigger version of Book One/Page Four/Panel One...Isabel kicking Calexa in the gut, knocking over the trashcan, etc. Obviously we can see Isabel's face in this version.

6/CALEXA: huffff huffff

7/ISABEL: Nosy little bitch.

Panel five: FLASHBACK—Calexa tries to rise, looking at her pleadingly.

8/CALEXA: Izzy...don't...

PAGE SEVENTY-TWO:

Panel one: FLASHBACK—Isabel punches her hard in the face, as in Book Two/Page Five/Panel One.

1/SFX: KRAKK!

Panel two: FLASHBACK—Calexa on the floor, moaning, one hand on her gut and the other wiping her bleeding mouth. Isabel has gone to a cabinet and taken out a plastic-wrapped syringe.

2/CALEXA: unnhhhh...

Panel three: FLASHBACK—Isabel is using the syringe, now unwrapped, to draw the fluid out of the tube.

3/ISABEL: I didn't intend to hurt you, "little sister"...but you shouldn't have eavesdropped on my conversation with Bryan.

Panel four: FLASHBACK—Isabel has turned toward Calexa again. Calexa is rising, as in Book Two/Page Five/Panel Two.

4/CALEXA: Why are...why would you...

5/ISABEL: I've worked too hard for this. Can't have you messing it all up for me now.

Panel five: FLASHBACK—Isabel brandishes the needle.

6/ISABEL: The drug's supposed to treat emotional disorders... like chemical shock treatment...only without the electric bills and people biting their tongues off.

7/ISABEL: What a massive dose might do...well, I think we can guess.

PAGE SEVENTY-THREE:

Panel one: FLASHBACK—Calexa, looking tough now, rising and wiping the blood from her chin.

1/CALEXA: All those times I said you were an evil bitch—

Panel two: FLASHBACK—Isabel coming toward her.

2/ISABEL: I'm not evil, kid. I just want what's mine...

Panel three: FLASHBACK—Calexa throws a punch but Isabel is dodging and Calexa's momentum is carrying her forward. (She's in pain from the beating thus far...)

Panel four: FLASHBACK—Isabel kicks her again and Calexa is going down.

3/ISABEL: Stay down!

Panel five: FLASHBACK to a shot in BOOK TWO in which Isabel (though we couldn't see who it was then and we can now) has a gloved hand over Calexa's mouth and is injecting her in the neck. (Pretty sure that's what was in the panel.) [NOTE: We don't have the art immediately to hand for book two—please check to see if this injection matches what has been shown in flashback before. We believe that the injection flashback in book one does NOT match the one in book two. We want it to match book two—so the person doing the injecting was behind Calexa, meaning that Calexa did not see her face at the time.]

4/CALEXA: Please, no...

PAGE SEVENTY-FOUR:

Panel one: Back in the present. Calexa is sitting behind the fallen tree, hair and jacket covered in snowflakes. Her eyes are wide with horror at this memory.

1/CALEXA: Isabel...

2/SALAZAR'S GHOST (off-panel): Kid, you've gotta run.

3/CALEXA (small letters, whispering): Tell me about my father... did he hire you?

Panel two: Salazar's ghost looms above her, urgent now.

4/SALAZAR: We'll swap stories later. Right now, you have to survive, and that means running!

Panel three: Calexa is climbing to her feet, the ghost behind her, and she's looking up in surprise at something off panel.

5/CALEXA: I'm going, okay? I'm—

6/CALEXA: Oh.

Panel four: Samuels is there, pointing his gun right at her, cocky and cruel as ever.

7/SAMUELS: End of the line, honey.

Panel five: Calexa drops down behind the fallen tree again. The ghost is sliding INTO HER.

8/CALEXA: Help me, Mr. Salazar!

9/SALAZAR: Open your mind, girl...see what I see...

PAGE SEVENTY-FIVE:

Panel one: Samuels looks irritated as he leans over the fallen tree, leading with his face and gun.

1/SAMUELS: What are you, five years old? You can't just hide. And Salazar can't help you. He's gone...

Panel two: From her spot behind the tree, Calexa is reaching up and grabbing him by the jacket with one hand and by the gun with the other, and pulling. Salazar's ghost is partly inside of Calexa, but out of synch, so it's like he's slightly to one side but otherwise superimposed over her.

2/CALEXA: He hasn't gone far!

Panel three: The gun goes off, but the bullet fires into the ground.

3/SFX: BLAMM!

Panel four: Calexa hauls Samuels over the fallen tree, struggling with him as she rips the gun from his grasp. The ghost of Salazar is still there, merged with her.

4/SAMUELS: Hunnfff

Panel five: Calexa smashes Samuels across the temple with his own gun.

5/SFX: SWAKKK!

PAGE SEVENTY-SIX:

Panel one: Samuels is trying to rise, reaching for her, sneering, blood coming from a gash on his temple. Calexa/Salazar is in the panel.

1/SAMUELS: ...little...bittcchhh...

Panel two: Calexa hits him with the gun again, even harder, blood flying.

2/SFX: SSWWAKKKK!

Panel three: In the snowy woods, McKee is rushing past trees, his gun out. He's heard the gunshot and is rushing to respond.

3/MCKEE: Samuels! Did you get her? Sing out, damn it!

Panel four: Calexa hiding behind a thick tree (this one standing, not fallen). The ghost has separated from her. They're near the fallen tree and we can see Samuels sprawled unconscious behind it.

4/SALAZAR: I can help you again...but McKee's not going to be so easily—

5/CALEXA (small letters, whispering): No worries. I've got this one...

Panel five: As McKee comes through some trees off to the right, catching sight of Samuels lying on the ground, Calexa darts out from cover to run left-and-away, back the way they all came in the first place, back toward the street.

6/MCKEE: Samuels, you stupid son of a—

7/MCKEE: HEY!

PAGE SEVENTY-SEVEN:

Panel one: Calexa bolting, top speed, through the trees and snow— which isn't easy with the snow.

Panel two: McKee has paused to shoot at her, firing his gun.

1/SFX: BLAMM BLAMM BLAMM!

Panel three: Calexa running as a bullet hits a nearby tree, sending splinters flying.

2/SFX: sshukkk

Panel four: McKee giving chase, gun in his fist, absolutely furious now. He can't wait to kill her.

3/MCKEE: Enough of this shit!

Panel five: Calexa looking over her shoulder, slowing down as if she's waiting for him.

4/CALEXA (small letters, whispering): C'mon, you bastard...catch up to me...you can do it...

Panel six: McKee HAS caught up with her...only maybe fifteen feet behind her as she goes around a big tree, running.

5/MCKEE: I can't wait to put a bullet in you...

PAGE SEVENTY-EIGHT:

Panel one: Calexa LEAPS over the ravine, arms flung wide...

1/CALEXA (small letters): huppp

Panel two: Calexa crashes down on the other side, tumbling in the snow.

2/CALEXA (small letters): whooofff

Panel three: McKee comes racing around the tree, noticing the ravine too late. He's trying to stop himself, but momentum is carrying him forward.

3/MCKEE: ohshitohshitohshitoh...
Panel four: As Calexa climbs to her feet on the other side, McKee is falling into the ravine.

4/MCKEE: sssssshhhhiiiiiiiiiii—

PAGE SEVENTY-NINE:

Panel one: Calexa stands in the snow, staring down into the darkness at the bottom of the ravine.

1/CALEXA: I hope it hurt, you son of a bitch.

Panel two: A snowplow moves along the road where Calexa's car has gone off the road, its headlights picking out the car.

2/SFX: RRRRMMMMMM

Panel three: Calexa stumbles out of the woods in front of the plow, waving her arms.

Panel four: Calexa's standing beneath the snowplow's window, pitiful and frozen, looking up at the bearded, burly driver.

3/DRIVER: That your car, sweetheart?

4/CALEXA: It used to be. Pretty sure my dad won't let me drive it again till I'm a thousand years old. Please, can you take me home?
Panel five: She's in the truck with him now and they're driving

away.

5/DRIVER: I'm not supposed to do this, but I figure in this weather, I'm your best bet.

6/CALEXA: You're a lifesaver. Seriously...you have no idea.

PAGE EIGHTY:

Panel one: We're looking at Calexa and the driver through the windshield. He's peering out at the road, which is hazardous. The snow is coming down. It's night. The headlights are on. But Calexa is smiling slightly, invigorated.

1/CALEXA/CAP: I'm so close to finding out who I am. Where I belong.

Panel two: We move in closer to Calexa, whose smile has faded.

2/CALEXA/CAP: I know my stepsister Isabel tried to kill me. In the lab of a company my father owns.

Panel three: She's looking down at the butt of a gun, which she's pulled up a little bit so that she can peek at it. It's in her right hand coat pocket, definitely NOT where the driver can see it.

3/CALEXA/CAP: I have a souvenir, to help keep me safe...

Panel four: Calexa looks grim, and now we see the ghost of Salazar is behind her seat in the truck, looking forward.

4/CALEXA/CAP: Mr. Salazar was trying to protect me, but I'm not going to let anyone else die for me.

5/CALEXA/CAP: This is my fight now.

Panel five: McKee is crawling up over the snowy edge of the ravine. His head is bloody and his clothes are torn. He is furious.

6/MCKEE: Oh, you little bitch...

PAGE EIGHTY-ONE:

Panel one: Exterior shot of the Kelner house. Night, snow falling.

1/KELNER (floating balloon): They took off with her before we could stop them, and this man Salazar went after them.

Panel two: Inside. There are two policemen in the living room with Kelner and Mason, both of whom look very troubled. Kelner and Cop One are in the foreground, Mason and Cop Two (a woman) in the background.

2/COP ONE: Salazar? I know a private eye, used to be a cop . . .

3/KELNER: That's him.

Panel three: Focus on Cop Two, who is censorious, frustrated with them. Mason is agitated.

4/COP TWO: This girl has been living in the cemetery? In this weather? You knew this?

5/MASON: If we'd reported it, she'd have taken off...

6/MASON: And we're more worried about her life right now!

Panel four: Cop One is busy with his phone, and Cop Two is looking around the room suspiciously. Kelner and Mason have moved close together.

7/KELNER: They'll find her, son. She won't make it easy for the guys who took her.

8/MASON: Men with guns? Dad . . . her only hope is Salazar. I wish we'd trusted him.

Panel five: They're still talking. We're closer to them.

9/KELNER: She's going to be furious when she finds out we've told the police about her.

Panel six: Cop One is putting his phone into his pocket. He looks very serious. Cop Two is looking at him. He has news, obviously.

10/COP ONE: That was the patrol car that made it up the mountain. Bad news, I'm afraid. They found Martin Salazar.

11/COP ONE: He's dead.

PAGE EIGHTY-TWO:

Panel one: Outside, Cop One and Cop Two are getting into their car in front of Kelner's hosue (Cop One is driving), and the Kelners are in their doorway. They are deflated with hopelessness.

1/KELNER: Thanks for your help. Please call us if you find her.

2/COP TWO: We'll call, either way.

Panel two: Inside, Mason and Kelner are making their way to the kitchen. They're depressed and exhausted.

3/KELNER: We better heat up some soup. I'm cold to the bone.

4/MASON: She's out in this, Dad.

Panel three: They're opening the swinging door into the kitchen. At the same time, Calexa is entering through the kitchen/side door. She is a mess. Her hair disheveled, her coat smeared with snow and dirt. It's torn, too. One side hangs heavy with the GUN in her pocket.

5/MASON: CALEXA!

6/KELNER: Oh, thank God.

Panel four: Calexa is smiling at them in a weary way, exhausted.

7/CALEXA: I'm so glad to see you. I didn't think I'd make it off the mountain.

8/KELNER: We want to hear all about it. But first we have to tell the police you're safe.

Panel five: Close up of Calexa, stunned.

9/CALEXA: You called the cops?

PAGE EIGHTY-THREE:

Panel one: Calexa has leaned against the fridge and has her hands on the top of her head, a little panicked. Mason and Kelner look on, concerned.

1/CALEXA: What am I going to do?

2/MASON: Calexa, I'm sorry, but we saw those guys abduct you. What were we supposed to do?

Panel two: Kelner has put a hand on her shoulder. She's lowering her hands, staring off at nothing as she comes to a realization.

3/KELNER: Calexa...

4/CALEXA: No. You know what?

Panel three: Calexa has tears on her face, but also the hint of a smile. Kelner still has a hand on her shoulder and Mason has his hands stuffed in his pockets, still worried.

5/CALEXA: It's...maybe it's okay.

6/CALEXA: A lot of horrible things happened today. Those ass-holes took me, kidnapped me or whatever. And Mr. Salazar...he died trying to save me.

Panel four: Close up on Calexa, intense and beautiful in spite of all she's been through.

7/CALEXA: But I started to remember who I am.

PAGE EIGHTY-FOUR:

Panel one: In the living room now. Mason is sitting close to Calexa, who has a steaming mug of something in her hand. She has taken off her torn jacket and is wrapped in a knitted afghan, the kind of thing Kelner's wife might have made. Kelner is perched on the arm of the sofa.

1/KELNER: That tea should warm you up. Now let's have it. What do you remember? Who dumped you here in the first place?

2/CALEXA: I don't have the whole picture yet. I'm just getting pieces of it so far.

Panel two: She's raised the cup to sip. Her eyes are narrowed with grim contemplation. The men are leaning forward, waiting to hear.

3/CALEXA: I have a sister . . .

4/MASON: Cool.

Panel three: Close on Calexa's face as she glances toward Mason (who is off panel).

5/CALEXA: . . . she's the one who tried to kill me.

Panel four: Mason has leaned back in his chair and thrown up his hands. Calexa is looking at Mason. Kelner is stroking his chin in contemplation.

6/MASON: But where were your parents? Why didn't someone look for you?

7/KELNER: That's the biggest question.

Panel five: Calexa has gotten up and gone to the window. The afghan is still around her shoulders and she still holds the tea cup—in both hands, warming her hands—as she gazes out the window sadly.

8/CALEXA: I don't have many of the answers, but I know this. My sister is a step-sister...

9/CALEXA: And my mother is dead.
Panel six: Close on Kelner, looking on with fatherly concern.

10/KELNER: Oh, honey. I'm sorry.

PAGE EIGHTY-FIVE:

Panel one: We're looking at Calexa from outside, through the window.

1/CALEXA: I think my dad might still be alive. He's really sick, though. At least, he was.

2/CALEXA: That's why Isabel sent those guys after me. She wants me dead so she can inherit everything. His house. His company.

Panel two: Calexa is setting the tea cup on a table.

3/CALEXA: All this time I wondered who tried to kill me, but now that I know, I wish I didn't.

4/CALEXA: I think I could have been happy living as Calexa Rose Dunhill forever.

Panel three: Mason has stood. Kelner still perches on the sofa arm. Calexa has taken off the afghan and is putting it on the sofa.

5/KELNER: We ought to phone the lawyer. Mr. Griggs.

6/MASON: He can make some calls about your dad.

Panel four: A shot of Calexa alone, the spirit of Salazar looming behind her, looking concerned. Calexa has closed her eyes.

7/SALAZAR: No lawyers. No police. Tell them.

8/CALEXA: Why?

Panel five: The Kelners are staring at Calexa, who has her eyes closed in concentration.

9/MASON: Calexa, who are you talking to?

Panel six: Calexa is in her "mindscape," facing Salazar, who has taken her hands in his. This must be clearly NOT the Kelners' house. Maybe they both look ghostly in this shot.

10/SALAZAR: Your father's very sick, but not just his body. He's mostly all there, but his paranoia is out of control. When you vanished, he refused to go to the police.

11/CALEXA: I don't understand. He didn't try to find me?

PAGE EIGHTY-SIX:

Panel one: Salazar in the old man's room. Calexa's father is in a chair but with an IV bag hooked up and a blanket over him, quite obviously a sick man receiving medical care.

1/SALAZAR/CAP: "Of course he did. He's had me searching for you all along, but quietly. Your sister was supposed to be doing the same thing, but we both know how that went."

2/SALAZAR/CAP: "He thought if word got out about his illness or your disappearance, he would look weak, and his company would suffer."

Panel two: Back in the present, Kelner is snapping his fingers in front of Calexa's face. She's opening her eyes suddenly.

3/KELNER: Calexa! Hey, kid, are you with us?

4/SFX: SNAPP SNAPP

Panel three: With Mason and Kelner looking on in concern, Calexa glances sadly at the floor.

5/CALEXA: Apparently my father's company is more important to him than his daughter.

Panel four: Salazar, alone on the mindscape. Ghostly.

6/SALAZAR: It isn't like that. He's been unraveling for years, mind and body. Just talking to him, it's obvious he loves you more than anything.

7/SALAZAR: I think the hope of seeing you again may be the only thing keeping him alive.

Panel five: In the living room, Salazar's ghost looms behind Calexa, whose expression has changed to one of surprise and concern.

8/SALAZAR: But he's not gonna stay alive long. When McKee gets back and tells her what's happened, she'll know it's only a matter of time before the police get involved.

9/SALAZAR: She'll lie, of course. She's good at it. But there's only one way for her to make sure your father doesn't contradict her.

Panel six: Calexa has grabbed Mason by the arm and is looking at Kelner, determined and worried.

10/MASON: Calexa, what—

11/CALEXA: I'll explain in the car, but we've gotta go...

PAGE EIGHTY-SEVEN:

Panel one: Establishing shot of the mansion, at night, lights on inside.

1/CALEXA/CAP: "...My father's in danger."

Panel two: Echoing the scene at Kelner's cottage, McKee is coming into the mansion's kitchen through a mud room. Though this part of the mansion is not as grand, the kitchen is clearly lavish. Isabel is standing by a counter, carrying a cell phone, and her body is tense and angry. McKee is obviously very much the worse for wear.

2/ISABEL: What did you do with Samuels?

3/MCKEE: Dropped him at Mercy General. Told him to say he'd slipped on some ice.

Panel three: Close up on Isabel, and she's furious.

4/ISABEL: You think they'll believe that? Won't call the police?

Panel four: Close up on McKee, who's tired, beaten, and angry himself.

5/MCKEE: I couldn't just dump him by the side of the road!

Panel five: Isabel and McKee. Isabel has turned away, worried now instead of angry. McKee is still miffed.

6/ISABEL: So...she's really been in that cemetery all this time? Why would she do that? Why not just call and talk to her father?

7/MCKEE: I'm telling you, she had no idea who she was. No idea you even existed, never mind that you were the one who dumped her there in the first place.

Panel six: Isabel is thoughtful. McKee is very curious.

8/ISABEL: That's perfect. We were going to market that drug as a chemical alternative to electroconvulsive therapy. Rewrite brain patterns to treat mental illness.

9/MCKEE: What do you mean you were going to? Not anymore?

PAGE EIGHTY-EIGHT:

Panel one: Isabel's smiling.

1/ISABEL: No, no. Too many unpleasant side effects, even in low doses. Of course, I gave my stepsister a dose big enough to melt and elephant's brain.

Panel two: McKee is exhausted, looking at her like she's crazy. Isabel is not happy.

2/MCKEE: But she's still alive.

3/ISABEL: You should go, McKee. Before you make an even bigger mess of this than you already have.

Panel three: Insulted, McKee is straightening up, smoothing his coat to look dignified.

4/MCKEE: The girl's out there. Only a matter of time before I find her again. And Salazar won't make any more trouble for us.
Panel four: Isabel has a lopsided grin, pleasantly surprised as she faces McKee.

5/ISABEL: He won't be coming back?

6/MCKEE: Not without voodoo or something. His lights are out for good.

Panel five: They're interrupted by the secretary, Brant. He's come into the kitchen from the hallway, still holding the door open with one hand, and is looking at both of them with some suspicion. Isabel is cold, barely looking at him, dismissive toward him.

7/BRANT: Excuse me for interrupting, Isabel, but your father is upset because he hasn't heard from Mr. Salazar. I don't suppose he's called you?

8/ISABEL: Don't get your panties in a wad, Brant. Salazar will call when he can.

PAGE EIGHTY-NINE:

Panel one: On the highway, in the snowstorm, Mason's car makes its way through the snow. The headlights are barely able to cut through and obviously things are moving pretty slowly. There are a couple of cars going to other direction (if we can even see that), but this is NOT a night when many people would be out.

1/MASON (from inside the car): So how much more do you remember?

Panel two: Mason and Calexa in the front seat of the car. He's driving. She's looking out the window. Snow covers the windshield except where the wipers have cleared it off. Mason is intent on driving carefully.

2/CALEXA: It started as a trickle, like someone put a little hole in the dam holding my memories back. Now they're flowing. Pretty soon it could be a flood.

3/CALEXA: But there's more to it than that. Salazar told me some things.

Panel three: Close on Mason, still focused on the road.

4/MASON: You said they killed Salazar.

Panel four: From behind Calexa, we see her profile and then her reflection in the window...and we see Salazar's reflection beside hers.
5/CALEXA: Yeah.

Panel five: Another angle shot of Mason and Calexa inside the car. We can see that she's got her hand on the gun in her pocket, like it's her lucky charm. Mason doesn't notice because he's driving.

6/MASON: Okay...

7/MASON: So what do you know? Tell me about your family. Maybe that'll help you remember the rest.

PAGE NINETY:

Panel one: The car is getting off the highway onto an off-ramp with a big EXIT sign that is partly obscured by snow.

1/CALEXA (balloon from car): My stepsister Isabel is a lawyer for DPC...the Dabney Palmetto Chemical Company.

Panel two: Looking across Mason, we can see Calexa beyond him, and Salazar's ghost reflected in the window, looking at Calexa.

2/CALEXA: Salazar tells...I mean told me that since my dad got really sick, DPC is being run by the board of directors. He's Chairman Emeritus or whatever, for as long as he lives.

3/CALEXA: Isabel is his legal proxy. She speaks for him.

Panel three: Mason glancing at her, frowning angrily.

4/MASON: But she's the one who tried to kill you!

Panel four: Calexa, wide-eyed, reaches toward the windshield.

5/CALEXA: Mason, look out!

Panel five: We see the car from the outside. Mason has drifted a bit on the curving ramp and the car is headed for the guardrail.

Panel six: Mason, inside the car, is jammed back against his seat as he frantically turns the wheel, trying to avoid a crash.

PAGE NINETY-ONE:

Panel one: The car's tires slew sideways, kicking up snow, the front end swinging the opposite direction.

1/SFX: SSSHHHSSSS

Panel two: The car skids the other way as it moves further along the off-ramp, but Mason is getting it under control.

2/SFX: SSSHHSHHSHS

Panel three: Mason has the wheel straight ahead, both arms stiff, staring through the windshield with wide eyes, shocked but relieved that he's managed not to crash them.

Panel four: The car rolls up to a stoplight at the end of the off-ramp, NO other traffic anywhere. In the storm, it's like the world is deserted.

Panel five: Inside the car, Mason is still straight-armed. Calexa has a hand on the dashboard, looking equally shocked.

3/MASON: Holy shit.

4/CALEXA: Yeah.

5/CALEXA: Maybe keep your eyes on the road.

PAGE NINETY-TWO:

Panel one: They're driving again, down a two-lane street now. This shot is from outside.

1/CALEXA (from inside car): Isabel made it look like I'd run away…

Panel two: FLASHBACK. Mr. Dabney (not looking nearly as sick as we've seen him) sits in a chair in a rumpled suit, one hand on his head in sorrow. The other hand holds a letter he believes is from Calexa.

2/CALEXA/CAP: "Isabel used my computer to write a note and forged my signature to it. The note said I'd never forgive my father for the way he treated my mother when she was alive…"

3/CALEXA/CAP: "…The letter told him not to look for me, that I never wanted to see him again."

Panel three: Inside the car, Mason looks over at Calexa sadly.

4/MASON: But why?

5/CALEXA: She's not his daughter. Not by blood. He was going to leave her plenty of money, but Isabel wants more than his money.

Panel four: On the mindscape. Calexa and Salazar, both ghostly, but now it's snowing on the mindscape.

6/SALAZAR: She wants the company.

Panel five: Back in the car. Calexa looking out the window at the snow as they're driving through a huge pair of wrought-iron gates. Salazar's reflection in the glass.

7/CALEXA: Once my father died, she'd be the executor of his estate. His share of the company would be held in trust until she could have me declared legally dead.

8/CALEXA: Then it would all belong to her.

PAGE NINETY-THREE:

Panel one: Calexa looking down at her hands. Mason has reached out to put his hand over hers, comforting and loving. Calexa is deeply sad.

1/CALEXA: I wanted so badly to remember, but this...it's awful. My father's not all there anymore. Salazar said he was unraveling.

2/CALEXA: But I just want to see him...let him see me, so he knows I didn't run away. That I'd never do that to him.

Panel two: Close on Calexa.

3/CALEXA: My memory is still spotty, but I know my feelings for him are complicated.

4/CALEXA: No matter what, though...I don't want him to die thinking that I hated him.

Panel three: Close on Mason behind the wheel, maybe seen through the windshield from outside.

5/MASON: You know, there's one thing you still haven't told me—your real name.

Panel four: Calexa looks determined and ready for a fight now, gazing straight out through the windshield.

6/CALEXA: No matter what I remember, or what Salazar told me, down inside I still feel like Calexa Rose Dunhill. That's who I am now.

7/CALEXA: You and your dad and Lucinda...you guys have been my family. Whatever happens, that won't change.

Panel five: Large panel of the car pulling up to the mansion in the snowstorm. It should look beautiful but also remote and ominous.

8/MASON (balloon from car): Calexa...

9/MASON (balloon from car) ...You're home.

PAGE NINETY-FOUR

Panel one: Inside the house, Brant is in a first floor office, banker's lamp on the desk. He's on his cell phone, leaning against the desk.

1/BRANT: I know, okay? I should have left before it got this bad. Isabel's offered me a bed for the night and I'm going to...

2/BRANT: No. Just stop. She's the last person you should be worried about. You want me to die trying to make it home tonight because you've got these delusions?

Panel two: A shot of a hand knocking hard on the front door, out in the dark and the snow.

3/SFX: NOKK NOKK NOKK

Panel three: Brant has looked up, frowning, surprised by the sound.

4/BRANT: Hey, look, honey, I've got to go. Someone's at the door.

Panel four: Brant walking out into the foyer, still on the phone. He looks irritated.

5/BRANT: Yes, in the middle of a blizzard. Could be the plow guy, I guess.

6/BRANT: You know what? Fine. You want me to try to drive home tonight, I'll do it, but if I get stuck in a snowbank, remember who's to blame.

Panel five: Brant is slipping his phone into his pocket.

7/BRANT: Man's gonna be the death of me.

Panel six: Brant's starting to open the door, snow whipping in through the already open portion.

PAGE NINETY-FIVE:

Panel one: From outside, we're looking at Brant silhouetted in the open doorway, snow skittering over the threshold. His eyes are wide with surprise.

1/BRANT (small letters): Oh my God.

Panel two: Closer on Brant, smiling in relief.

2/BRANT: Oh my God!

Panel three: Brant is getting out of the way so Calexa and Mason can enter. Calexa looks grim, Mason nervous. Brant is still smiling.

3/BRANT: Come in. I just can't believe you're here. Your father is going to be so relieved.

4/CALEXA: He's alive, then.

Panel four: Brant is closing the door, the two of them standing in the foyer behind them. Mason is looking around, impressed, but Calexa has her hand stuffed into the jacket pocket where she's been keeping the gun.

5/BRANT: Holding on. He's holding on. Let me just lock up and I'll go up and get Isabel.

Panel five: Brant has turned toward them. Calexa has the gun aimed at his chest. Brant is wide-eyed, hands partly raised. Mason is staring at her. The ghost of Salazar, just a suggestion or hint of him, looms behind Calexa.

6/CALEXA: You'll do no such thing. Let's go into the office.

7/BRANT: Oh.

8/MASON: Calexa, don't. We came here to help your father.

Panel six: Brant, frowning.

9/BRANT (small letters): Who's Calexa?

PAGE NINETY-SIX:

Panel one: Almost at the top of the stairs, Isabel stands looking down toward the foyer (we don't see the foyer or the people in it). McKee is behind her on the stairs.

1/ISABEL: That's a good question, Brant. My guess is the Calexa is the name of the Ghost of Dunhill Cemetery.

2/ISABEL: Am I warm?

Panel two: Close on Isabel's face, smug.

3/ISABEL: Hello, Charlotte. Welcome home.

Panel three: The rest of the page. Calexa has turned to point the gun up the stairs at her sister and McKee. Mason is holding up a hand toward Brant, silently urging him to stay in place. This is a tense moment and he doesn't want Brant to set Calexa off.

4/CALEXA: That's not my name. Not anymore.

5/CALEXA: Come downstairs, both of you.

PAGE NINETY-SEVEN:

Panel one: Calexa has her back to the wall (or the open office door), covering Isabel and McKee as they reach the bottom of the stairs and are stepping to one side in the foyer, which is growing crowded.

1/ISABEL: I'm sure Daddy will be happy to hear you're casting aside the name he gave you, Charlotte.

2/CALEXA: Don't call him that. He tried to be a father to you, but you've thrown away the right to call him yours.

Panel two: Calexa has aimed the gun at McKee now, and the panel should be tighter, including either just the two of them or just them and Isabel. McKee looks cruel, ready for trouble.

3/CALEXA: Sorry to see you here, Mr. McKee. I'd been hoping you had broken your neck at the bottom of that ravine.

4/MCKEE: Don't worry, kid. It's the last time you'll see me. I can promise you that.

Panel three: Calexa is still pointing the gun at Isabel and McKee. Perhaps this panel is from a POV up on the stairs, looking down on them at an angle.

5/CALEXA: Brant...I want you to call the police. Right now, please. Say whatever you want, but just so you know, Izzy tried to murder me, and then she sent McKee to finish the job.

6/CALEXA: Mason, I'd like to see my father now. I've waited long enough. You need to keep them here.

Panel four: Close on Mason, frowning.

7/MASON: How am I supposed to do that?

Panel five: Brant is on the phone in the corner.

8/BRANT: Yes, I'd like to report...I mean there's been...They're talking about murder.

Panel six: Calexa still has the gun pointed at them. Mason has come up behind Calexa, reaching around, about to take the gun from her hand.

9/CALEXA: Take the gun. If they try to leave or come after me, just remember what they've done to me. Both of them.

10/MASON: I won't forget.

PAGE NINETY-EIGHT:

Panel one: McKee lunges for the gun as Calexa passes it to Mason. It's in Mason's hand but Calexa has barely let go of it. McKee is about to tackle Mason, reaching for the gun.

1/MCKEE: Isabel, get out of here!

Panel two: Isabel shouting furiously, pointing at Mason and McKee, who are slamming against a wall, grappling. McKee has a hand on the gun barrel but Mason still holds it.

2/ISABEL: I'm not going anywhere! Get the damn gun and shoot them both!

3/SFX: THUMPP!

Panel three: Calexa is rushing to help Mason but Isabel has grabbed a handful of her hair and is about to yank backward.

4/CALEXA: Mason!

5/ISABEL: That's far enough—

Panel four: Isabel yanks her head back by the hair.
6/ISABEL: --little sister!

7/CALEXA: aagghh!

Panel five: Calexa's face in closeup, in pain, remembering.

8/CALEXA: Let go of me! Let—

PAGE NINETY-NINE:

Panel one: Again, we FLASHBACK to a shot in BOOK TWO in which Isabel (though we couldn't see who it was then and we can now) has a gloved hand over Calexa's mouth and is injecting her in the neck.

1/CALEXA: mmfffhh

Panel two: Back to the present. Calexa has ducked down and is backing up, going with the backward momentum, slamming an elbow into Isabel's gut. Isabel's grip on her hair has opened.

2/CALEXA: --GO!

3/ISABEL: oooff

Panel three: As Mason and McKee (also in this panel) continue to struggle for the gun, it goes off, firing a bullet into the ceiling. Calexa has turned and is halfway through the process of throwing a punch at her sister's face. SALAZAR'S GHOST is behind her, egging her on.

4/SFX: BLAMMM!

5/SALAZAR: That's it! Swing from the hip! Put your weight behind it!

Panel four: Calexa smashes a fist into Isabel's face.

6/SFX: KRAKK!

Panel five: The nurse is running down the stairs toward them. Calexa is looking up at her, has stepped back away from Isabel and is waving at the nurse, trying to tell her not to come down any further. The nurse looks horrified. Isabel looks furious, staring directly at Calexa.

7/NURSE: What the hell is going on? You people are—

8/CALEXA: Go back upstairs! Are you crazy? Didn't you hear the gunshot?

PAGE ONE HUNDRED:

Page one: McKee and Mason are still fighting, but now their arms are lowered to one side, the gun clearly pointing in a horizontal way, and Mason fires again.

1/MCKEE: Son of a bitch, let go of the—

2/SFX: BLAM!!

Panel two: Isabel, in shock as she stares down at the hole in her abdomen, slightly to one side, where blood has already started to soak into her shirt a little. She's been shot, obviously.

3/ISABEL (small letters): oh...

Panel three: As Isabel slumps against the wall, sliding down it, leaving a streak of blood on the wall, the nurse pushes past Calexa, rushing toward Isabel, wanting to help. The blood stain is spreading much wider on Isabel's blouse. (She's not going to die, but it'll be a near thing.)

4/NURSE: Oh my God! Isabel!

Panel four: Mason rips the gun away from McKee, finally winning the struggle over it.

5/MASON: That's it!

Panel five: Mason smashes McKee across the face with the gun, a blow that will knock him down.

6/MASON: You're done!

7/SFX: KRAKK!

PAGE ONE HUNDRED AND ONE:

Panel one: Splash page. (or a vertical triptych with Calexa left, nurse and Isabel center, and Mason and McKee left.) Calexa is at the bottom of the stairs, her body language saying she wants to go up, but she's looking back at Mason, who is holding his side (where he was stabbed in book two), wincing in pain, but still aiming the gun at McKee, who has backed off, hands slightly raised in surrender. On the floor between them is Isabel, lying on the floor with the nurse kneeling by her, pressing her hands over Isabel's wound. The nurse is angry at them, shouting at them for someone to call 911.

1/NURSE: Someone, please! Call 911!

2/MASON: Go, Calexa. Go see your father.

3/MASON: I've got this.

PAGE ONE HUNDRED AND TWO:

Panel one: Brant, the secretary, appears from a side room with a phone in his hand. He's already been on the phone with the police.

1/BRANT: I've called the police...but I wasn't the first. They were already on their way here.

Panel two: McKee is glancing toward the door (is there a window by the door, or are there sidelights on either side of it?). There are blue lights flashing out there. (Or maybe the door has been open this entire time?) Somehow the police are already here. Mason is also in this panel.

2/MCKEE: Shit.

3/MASON: That'd be my father...

Panel three: The police outside—three cars—with several cops rushing toward the door with their guns drawn.

4/MASON/CAP: "...No way was he going to let this all happen without calling the cops."

Panel four: Calexa runs up the stairs, desperate now. She's this close to her father and she's not going to wait another minute. Salazar's ghost is on the stairs up ahead, pointing the way.

5/SALAZAR: He's this way, kid. You're almost—

6/CALEXA: Thank you. Thank you so much...

Panel five: Calexa turning the corner at the top of the stairs, about to head down the hall, and we can see that she's frowning because she KNOWS the way. The ghost is behind her, smiling happily.

7/CALEXA: ...But I know the way...

PAGE ONE HUNDRED AND THREE:

Panel one: Calexa is walking down the hall now, tracing her fingers along the wall. There's a painting on the wall (doesn't matter what of) and she's got that same frown on her face. Salazar is behind her, the ghost still smiling as he rises up toward the ceiling.

1/CALEXA: ...I remember.

2/SALAZAR: Then you don't need me anymore.

3/CALEXA: Thank you, Mr. Salazar. Thank you so much.

Panel two: FLASHBACK to Calexa at about six years old, moving down the same hall, tracing her fingers along the same wall, but much lower on the wall because of her size and age. The same painting is there, up on the wall. Young Calexa is smiling sweetly.

Panel three: Downstairs, in the present, the police are coming through the front door, guns drawn, and everyone who CAN raise their hands has raised their hands. Mason has one hand raised and with the other he is setting the gun on the floor. Cops have their guns aimed at everyone there.

4/COP: Put the gun on the floor and back away!

5/MASON: Doing it now!

6/COP: We got a call about a girl in danger! Calexa Dunhill. Where is she?

Panel four: Brant is pointing upstairs and the cops have started to look up that way.

7/BRANT: She went upstairs, officer. To see her father. But...

Panel five: FLASHBACK to Young Calexa at her father's bedroom door. She's turning the knob and the door is slightly open as she begins to enter the room.

8/BRANT/CAP: "...that's not her name."

PAGE ONE HUNDRED AND FOUR:

Panel one: Present day Calexa, wearing the smile of the young Calexa, is pushing her way into the bedroom of her father. We're looking at her, not at the interior of the room, but it's gloomy in there, one light on.

1/CALEXA: Daddy?
Panel two: FLASHBACK to little Calexa, standing in the same place.

2/CALEXA: Daddy?

Panel three: FLASHBACK. Her father twelve years ago, already old but handsome and rich and healthy, standing in front of a mirror tying his necktie. He's smiling into the mirror (and in the reflection, we can see little Calexa).

3/DABNEY: There's my little girl. Come and give your dad a hug!
Panel four: Present day. The much uglier reality. Her father is lying in his bed, near death, machines beeping nearby that monitor his vitals. A fluid bag standing next to the bed. He's rolled his head

toward her and is frowning, unsure of what he's looking at.

4/DABNEY: Who is it? Who's there?

Panel five: Close on Calexa's face, full of emotion at this reunion and at the horrible sight of her dying father.

5/CALEXA: It's me, Dad.

PAGE ONE HUNDRED AND FIVE:

Panel one: Smallish panel in upper left. She's sitting on the edge of the bed, taking his hand.

1/CALEXA: It's Charlotte.

Panel two: The rest of the page. She has laid her head on his chest/shoulder, reunited at last. The machines beep. Tears stream down his face and hers as well.

2/CALEXA: I'm home.

PAGE ONE HUNDRED AND SIX:

Panel one: Later. A bright sunny morning in front of Dunhill Cemetery. This is an establishing shot, so let's see the front gate in this panel. Some traces of snow, but most of it has melted.

1/CAP: Three weeks later.

Panel two: A car is parked in front of Kelner's house. A Lexus or something similarly expensive. Kelner's truck is also parked there. Kelner is standing outside (wearing a jacket—it's cold but not frigid), cup of steaming coffee in hand.

Panel three: Mason stands outside Calexa's crypt. The door is open. He looks healthy, healed.

2/MASON: So here's my big question. What do we call you now?
Panel four: Inside the crypt, Calexa is putting the stuff she still cares about in a cardboard box. Photos. Newspaper clippings. Candles.

3/CALEXA: That's your big question?

4/CALEXA: I'm Charlotte at home, obviously. But to you and your dad and Mr. Griggs, I'll always be Calexa. Hell, in my own head I think of myself as Calexa.

Panel five: Mason stands in the open doorway of the crypt, smiling at her.

5/MASON: I hate to say it, but I'm sort of glad. I know Calexa. I never met Charlotte.

PAGE ONE HUNDRED AND SEVEN:

Panel one: Calexa is looking at the folded clothes that are on a shelf inside the crypt. There aren't many, but we do see the veiled hat that she wore to funerals in book one.

1/CALEXA: I'm with you. Pieces of my memory keep coming back, but it all feels like something I dreamt once instead of something I lived.

2/CALEXA: Listen...Are you guys sure you don't mind getting rid of the rest of this stuff for me?

Panel two: Close on Mason, smiling.

3/MASON: Not at all. We'll donate the clothes and toss out everything else. If you're sure you can really part with it all.
Panel three: Calexa has turned toward him, holding the veiled hat in her hands.

4/CALEXA: I'm taking some mementos, but most everything that matters is over at Lucinda's house.

Panel four: Mason stands aside as she comes out of the crypt carrying the box. The hat is on top of the stuff in the box.

5/MASON: It must feel pretty surreal, going from hiding in a crypt to living in a mansion with staff to look after you.

Panel five: The two of them are walking back through the cemetery, and it's beautiful. Calexa has a sad smile on her face.

6/CALEXA: There are perks. I don't have to do my own laundry, or steal clothes from mourners at funerals. But I miss the cemetery, honestly. I miss Lucinda's house.

7/MASON: She'd be proud of you. Happy for you.

PAGE ONE HUNDRED AND EIGHT:

Panel one: Mason and Calexa are walking past the stone angels we've seen before.

1/CALEXA: I know that. I do. I miss being here, and having real friends. Friends I earned. I'm not the girl I was before Dunhill. I'm the person I became here. The person I made.

2/MASON: That person is not going anywhere. No matter what name she uses.

Panel two: They're passing trees and walking toward the fountain that we've seen before, particularly in book one.

3/CALEXA: Can we just sit for a minute?

4/MASON: Sure.

Panel three: A broad shot of the cemetery in all its glory, an aerial view.

5/CALEXA (floating balloon): Old friends...Charlotte's friends... have been coming around.

6/CALEXA: (floating balloon): But I feel this huge distance from them and I know they feel the same. I don't know them anymore, and they definitely don't know me. I'm starting over...

Panel four: The box is at her feet. They sit on the edge of the fountain, very close to each other but not touching. Calexa is looking around, taking it all in. Mason is gazing at her with understanding.

7/CALEXA: The most important thing right now is that I be there to help care for my father.

8/CALEXA: The doctors give him two or three months and I want to spend every one of those days with him...

Panel five: A shot of Calexa's father in bed, machines beeping around him.

9/CALEXA/CAP: "...The media is going wild with the story. Sister attempts to murder sister out of greed. Throw in wealth and the urban legend of the Ghost of Dunhill Cemetery..."

10/CALEXA/CAP: "...It's on TV and in the papers constantly, and I have to protect Daddy from that. I can't let him learn what's happened to his legacy. He'd die broken-hearted."

PAGE ONE HUNDRED AND NINE:

Panel one: Calexa's head is down. Mason is looking at her, a little sad.

1/MASON: He thought you were dead. Having you back...I suspect that's the only legacy he needs.

2/CALEXA: Maybe you're right.

Panel two: Calexa has looked up at him, smiling softly.

3/CALEXA: You know...I won't always be this busy.

Panel three: Mason has gotten up and is reaching for the box, about to pick it up.

4/MASON: You just worry about your father. You can come and visit us when you get the time. I'm out for the whole semester, so I'll be here.

Panel four: Calexa has a hand on his arm, stopping him from pickingup the box, and he's glancing back at her, smiling.

5/CALEXA: Mason...

6/MASON: I know, I know. You don't need a guy to carry your stuff.

Panel five:
Mason has turned around. She still has one hand on his arm but

she's lifted the other hand and is touching his face gently, gazing into his eyes.

7/CALEXA: That's true. But it's not why I stopped you...

PAGE ONE HUNDRED AND TEN:

Splash Page: Calexa and Mason in an embrace in front of the fountain, locked in a passionate kiss.

PAGE ONE HUNDRED AND ELEVEN:
Panel one: Calexa has pulled back from him and is smiling, flush. Mason is obviously dumbstruck by the kiss.

1/CALEXA: As I was saying...I don't NEED you to carry my stuff. But I'm not gonna stop you, either.

2/CALEXA: You know, you could visit me, too. If you're willing to make the drive.

Panel two: She's holding his hand. He's got the box under one arm. They're walking toward Kelner's cottage, where her car is parked. Kelner is leaning against his truck drinking his coffee (though we're still a distance from the house).

2/MASON: I am. I definitely am.

Panel three: As they approach the house, Kelner is watching them, smiling, holding his coffee cup as he greets them. Mason and Calexa are still holding hands.

3/KELNER: Took you kids long enough. Thought you might need a hand, but I didn't want to crowd you. Looks like I made the right call.

4/CALEXA: You always seem to.
Panel four: As Mason puts the box in the back seat of her car, Calexa kisses Kelner on the cheek.

5/CALEXA: Thank you, Mr. Kelner. Thank you for everything.

Panel five: Kelner holds her by the arm, looking at her very seriously. He wants her to know she always has friends here. Calexa's wiping at one eye, tears welling up but not falling, even though she is smiling.

6/KELNER: You just remember, kid. You've always got friends here. This is home, too.

7/CALEXA: I won't forget.

PAGE ONE HUNDRED AND TWELVE:

Panel one: She's walking toward her car. Mason is holding the door open for her. Calexa is wiping at her eyes but she's okay. She's going to be fine.

1/MASON: So now that you're back home, what are you going to do with Lucinda's house? I mean, it's your house. Are you going to sell it?

2/CALEXA: I've been talking to Mr. Griggs about that. I think I'm going to fix it up, have it painted, replace the old wiring.

Panel two: Mason has shut the car door. Calexa is behind the wheel. She is looking at him, smiling, wanting to make sure that her words are being understood.

3/CALEXA: But I'm not going to sell it. I figure someday I'll have a family of my own and maybe we'll want to live there.

4/CALEXA: Of course, that's a long way off... Right now, I'm taking one day at a time. Taking advantage of the fact that, for the moment, nobody's trying to kill me.

Panel three: Mason and Kelner stand together, watching her drive toward the front gates. Mason has a smile on his face. Kelner wears a knowing, lopsided grin.

5/KELNER: Sweet girl.

6/MASON: She is.

7/KELNER: Wants a family of her own, someday.

8/MASON: Not another word, old man.

Panel four: From one side, we can see Calexa's car exiting the cemetery.

9/MASON (floating balloon): Not another word.

Panel five: From inside the car, we can see her smiling as she looks in the rearview mirror.

10/CALEXA/CAP: I say a silent goodbye to my friends in the cemetery, living and dead. Both have helped me get to this day.

PAGE ONE HUNDRED AND THIRTEEN:

Splash page: As the car drives toward us, away from the gates (and we can clearly read the DUNHILL CEMETERY arched over the gates), we also see the huge ghostly image floating above the cemetery of Calexa, younger, standing in the midst of tombstones. Her memory of her time here. (Essentially, this image is a ghostly version of the frontispiece used in book one). No matter where she goes, she knows she will always carry the Ghost of Dunhill Cemetery with her. She'll always be the Cemetery Girl.

1/CALEXA/CAP: It may be that one day another lost soul will seek my help the way Marla's ghost did. The way Lucinda's did, and Salazar's.

2/CALEXA/CAP: If that day comes, I'll do whatever I can to ease the pain and confusion of their passing.

3/CALEXA/CAP: It's the least I can do. The ghosts of Dunhill Cemetery saved my life more than once. They did far more for me than I did for them.

4/CALEXA/CAP: For so long, I couldn't remember who I really was. Now I finally understand what I should've known all along.

5/CALEXA/CAP: It's up to me. I get to choose.

6/CALEXA/CAP: Whatever the future brings, in my heart I'll always be Calexa Rose Dunhill.

7/CALEXA/CAP: I'll always be the Cemetery Girl.

THE END